Pembroke

Regional map of
Pembroke Township.
Created by author.

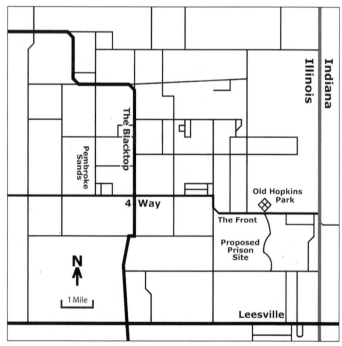

Local map of Pembroke Township. *Created by author.*

PEMBROKE

A RURAL, BLACK COMMUNITY ON THE ILLINOIS DUNES

DAVE BARON

Lester and Norma,
Thank you so much
for being here today — and
particularly for bringing the
articles! I really appreciate
it.
— Dave Bar

Southern Illinois University Press * Carbondale

Southern Illinois University Press
www.siupress.com

19 18 17 16   4 3 2

Cover illustration: Johari Cole-Kweli. *Photograph by author.*

Library of Congress Cataloging-in-Publication Data
Names: Baron, Dave (David M.), author.
Title: Pembroke : a rural, black community on the Illinois dunes / Dave
    Baron.
Description: Carbondale : Southern Illinois University Press, 2016. |
    Includes bibliographical references and index.
Identifiers: LCCN 2015044747 | ISBN 9780809335022 (pbk. : alk. paper) |
    ISBN 9780809335039 (e-book)
Subjects: LCSH: Pembroke (Ill. : Township)—History. | African
    Americans—Illinois—Pembroke (Township)—History. | Kankakee
    County (Ill.)—History, Local.
Classification: LCC F549.P38 B37 2016 | DDC 977.3/63—dc23 LC record
    available at http://lccn.loc.gov/2015044747

Contents

Maps and Tables

Maps

Tables

Acknowledgments

First and foremost, I am deeply grateful to the people of Pembroke Township for their hospitality and contagious spirit, which made it easy to gather and share the community's stories. In particular I thank Johari Cole-Kweli, Basu, Pam Basu, Ardella Perry, Genova Singleton, Samuel Payton, Sharon White, Sister Mary Beth Clements, and numerous others who opened their hearts and lives to me. While conducting my research I also benefited from the considerable information compiled by the Kankakee County Historical Society, the Roman Catholic Diocese of Joliet, the *Daily Journal*, and especially *Journal* reporter Robert Themer who offered his decades of experience covering the Pembroke beat.

I am very thankful to Emily Caveness, Jackie Pruitt, Vince Guider, and Nick Guzmán, who each took considerable time to edit early drafts of my manuscript, and to Joe and Amy Meginnes, Cate and Nick DeJulio, Diana Banks, and Sarah Ames for their guidance on particular chapters. I also thank Southern Illinois University Press's Karl Kageff, Wayne Larsen, Lynanne Page, and Linda Buhman, as well as copy editor Ryan Masteller, who all helped to shepherd a manuscript into this finished work. To Professor Randall Kennedy, Father Jim King, Sharon and Steve Fiffer, Gary Moore, Jeff Carroll, and Nena Madonia for sharing their experience in the literary world with a first-time author; to Peggy Heck, Neely Benn, and Ben Kurstin, whose talents behind a camera have captured another element of Pembroke's exceptional beauty; to the attorneys at Sidley Austin LLP who let me step away from billable hour requirements for a few weeks to complete the first draft of my manuscript; and to Judge Ann Claire Williams, Claire Stewart, Tony and Brenda Ortiz, Ken and Michelle Barrie, and Zac Madonia for their ongoing interest in my project—I owe my sincere appreciation.

My gratitude also goes to my sister, Denise Baron, and my fiancée, Anya Hurtado: both provided insights on my manuscript and motivation to prepare a compelling story. Finally, to my parents, Dennis and Debi Baron, who not only encouraged me while writing this book but also primed me for my Pembroke experience since childhood, thank you. You taught me to seek out the unexpected virtues and the hidden injustices that exist in the world around me, to appreciate the former and to act on the latter.

Pembroke

Introduction: The Paradox of Pembroke

"When the Spirit is inside you, you just can't help but let it out," Gertrude Higginbottom spoke to people in church pews before her. "You feel it, children. You feel God inside you, and you should let everyone outside feel it as well." She stood at a simple lectern with no microphone. The pews echoed back, "Amen, Amen."

The year was 1999, but the small, peaceful church looked much like it did when it was built over half a century before. No more than sixty or seventy people could fit comfortably inside. On the wood paneling of the walls hung crosses, small sculptures, and framed pictures—one of which portrayed a young black woman wearing a sky blue African robe and headdress. She looked at the face of her child, smiling contently in her arms, and both of them had the golden halos of the Holy Family encircling their heads. The picture needed nothing but sunlight to illuminate it, which shone through the sanctuary's many windows. Looking outward, one could see the neighborhood surrounding the church. It was not colored in the gray of urban concrete, but the irregular greens and browns of a lush forest.

Gertrude's church wasn't in Harlem or South Central Los Angeles. It wasn't in the South Side of Chicago; in fact, it wasn't in a major metropolitan city at all. Nor was it in the rural Deep South, although a sizable black population lives in such areas as the Mississippi Delta and the Pee Dee region of South Carolina. It sat in the middle of Mid-America—sixty-five miles south of Chicago and one mile west of the Illinois-Indiana state line.

Gertrude Higginbottom lived in Pembroke Township, Kankakee County, Illinois. Her house of worship was located in a small "subdivision" along with a few other structures including another church, a school, a re-sale

1

shop, inhabited homes, and abandoned walls and foundations that were once homes. These buildings were surrounded by a thin, yet dense and aggressive, patch of oak forest that crept right up to their facades, openly threatening to retake the land and revert the structures to their component materials. But outside that ring of foliage, less than a hundred feet from Gertrude's church, grew the ubiquitous crops of Illinois. Rows of corn and soybeans fought to take root in a light, porous, and sandy soil.

At seventy-eight years old, Gertrude had lived nearly her entire life in Pembroke on the same piece of land that she inherited from her parents, who had also been born in the town. Gertrude's great-grandparents, Joseph "Pap" Tetter and Mary Eliza Tetter, were the first black settlers in the area. They arrived in Pembroke from North Carolina around 1861, and they began to farm and build a family on land close to both Gertrude's home and the church where she now spoke.

Gertrude used several vivid, personal anecdotes to introduce the daily reading, and even when she began reciting from the Bible below her, Gertrude injected her own sentiments throughout the ancient passage. "And this next part is so important, children," she said before discussing the spiritual directive to thank God always. As Gertrude came to the end of the scriptural text, she concluded with five words from the official liturgy of the Roman Catholic Church: "The Word of the Lord." The assembly responded, "Thanks be to God."

Over 20 percent of the U.S. population belongs to the Catholic Church, but only 3 percent of those who make up that statistic is black—as compared to the U.S. population overall which is 13 percent black.[1] As a young girl Gertrude lived on the northern end of Pembroke Township, closer to the predominantly white town of Momence. Her parents raised her Catholic, and they attended mass at St. Patrick's Parish there. But in 1939 when St. Patrick's opened Sacred Heart Mission, a satellite church in Pembroke, she quickly found a new place to pray.

> When Sister Mary Adelaide started going around knocking door to door, then we started going to this church. This was a little all-black church, and I felt more comfortable in my little, black church. Not that I wasn't welcome out there, now don't get me wrong. But you know, it seemed more homelike to me here. And then I could get up, you know, and try to do my thing.[2]

Gertrude became a leader in the faith community, helping the small mission church grow into a formal parish, Sacred Heart Catholic Church, in 1968.

Gertrude was also a dedicated mother, a tireless force who took on an exhausting daily routine in order to provide for her family. She and her husband Orland had five children, and Gertrude once said, "I wanted my children to have a little bit more. Of course, my husband wanted me to be a housewife, but I went out and worked." Gertrude spent thirty years at her job with a mental health hospital twenty-five miles away in northern Kankakee County, mostly doing midnight shifts.

Lana Higginbottom, one of Gertrude's daughters, described her mother's usual schedule: "When she got home from the hospital in the morning, Dad had already gone to work. So she transported us to school." The Momence school bus did not provide service in Pembroke, so Gertrude would drive them to the Catholic grade school in Momence. It was no easy task to afford the tuition, but Gertrude and her husband made the extra effort. Because Lana went to private school, many in Pembroke thought the Higginbottoms were wealthy. This perception would affect Lana when she continued her education at the local public high school, which was located in St. Anne, another principally white town a few miles west of Pembroke. Teenagers from both St. Anne and Pembroke attended this racially integrated school, but Lana felt alienated from both groups: "I was an outsider to them, to both the whites of St. Anne and the black students of Pembroke." According to Lana, the color of her skin excluded her from one crowd, and the perception of wealth kept her from the other. "They thought we had money, but we didn't."[3]

When the children returned from school each day, Gertrude was prepared: "The dinner would be on the table. That's when we would have our discussion." Soon after the meal Gertrude would head north on Pembroke's shoddy dirt roads to the state hospital. It is not clear when she found time to sleep. Maybe she dozed for a few hours while the children were at school, but life in a country home likely provided ample distractions to keep her from resting.

Gertrude continued to attend weekly mass at Sacred Heart and to preach to the community as a lector until she passed away in 2001 at the age of seventy-nine, leaving to her children the same land that had belonged to her parents. Lana, who has children and grandchildren of her own, now lives on the family estate in a yellow bi-level home, which is set back from the public road by a driveway lined with stalks of corn. Lana leases these few acres to a farmer from Momence. The house sits in the middle of a grassy yard, and oak forests rise behind it. In the yard is a large swing set next to an ornamental plastic turkey bearing the words, "Be thankful."

Also close to the playground equipment are a few piles of discarded refuse, a dilapidated car underneath a brown drop cloth, and two metal barrels bearing scars from burning trash. Finally, a large box trailer stands before the forest wall so that anyone coming up the driveway can see the message in big, blue, hand-painted letters on the trailer: "Welcome to Higginbottom Heaven. Praise the Lord."

Lana's own health has declined in recent years, but several of her siblings have returned home to serve as caretakers for her and the family land.[4] To them, the land is more than its property value, more than the structures and crops upon it, and even more than their home. "We'll have this place until after we're dead and gone. We'll pay the taxes," explained Lana. "It's a testament to Mom and Dad. They put their whole lives into this land."

In many ways, Gertrude Higginbottom's very identity challenged social conventions and expectations. She was a rural, midwestern, Catholic, black woman. Gertrude, her family, and her neighbors indeed built Pembroke as a community that contradicts demographic trends, migration patterns, cultural expectations, economic developments, and environmental norms. Pembroke turns each on its head.

The fifty-two square miles that make up Pembroke Township are found in the extreme southeast corner of downstate Kankakee County. Within Pembroke is the township's sole municipality, the Village of Hopkins Park. According to the 2010 Census, the population of Pembroke Township was 2,140, and that of Hopkins Park was 603. It is far from certain, however, that these numbers are accurate.[5] Response rates in Pembroke are regularly lower than prevailing averages elsewhere, and it is doubtful that the census successfully reaches those living in tents, shacks, and lean-tos in the backwoods of the township. Local officials attest to their presence, but despite considerable efforts to ensure census workers knew where to look in 2010, accuracy of the count remains tenuous.[6]

Despite these relatively small numbers, Pembroke is one of the largest rural, black communities north of the Mason-Dixon Line. Gertrude's great-grandparents first arrived in Pembroke in the mid-nineteenth century, but the community did not become almost exclusively black until after World War II. Many who first journeyed north from Mississippi and Alabama during the Great Migration in the early twentieth century did not find the opportunities they expected in Chicago. Instead, they discovered a crowded, expensive, and inhospitable environment, so they left to search for the tranquil country setting that they had known.

They may have found their space and solitude, but economic opportunity remained elusive. Today Pembroke is one of the poorest communities in Illinois, and in the nation. Many who live in the backwoods choose to do so, but some do because they must. Recent surveys indicate that the median income per household is $25,466, which compares to a state median of $57,166 and a national median of $53,482.[7] Unemployment numbers generally soar above the national and Illinois averages. During the years surrounding the recent economic downturn beginning in 2008 and 2009, when unemployment was estimated nationwide at 9.7 percent, that figure in Pembroke was estimated at 34.3 percent. That statistic is even more staggering considering that unemployment rates represent the number of people unemployed divided by the number of people in the labor force. At the time, only 48.6 percent of the township's total population was represented in the labor force, as compared to 64.3 percent nationwide. Those outside of the labor force consist of children, the retired, or those not actively seeking work, meaning that only 31.9 percent of people in Pembroke (compared to 57.6 percent of people nationally) were actually employed.[8]

Even Pembroke's terrain deviates from midwestern norms—a fact that has helped shape Pembroke's human development. Most land in the Great Lakes region was made flat by glaciers that rolled over the land and left a rich, black topsoil that caters to commercial agriculture. The surface of Pembroke, however, is not flat. When the glaciers melted ten thousand years ago, they deposited sand and other sediment into the area, and wind quickly swept the materials into tall dune formations. Unique ecosystems, not found anywhere else in the region, developed on top of these Illinois dunes. In particular, Pembroke is home to a large concentration of black oak savannas, a transition ecosystem where some tall trees grow, but not enough to block sunlight reaching prairie grasses below. Although the elevated, dry, sandy soil lacks the nutrients for ideal farming, it is hospitable for black oak trees, a species far less common than the related white oak or pin oak. Nonetheless, because corn and soybean yields typically fall well below those of others elsewhere in the area, so do property values. Thus, individuals with limited financial means have been able to buy the land and build their own village among the black oaks.

Gertrude Higginbottom lived here as one of the town's grand matriarchs. She was a leader in a community that was, according to certain outside standards, an anomaly. Indeed, Pembroke's continued existence resists conventional wisdom. Despite obstacles of poverty, isolation, substandard infrastructure, poor soil quality, and racial prejudice, Pembroke remains. Where one might expect a ghost town, Pembroke endures.

Boundaries defined by expectations, conventions, and their problematic relative, stereotypes, are often broken. They shatter in a cathartic moment, leaving us to see the world with new eyes. We come to see that things are not necessarily what we believed them to be. Such realizations can incur a crisis of confidence if we are unable or unwilling to change our worldviews. But alternatively, breaking through the expected can be an opportunity. We are afforded a new perspective and basis from which to approach the world and the people in it. We can widen our limited view and come slightly closer to truth. Following these paradigm shifts we discover new insights into the surrounding world, but we are also able to see ourselves through a new lens. In that sense, we come to a more accurate self-understanding. By remaining open to these moments, rather than clinging to our previous assumptions, we can arrive at a clearer, more confident sense of identity and purpose. These are moments of paradox.

Seventeen years ago, I experienced my first such moment in Pembroke Township. On Sunday, August 1, 1999, I arrived in Pembroke as a participant of Project Hearts of Hope, a service trip organized by my church's teen group. There were forty of us in all, and for one week we assisted with home improvement projects for the people of Pembroke, interviewed Sacred Heart parishioners, took part in a nightly spiritual revival of song and prayer, and reflected on our experiences in journals.

Many initiatives like this are meant to extract people from the familiar and place them in new situations. Often groups journey across the country or even across the world—to the lake villages of Uganda, border cities in Mexico, or coal communities of Appalachia. I did not need to travel that far to find a world radically different from my own. Pembroke is less than twenty miles from Kankakee, where I grew up.

Kankakee is its county seat and home to almost thirty thousand people. From the big-city perspective of Chicagoans, Kankakee is a small town off Interstate 57 where people stop on the way to the University of Illinois. But for many in Pembroke, Kankakee is an urban metropolis. Eva Grant, as a forty-seven-year-old lifelong resident of Pembroke, spoke about her visits to Kankakee: "When you went out a back door, you were looking at someone else's back door. When you went out a front door, you were looking at someone else's front door. When you look out your window, you're looking into someone else's window. And it's even worse in Chicago."[9]

My family is not new to Kankakee, having lived in the area for five generations. I grew up in a house only a block from my father's childhood home. I was born in the same hospital that he was and attended the same grade school that he did, and at the time of Project Hearts of Hope, I had just completed my freshman year at the same high school my father had attended. It was a fortunate life. I always assumed that we would have food, clothing, housing, and education, as well as a close-knit family. According to Chicago standards, we were not rich, but by Kankakee standards, we were plenty well off.

Even before Project Hearts of Hope, my parents had taken me out to Pembroke a few times in conjunction with their own involvement in the community. I knew it was poor and primarily black, but little else. Although my parents sometimes mentioned the strength and resilience of the community, I was also aware of its less favorable reputation. Many Kankakee residents saw Pembroke as backward. It was crime-ridden, dirt-poor, and somewhere to avoid. People told shadowy stories of shootings and other terrible events—though usually based on second- or third-hand accounts. Although I sensed this reputation was exaggerated, it remained heavy in my mind as I left for our week in Pembroke.

Upon arriving at Sacred Heart, I was quickly introduced to Gertrude Higginbottom, who I encountered at the very first session of the spiritual revival service. Indeed, her sermon recounted above is how I remember Gertrude's readings and commentary that Sunday evening in 1999. She described that she couldn't help but let inhibitions go when she feels the Spirit. As I listened to her and the other Sacred Heart parishioners around me, I quickly realized that this was not the type of Catholic mass to which I was accustomed. All throughout the service, parishioners punctuated the words of the priest with "Thank you, Jesus." Then moments later they would follow with an enthusiastic "Amen, Amen!" Gertrude sang wholeheartedly, maintaining a smile from the beginning of the revival to the end.

I was struck by Gertrude and her style of worship. At no point during the revival was she merely present in the church. She was perpetually engaged as a vocal participant, savoring each step of the mass. For example, Gertrude was the loudest when reciting the Apostles' Creed and the first to start clapping during the service's closing hymn. Obviously I witnessed the rituals of a mass every Sunday at my own parish, and I knew what words to repeat, but nothing for Gertrude was repetitive or automatic. It was clear that the actual meaning behind these practices did not escape her. Rather, with each exclamation, she commemorated the very reasons that we Catholics deem these things important enough to do week after week.

I seldom prayed like she did—in fact I could not do it. I could never talk before a crowd like that. Earlier that year I declined to run for a leadership role on the student council because, even though I probably gave some excuse about not having enough time, I was scared to deliver a speech in front of my class before the election. The idea of public speaking in front of that group made me sweat. So I sat it out.

When Gertrude rose to deliver the first reading and talked about the Spirit inside her, it was as if she was speaking directly to me. She said later in an interview with the Hearts of Hope group,

> Now if the Spirit sticks me though, I gotta tell you! You know, I'll tell you! Because there are some words, if you just listen to the Spirit, they'll come out. They just come to you. You don't have to say nothing. You'll just be like, wha- wha- what happened? Then it comes to you. Yeah, it really do.

During the days that followed, I came to better understand what Gertrude Higginbottom meant. My encounter with Gertrude was only one of several moments where my assumptions were tested and broken, where I saw beneath appearances and sensed the reality of the community.

That week we heard from Father Anthony "Tony" Taschetta. Father Tony was a familiar face, serving as the current pastor of a parish in Kankakee, but from 1976 to 1982, he had been a resident priest and pastor at Sacred Heart. Taking us on a tour of the church's subdivision, now known as Old Hopkins Park, Father Tony showed us the abandoned house where he once lived and the tree that had since fallen through the roof and into his former living room. He also showed us the re-sale shop, which offered furniture, clothes, and just about everything else to the people of Pembroke who had limited desire or means to travel to the sometimes unfriendly shops in St. Anne and Momence.

We met with Robert Hayes, who had been a long-serving township supervisor, the top elected position in the area, and he told us about the difficulties faced and overcome by the people of Pembroke. He described the condition of the dirt roads throughout the township and noted that some were absolutely impassable in the spring. He also talked about the Catholic Church broadly, readily willing to offer a critical but sincere comment about the enduring existence of prejudice in an institution he nonetheless loved dearly.

And we came to know Duke, a young basketball fan whose home and school were both just around the corner in Old Hopkins Park. Like many ten-year-olds during the summer months, he had little to do, and the arrival of forty new people captured his interest. I never learned his last name, but Duke was always around, helping us while we worked and hanging out during the down times.

That week my paradigm shifted, and I came upon a new understanding of myself. I clapped and sang with the rest of the congregation at Sacred Heart, and at the week's final mass, this white kid from downstate Illinois was even offering his own "Thank you, Jesus" during the middle of a sermon. I later wrote in an article for my school newspaper: "The teens realized their lives had been changed. No one thought he or she could go back to the old lives of television, gossip, and $160 shoes. . . . For the short time, the teens were there, they were content with what they had."[10]

With these feelings came a new sense of confidence. I have since gotten up and spoken before thousands of people, and I went to law school to pursue a profession rooted in public speaking and advocacy. I recognize a direct link from these aspects of my current identity to my experiences in Pembroke and the message of Gertrude Higginbottom.

In September 2009, I was supposed to begin my employment with a large Chicago law firm. Because of the recession, however, my start date was pushed back three months, and I moved home with my parents in Kankakee during that time to save money. I spent much of that period pondering my experience in Pembroke Township. How did Pembroke become the community it is today? How had it survived so many obstacles? What is next for Pembroke? Why did it have such a deep impact on me, and why does it continue to do so?

My desire for answers led me to prepare this cultural and economic history of Pembroke Township. During those three months I traveled to Pembroke nearly every day to interview people there. I attended village board meetings, township board meetings, school board meetings, church services, and community events where I listened and asked questions. Since then I have searched for any materials about Pembroke that I could find—local newspaper articles, letters, reports, and studies—often coming upon new tales that caused me once again to readjust my assumptions. I then drew my own conclusions about the unrecorded history as best I could. Although my analysis touches upon several academic fields, including sociology, anthropology, geography, political science, and law, it does not purport to be a formal piece of scholarship, which would require further examination of the comparable academic literature in the relevant areas.

As I conducted my research, I faced some clear and significant limitations. I was a white man attempting to understand the heart of a black community, and there were inevitably mistakes of translation when listening to the black experience with white ears. Moreover, I was a *random* white man asking people to share their private lives and history with me. Even without the racial component, a barrier of distrust may have prevented open and honest communication, and I recognize that responses to my interview questions might have been guarded or screened in some cases. More than once, I sensed that an interviewee held back from telling me about a time when he or she endured prejudice or unjust treatment by a white man. That barrier can be deconstructed, but it takes effort and, most of all, time. A few months are hardly sufficient. I have endeavored to be aware of these instances, and I apologize for any incongruities.

I did not, however, shy away from talking about matters of race when preparing or writing this analysis. As Barack Obama, then a U.S. senator from Illinois, stated in March 2008, we cannot be fearful of "the complexities of race in this country that we've never really worked through—a part of our union that we have not yet made perfect. And if we walk away now, if we simply retreat to our respective corners, we will never be able to come together and solve challenges. . . ."[11] I have taken these words to heart, by trying to maintain first, a sense of the historical import of race, and second, a belief in the ever-present need for respect in such discussions.

During my interviews I often asked what the rest of the world should know about life in Pembroke. A common answer surfaced. Several people expressed a concern that the only stories printed about the community were negative tales of plight, vice, and despair. According to Pat Eckles, who moved to Hopkins Park in 1984, "We're here. We're not the forgotten zone. That's what people think. But we're right here."[12] There is no doubt that there are real problems in Pembroke, many of which are due in part to the community's own missteps. Nonetheless, these problems are not the only story to tell. As an elderly resident once told my mother, "Pembroke can be the closest thing to hell on earth, and the closest thing to heaven on earth, depending on where you're standing."

To that end, I sought to learn more about Pembroke's grand matriarchs and patriarchs. I strove to tell the community's many tales of kindness, selflessness, and achievement. At the same time, fully ignoring the negatives would not only be inaccurate; it would curtail the complete richness of Pembroke's story. The people of the community have also exhibited virtues of strength, perseverance, and resilience by overcoming the many obstacles experienced throughout the township's history. Much like how the black oak embeds itself in the sandy terrain and prevents the ground from blowing away, steadfast individuals like Gertrude Higginbottom anchored the community and enabled it to defy expectations.

This book presents a history of Pembroke Township, offering an answer to my initial question about how Pembroke became the community it is today. I found that the rare, natural features of Pembroke's black oak savannas made the land difficult to farm but allowed poor, African American migrants the chance to purchase their own property. Although they lacked capital to develop their holdings, the migrants built a distinctively rural and black community there in which connections to the land and the desire for self-determination are central to the township's identity and future direction.

The chapters that follow support and expand on this answer. After reviewing the geological events that created the black oak savannas and the early human settlement nearby that left the savannas intact, I discuss black migration to the area. The next chapters detail various aspects of Pembroke's history: politics, commerce, crime, faith, education, and others that reflect an African American take on rural, midwestern life. I then turn to the unsuccessful attempts to spur economic development and eliminate poverty in Pembroke. I specifically consider two controversial efforts in which control of the land became a contentious issue—a proposed women's prison pushed by former governor George Ryan around the turn of the millennium and ongoing conservation efforts to protect the black oaks and their surrounding savanna ecosystem. I conclude by positing how people inside and outside of the community might deal with differing visions of the ideal Pembroke going forward.

Intertwined with this telling of Pembroke's story is my own personal encounter with the community. Each chapter begins with a brief, first-person narrative based upon my week in Pembroke during Project Hearts of Hope in 1999. These passages also serve to introduce the subject matter of the chapter.

They show that I found my voice seventeen years ago while in a community built over fault lines of rich-poor, black-white, rural-urban, and powerful-powerless. I observed general virtues, like endurance, valor, poise, and grace, but I was also introduced to more specific and complicated matters of contemporary American race relations, identity within the Catholic Church, and viable economic development strategies that enable a community to chart and advance its own course. One week in Pembroke years ago awakened and compelled me to keep exploring these lessons. Neither the community nor I have come to final resolutions (and indeed I hope this book inspires further investigation and analysis), but I am convinced that the experiences of Pembroke and its black oaks carry significance for individuals and communities outside of the township's boundaries.

Mskoda

We headed eastbound on Illinois Route 17. The flat landscape allowed for a view spanning all 180 degrees of the horizon, and the seemingly enormous late-afternoon August sun beat down on cornstalks as tall as my younger sister, who sat next to me. It was hot out there, but we sat in the cool security of air conditioning.

Given the even terrain and few natural obstacles, roads can run in nearly straight lines across the width of Illinois and into Indiana. For the most part, Route 17 behaves this way, but about seven miles outside of Momence, the highway unexpectedly curves to the north. Travelers can take the turn without slowing down, as most do, or they can continue going straight, following a tiny green sign with an arrow toward the Village of Hopkins Park. Today my family and I took the latter.

I had made this drive before—several times, in fact, when accompanying my parents to one community event or another. My parents, in the front seat, talked about those experiences. Unfortunately, my memory of those trips had wilted by the time I reached fifteen years of age. My attention remained fixed outside the windows where I could perceive the slow change from the perfectly linear row crops associated with commercial agriculture to fields and hedges that were more irregular, more natural.

We turned right and passed a white wooden real estate sign stenciled with block blue letters: "We Buy, Sell, or Trade Lots, Acres, Farms, Homes. Financing Available. $50 Down. Moscickis Realty." We turned *left and drove past an old farmhouse, its yard filled with a half dozen husks of old, rusted automobiles. We turned right again toward a tree-lined horizon that was no longer flat, but noticeably bumpy. The soil all around us was not black anymore, but beige and sandy.*

Before driving beneath the light canopy of trees, we came upon another green sign: "Hopkins Park, 800." According to my Mom, we were now on the "Blacktop." The village's main artery ran for about two miles with well-worn structures on both sides of the road. Mobile trailers had been transformed into residences, restaurants, and re-sale shops, several of which bore the telltale black scars of fires. Many churches appeared along the road, including one whose simple marquee proclaimed "JESUS" both across and down a cross-shaped sign, interlocking the two words at the middle "S" like a crossword puzzle. All along the Blacktop, people walked on a sidewalk of sorts—the gravel space in between the asphalt and the ditch. A few were on bikes, and three boys sat atop a single ATV. Each of them waved to us as our car drove past. We approached a stop sign, which Mom explained to me was called the "4-Way," and we turned left, past the village hall and the tallest manmade structure in Hopkins Park, a rusting, faded water tower. Eventually we emerged from the trees and continued east. We passed more fields, as well as modest country homes and numerous buildings with electric signs indicating that Pabst Blue Ribbon was sold there, or at least it used to be.

Our car slowed as we approached three signs—Baker's Auto Parts, School, and Sacred Heart Catholic Church. We turned left toward the church and I saw my home for the upcoming week. Sacred Heart was painted white with brown trim. It stood on a small, grassy knoll.

We drove around to the back where other members of my youth group, including its leaders, Ken and Michelle Barrie, had already arrived. I slowly climbed out of the car and took my things from the trunk. Michelle immediately and enthusiastically asked if I knew how to drive a Bobcat. Before I could respond (or ask what a Bobcat was—a brand of small skid loader, it turned out), she told me that trucks were coming to haul hundreds of pounds of rich, black soil to the church, so we would need shovels, rakes, and someone to push the dirt around in a Bobcat. In time I also learned that Sister Pat, one of the two nuns living at Sacred Heart, wanted to build a prayer garden, but that nothing could grow in the sandy soil currently there. Michelle explained that each of our tasks this week would have a particular name. Our first was dubbed "Black Gold."

* * *

As a young man, Will Carter lived around the manufacturing capitals of Pittsburgh and Chicago, but he felt something lacking in the clamor and complications of mid-twentieth-century urban life. So he turned to the wisdom of earlier centuries for insight. After researching his family genealogy, Carter adopted the name of Basu, a one-word name shared by his great-grandfather and derived from the Basula tribe in the Zaire region of Central Africa of which his ancestors were members.[1] He decided to emulate them further by relocating to the country, so in the early 1980s he and his wife, Pamela Ward Basu, moved to her hometown of Hopkins Park.[2] Basu continued to work in Chicago for a while, including for Moscickis Realty by promoting and selling parcels in Pembroke Township to black families living in Chicago's South Side.[3] Eventually he and Pam made a decision to "wean ourselves off the city . . . off of dependency altogether."[4]

Now they own Basu Natural Farms, a sustainable agricultural operation located on forty-three acres immediately north of Hopkins Park. The Basus do not use any chemicals on their land, but refresh its nutrients by rotating more traditional crops like corn with legumes, sweet potatoes, peanuts, and several other less common fruits and vegetables—all of which are weeded and harvested by hand. According to Basu, who encourages customers to pick their own vegetables from his fields, "You've got to treat the earth like your mother. Would you dip your mother in chemicals?"

Basu also recognizes a kinship with another tribe, the Potawatomi, who used to inhabit this area of the Midwest and called their surroundings "Mskoda," a word for prairie. "Nobody needed to tell Native Americans to maintain the land, they were already doing it. They were doing it. So are we," he explained. To that end, Basu and Pam have gone beyond organic farming and embraced other methods for living sustainably. No power lines connect to Basu Natural Farms; instead, the Basus use solar panels to light their residence, and they burn corn pelt for heating. "A field of corn can provide you with food, but also enough heat for the whole winter," said Basu, who also maintains the old Potawatomi trails on his property and collects tribal artifacts he finds there, including arrowheads, pottery, and campfire stones. "We are the new Potawatomi."

Basu expresses his frustration when he hears of stories that solely discuss the negatives of life in Pembroke. "Only crime, prostitution, distilleries, and moonshine . . . it seems to be the only thing presented. You never hear about the master's degrees and PhDs of people living here according to their choice." He continued, "We have history in Pembroke. We choose to live this lifestyle. We've come here for a reason. We want to be people in the country."[5]

The Basus and other "people in the country" have embraced a philosophy of sustainability and self-sufficiency. Dozens of families in Pembroke have signed up for classes taught jointly by the Basus and the University of Illinois Extension Service on crop rotations and the certification process for organic farming. Others work to develop their own ways of living sustainably.[6] A deep green streak runs through the personality of Pembroke, and in order to understand the community today and its fundamental regard for the land, it is necessary to look centuries, even millennia, into the past to see how the land became worth protecting.

According to this natural history, glaciers flattened most of the Midwest into a sweeping prairie, but in the area that would become Pembroke, the masses of ice created swamps and sand dunes that attracted plants and wildlife unseen throughout the rest of the region. For over ten thousand years, a delicate balance of growth, destruction by blazing wildfires, and regrowth gave rise to the beautiful, extraordinary habitat known as the black oak savanna.

The arrival of humanity to the area did not disturb the local ecosystem. Early inhabitants like the Potawatomi hunted and pulled what they could from the ground, but they operated in sync with the prevailing natural patterns. During the eighteenth century landowners used new technologies to alter those patterns and transform the land for mass agriculture. Across the state line in Indiana, swamps were drained and dunes were leveled. However, for a number of political and economic reasons unrelated to the land or people in Pembroke, the artificial modifications were not made in Illinois. Thus, the steamroller of progress would miss Pembroke, which largely remained in its original state. Pembroke's early history was a series of common natural events and ordinary human actions that interacted in uncommon, unordinary ways to distinguish the land from its surroundings and make it a sanctuary for individuals like Basu.

In the last million years, Pembroke was often covered by more than black soil or beige sand. Indeed, white ice lay atop much of North America at four separate times during this period. Prevailing average temperatures dropped for millennia at a time, allowing huge glaciers to form and roll across the continent. The solid yet mobile glacial ice traveled with intense erosive forces. The extreme pressure created by accumulation and gravity caused the ice sheets to expand and scrape across the bedrock underneath. The glaciers often took several feet of the rock along with them, resulting in an ice-gravel mix above and leaving a flat—almost polished—surface beneath.[7]

Four named glaciers traveled across the region: the Nebraskan, the Kansan, the Illinoian, and the Wisconsinan, from earliest to most recent. In some ways, a glacier merely enhanced the topographical impact of those previous. For example, the repeated scraping of the landscape generated the Midwest's uniform, level terrain. Also the Great Lakes, which existed as thin river valleys before the glacial period, deepened through a regular pattern of glacial formation. The lakes were created when snow first accumulated in Newfoundland, hardened into ice, and flowed down into New England, continuing in a southwestern direction until being slowed by the hills of New York and Pennsylvania. Eventually the ice overtook the Appalachian Mountains and entered the open territory of the Midwest. The four glaciers traveled in common paths that carved deeper into soft rock beds that have become the modern Great Lakes.[8]

In other areas, each glacier exerted its own unique impact on the midwestern landscape. Although many changes were wiped away during the subsequent ice age, the effects of the Wisconsinan glacier, the most recent, remain visible.[9] These include the swampy marshland and sand dunes that populate the otherwise level, fertile surface near the northern Illinois–Indiana border.

At its zenith approximately twenty-four thousand years ago, the Wisconsinan glacier extended to the area just south of Lake Michigan.[10] Forces within the ice sheet pushed the drift material of rocks, sand, and dirt toward the edge, where it collected. The seasonal variation of temperature caused the perimeter to expand and shrink annually, forming moraines, or ridges of ice-gravel parallel to the glacier's edge.[11] When the Wisconsinan began to melt approximately seventeen thousand years ago, it did not do so evenly. Huge ponds and streams collected on top of the glacier as well as inside and underneath it. The large amounts of water eventually escaped and rushed from the moraines onto the flat land below.[12]

Just south of the Wisconsinan glacier flowed the Kankakee River, a remnant of earlier glaciers that predated the Great Lakes and served as a runoff to several surrounding river basins.[13] However, the melting of the

Wisconsinan glacier pushed the river well beyond its limit. An enduring ice sheet to the east prevented melting Wisconsinan water from escaping in that direction, so the water flowed south and west into the Kankakee, Vermillion, and Fox River Valleys.[14] The melting ice also reduced the massive load on the land beneath Lake Michigan, causing the lake's bottom to expand upward and empty even more water into the surrounding area.[15] These flood events created the Kankakee Torrent, which was ten times the normal size of the river.[16]

Before the floodwaters swept down from the moraines, they picked up much of the sand, gravel, rock, and other sediment that had accumulated at the glacier's edge. Once the waters hit the flat land, they slowed and dropped their cargo.[17] In this fashion, large amounts of otherwise anomalous drift material fell in a semicircle around the southern edge of Lake Michigan.[18]

For the most part, the Kankakee River runs parallel to the southern curve of Lake Michigan, generally between thirty-five and forty-five miles south of it. The river begins near modern-day South Bend, Indiana, and travels southeast to the city of Kankakee before turning northward and ultimately emptying into the Illinois River. As a result of the torrent and the massive amounts of sediment that settled to the ground, the eastern half of the Kankakee River Valley became a swamp.[19] Here the floodwaters destroyed the river's ability to hold its contents within any defined banks. Instead, the river became more of a network of streams and creeks that meandered through marshy wetland.[20] Where a straight line between certain points of the river would be 80 miles on a map, its curves and bends extended the distance between those points on the river's actual course to 240 miles.[21] This area, which became known as the Grand Kankakee Marsh, was the country's second largest wetlands behind the Everglades.[22]

Some of the sediment was deposited differently, creating tall sand dunes and unique ecosystems. After the rush of the Kankakee Torrent, the land drained relatively quickly through several small streams. As the sand dried, winds collected it into small piles that eventually grew into dunes hundreds of feet tall.[23] Such dunes are unstable until vegetative growth takes root within them. However, only certain types of grasses, shrubs, bushes, and trees can withstand the difficult growing conditions of dunes. Although the elevated sands receive the same temperature, light, rain, and wind as the surrounding marshland and prairies, where plant life readily grows, the dunes have a limited capacity to hold water and heat. This causes the temperature to vary greatly between day and night.[24] The sand also lacks many of the nutrients found in black topsoil—particularly nitrogen—that enable lush growth. Moreover, biodegrading leaves, dropped annually by plants, cause the sand to become more acidic, which makes the nutrients more soluble and allows them to wash away more easily. The system eventually finds a balance between what enters and exits the sand, but dune vegetation nonetheless must be efficient in the face of limited resources.[25]

The sands of Pembroke became, and remain today, a savanna, a type of transition ecosystem between prairies and forests—meaning they contain both large trees and open, grassy spaces.[26] Fires that occur every two or three years sustain the balance of plant life. They often occur naturally as the result of lightning strikes, and they are contained by swales between dunes that serve as natural firebreaks.[27] The blazes kill grasses, shrubs, and young tree saplings, but older trees are able to survive. Where the average period between fires is less than two years, no trees can take root. Low-lying plants reestablish themselves more quickly, thereby turning the land into a prairie. Where the average period between fires exceeds three years, the trees grow and crowd out the smaller plants. In these situations, the savanna eventually becomes a forest.[28]

In several respects, the ecosystem of Pembroke resembles an island. The Grand Kankakee Marsh is itself unusual compared to the prairies of Illinois and Indiana, and the dunes represent an additional type of isolation. As a result, Pembroke is home to over thirty species of plants and animals that do not inhabit the surrounding area of Illinois or Indiana.[29] In addition, the species themselves are uncommon. Twenty-two plant species that inhabit Pembroke have been classified as rare. Pembroke is the only known location of the yellow false indigo in Illinois.[30] The orange-fringed orchid grows in low numbers in the Mid-Atlantic, Southeast, and a small strip of land through Michigan, but Pembroke contains a large concentration of this endangered, long-stemmed, and spurred flower.[31] Other unusual plants in the area include the wild lupine, cinnamon fern, starry false Solomon's seal, black chokecherry, low-bush blueberry, black huckleberry, and lance-leaved violet.[32]

The signature plant species of the Pembroke sands, though, is the black oak, whose leaves are identified by pointed, bristle-tipped lobes. According to the Nature Conservancy, Pembroke holds the world's largest concentration of high-quality black oaks, which thrive in the dry sand savanna.[33] Before the arrival of European settlers, approximately 27 million to 32 million acres of oak savanna grew in the Midwest, but by 1985 only 6,400 such acres existed—just 0.02 percent of the original acreage.[34] An even smaller portion of this land contains black oak savanna like that found in Pembroke.

The wildlife of Pembroke is similarly uncommon. Although the ornate box turtle primarily lives in the territory from Texas to the southern Great Plains, many live in a narrow swath across northeastern Illinois and northwestern Indiana. This turtle has a brown shell with yellow bands that differs from that of the more common eastern box turtle. Pembroke's regal fritillary is a large orange and black butterfly that resembles the monarch but exists in far fewer numbers. The western glass lizard is a legless reptile that differs from a snake in that it has moveable eyelids, external ear openings, and a tail that readily breaks off from its body. It primarily inhabits territory in the American South around the Mississippi River, as well as Pembroke. The pocket plains gopher resides in the column of states from Texas up to Minnesota, but it also lives in Pembroke where it digs a labyrinth of prominent underground tunnels. Other rare animals in Pembroke include the greater prairie chicken, red-tailed hawk, American kestrel, red-headed woodpecker, grasshopper sparrow, meadow vole, blue racer snake, coyote, badger, and until relatively recently, American buffalo.[35]

Although some spots within Pembroke still appear untouched by humanity, the first humans to visit the region were Paleoindians, who came to the area over ten thousand years ago and hunted mammoth, elk, and caribou. Nomadic groups continued to hunt the land until approximately three thousand years ago, when Early Woodland people began to supplement their game by growing squash, gourds, sunflowers, and eventually corn. Over sixty permanent sites of the Upper Mississippian people have been uncovered in the area and dated as early as the eleventh century. Members of the Miami, Mascouten, and Kickapoo tribes settled in Pembroke as well.[36]

By the seventeenth century, the most prominent and powerful tribe of the region was the Potawatomi, whose name means "People of the Place of Fire." The tribe originated in the Northeast but migrated further inland during the fifteenth century to what would become northern Illinois.[37] Relations with the earlier tribes of the region were usually frayed because those tribes viewed the Potawatomi as squatters with no legitimate claim to the land. Nonetheless, the Potawatomi put down settlements in the Mskoda of what is now Chicago and along the Illinois, Kankakee, and Iroquois Rivers.[38]

The Potawatomi were self-sufficient and independent. Even among themselves, they confederated loosely as a tribe with constantly changing alliances. They lived in small, autonomous groups that joined together only once a year for a large buffalo hunt. Otherwise, the Potawatomi cultivated squash, corn, and beans. They resided in bark-covered lodges during the summers and dome-shaped wigwams during winters.[39]

The first Europeans to explore the Midwest, and particularly northeastern Illinois, were the French. In 1673 the team of Louis Joliet and Father Jacques Marquette traversed the Illinois and Des Plaines Rivers on their return trip from "discovering" the Mississippi River. They came back to the region two years later, this time likely using the Kankakee River.[40] In 1679 René-Robert Cavelier, Sieur de la Salle (Cavelier de la Salle) explored the region, claiming the entire Mississippi basin for France.[41]

During the early eighteenth century, settlement in Illinois was concentrated to the south along the Ohio River, but the abundant wildlife soon attracted French and English fur traders to the north. These traders eventually moved to the region to establish limited commercial trails. Immediately after the Constitutional Convention, Congress passed the Northwest Ordinance of 1787, which established the Northwest Territory, set its borders, and prohibited slavery therein.[42] More Americans then migrated from the Northeast and Mid-Atlantic in order to take advantage of the fur trade. John Jacob Astor, one of America's first multimillionaires, founded the American Fur Company in 1808.[43] He quickly set up and expanded operations around the Great Lakes, including in the Kankakee River Valley. Surrounding the War of 1812, the United States enacted a series of protectionist measures, including a prohibition of fur trading with Europeans. As a result, Astor and his company grew and developed a strong control of the industry.[44]

One young man employed by Astor as an apprentice clerk was Gurdon S. Hubbard. In late 1821 Astor assigned the nineteen-year-old Hubbard to a post on the Iroquois River, which originates from the Kankakee River and flows south. The following year Hubbard and Noel LeVasseur, another employee of the American Fur Company, set up a trading post on the Iroquois. Hubbard interacted and traded with the Potawatomi and Kickapoo tribes, learning to speak their languages and marrying the daughter of Chief Waba of the Kickapoo, thereby becoming the chief's adopted son.[45]

Hubbard developed a series of trails while trapping, including the longest and most prominent one stretching from Vincennes, Indiana, to Fort Dearborn, the U.S. military outpost at the site of modern-day Chicago. This trail, which became known as Hubbard's Trace, cut directly through modern-day Pembroke Township where, as Hubbard wrote in his autobiography, he used to hunt the abundant geese and ducks.[46] Hubbard's trade and personal wealth expanded considerably. In 1834 he moved north to the community quickly growing at the site of former Fort Dearborn. Here Hubbard became a wealthy warehouse and stockyard merchant, as well as one of the early trustees of the Village of Chicago.[47]

Other fur trappers provided detailed, yet at times contradictory, descriptions of what is now Pembroke Township. In 1827 Hezekiah Cunningham marched with Hubbard from Danville to Chicago, and he wrote:

> The only good water we got going out or coming back was at a remarkable spring bursting out of the top of a little mound in the midst of a slough, a few miles south of the Kankakee. I shall never forget this spring; it was a curiosity, found in the situation I have described.[48]

Solon Robinson, who moved with his family to a nearby location in Indiana in 1834, had a different perspective:

> A very erroneous impression has been long impressed upon the public in regard to the country purchased of the Potawatamies in 1832, lying within this state. It has ever been represented upon the map of the state as one immense swamp—But instead of that being the fact, it is directly the contrary. Ten thousand acres of high dry Prairie, to one of swamp, is more correct.[49]

Although their accounts diverge, both Cunningham and Robinson evince their surprise at what they found in lands around Pembroke.

The fur trappers operated in the relatively lawless environment of unsettled Illinois. In *Tales from a Vanishing River*, Earl Reed described the area as a remote and rustic swampland, filled with muskrat trappers and land squatters. Many of the trappers did not actually live in the area; instead, they took temporary residence in one of the many local tavern-hotels.[50] As written in an early twentieth-century history of Kankakee County, "The very early pioneers were tavern keepers, who located on the great thoroughfare leading to the metropolis of the west."[51] The name Pembroke itself comes from the name of one of the taverns along Hubbard's Trace.[52]

Some of the trappers, like Hubbard, maintained (and profited from) good relations with the native people. However, other facts suggest a history of distrust and animosity. In fact, the sacking of Fort Dearborn during the War of 1812 was planned and launched from Pembroke. Although the Potawatomi normally lived in entirely separate groups, Potawatomi chiefs Neskotnemek and Main Poche convinced chiefs Shabonna and Waubanse to join with the British and attack the American military installation. The Potawatomi warriors departed from Pembroke and traveled northward.

As a result of the attack, 148 people were killed and the fort was burned to the ground.[53]

By 1830 the Potawatomi resided on small tracts of land in and near Pembroke. Although a treaty expressly ceded land to them in 1833, the United States soon extinguished the Potawatomi's title to it.[54] According to Solon Robinson in 1834, "There appears to be but few Indians now in the country," and "they are frequently at my house to swap. . . ."[55] In 1836 the United States gave the Potawatomi two years to leave the state. Most did so, but many remained. According to one historian, the "stragglers remained on the fringes of white settlements and society while other integrated themselves into the now dominant culture."[56]

The area remained relatively undeveloped until 1850, when construction of the Illinois Central Railroad fundamentally altered the region. As William Ferguson wrote in his 1855 account of riding the Illinois Central, "Until this railway was made, this part of the state was quite inaccessible."[57] People could now move farther into the prairies and transport their crops using the rail instead of being limited to waterway settlements. On February 11, 1853, Kankakee County, one of Illinois' last to be formed, was organized from lands of Will and Iroquois Counties.[58]

In 1871 a second railroad became operational through Kankakee County: the Chicago, Danville & Vincennes Railroad, which would later become the Chicago & Eastern Illinois Railroad (C&EI). The line largely paralleled Hubbard's Trace, including its path through Pembroke.[59] On February 17, 1877, the 26,240 acres in the southeast corner of Kankakee County were organized into Pembroke Township, townships being defined in Illinois law as a level of governance beneath the county with certain limited areas of jurisdiction.[60] By 1883 the township had 223 inhabitants.[61] Five years later two of those inhabitants, John and Cary Hopkins deeded forty acres for the purpose of building a town. They also sold land to the C&EI Railroad, which began providing service to the new community of Hopkins Park.[62]

Pembroke's reputation for quality hunting continued to grow. Although some fur trapping and commercial hunting continued, the recreational pursuit of Pembroke's waterfowl, prairie chicken, pheasants, squirrels, foxes, and minx became particularly popular among the elite of Chicago and the East Coast.[63] During the 1880s both Grover Cleveland and Theodore Roosevelt hunted in Pembroke before advancing to the White House.[64] The hunters, sometimes accompanied by their families who picked blueberries, blackberries, and other wild fruit in the scenic environment, typically rode the train from Chicago to Hopkins Park in the morning and returned to the city by nightfall.[65]

Railroads were not the only technological advancement that permitted midwestern agriculture to develop. In 1837 John Deere perfected a cast-steel plow that reduced the time and effort needed for farming and incited a growing demand for open, agricultural land. While the prairie possessed good soil and required little effort to cultivate, the same could not be said for the swampy marshlands or the sandy dunes. In Indiana, however, the natural obstacle of the Grand Kankakee Marsh did not thwart the drive for agricultural progress. Some individuals bought land in order to transform it from "a haven for cranes to a home for corn," as Robert Reber described it. The largest land baron was Lemuel Milk, who acquired twenty-five thousand acres in Iroquois County and forty thousand acres in Newton County (immediately across the state line from Pembroke). Using his personal wealth, Milk drained over nine thousand acres of wetland.[66]

The State of Indiana also financed the conversion of its portion of the marsh. In 1853 Indiana unsuccessfully tried to drain the sixteen thousand acres of open water at Beaver Lake by digging a ditch from the lake to the Kankakee River. In 1882 John Campbell, Indiana's chief engineer, suggested in a report that the state should drain the marsh by channeling the winding Kankakee River into a uniform drainage ditch. The project began when Newton County's first steam-powered dredge became operational in 1884.[67] These dredges transformed the curving, swampy path of the river into a clear, defined canal. There the water could collect quickly and continue downstream, thereby reducing the risk of incessant flooding.

Although draining the swamp was good for farming, it severely disrupted the rare ecosystem. Reverend Timothy Ball described the impact in his nineteenth-century history of northwest Indiana:

> Now, nearly all is changed by the spade and the dredging machine of man's invention. The water in springtime runs off in straight lines, man's object being to get it from the land into the river and ocean as quickly as possible. He wants the use of all the land surface. And so thousands and thousands of acres where once the wild fowls had their resorts and where muskrats and mink and otter had their homes, are now pasture land and oat fields, and corn fields and the ditches mar the landscape's beauty.[68]

Illinois stood to achieve fewer benefits than Indiana from draining its portion of the marsh or straightening its half of the river. Although drainage would have opened up some land, particularly in Pembroke, the amount was considerably less than in Indiana. Further, draining the marsh in Indiana actually caused greater harm to Illinois fields downstream because the project decreased the buffering capacity of the Kankakee River. This increased flow of water led to floods further west in Illinois. A few private landowners in Pembroke bought their own dredges and cut approximately thirty miles of drainage ditches, but the Illinois government refused to sponsor the same sorts of large-scale dredging projects as Indiana.[69] After considerable effort, Indiana completed the transformation by draining Beaver Lake in 1916 and straightening its portion of the Kankakee River in 1918.[70]

The differences on the issue of drainage between Indiana and Illinois manifest themselves most clearly where the Kankakee River crosses the state line. On the eastern side, the river is wide and perfectly straight as it cuts neatly across the agricultural grid of Indiana. On the western side, the river immediately resumes its natural, snakelike course through Illinois. Several tiny creeks separate from the river. Some rejoin the river downstream, but others meander to their own destinations.

Thus, Pembroke Township remained relatively untouched—inhospitable to corn, soybeans, and mechanical tractors, but welcoming to the black oaks. After walking through a portion of the savanna in 2006, naturalist Michael Jeffords offered this description:

> I see no human disturbances, only rolling, sandy hills punctuated with black oaks and the occasional pin and Hill's oak. Ornate box turtles corkscrew themselves into the sand to regulate their body temperature, regal fritillary males flit low through the vegetation, awaiting the later emerging females, and a blur across the sand materializes into a slender glass lizard. Everywhere the mounds of pocket gophers appear like tiny ancient volcanoes, long dormant with their vents sealed over.

In Jeffords's words, "Hiking through this landscape is like going back in time."[71]

2

Pap and Mary Tetter

There was no time to start working on "Black Gold," our first project. No time to get a better sense of my bearings or to find exactly where I would be sleeping in the church basement. Just half an hour after arriving in Pembroke, we all piled into Sacred Heart's small sanctuary. I admit groaning a bit when Ken and Michelle told us that we were going to church for a revival. The Sacred Heart community had organized a series of communal, spiritual services for our first few evenings in town. The composition of the gathered assembly consisted of elders and teens, hosts and guests, black and white.

Father Tony Taschetta stood at the front of the church to lead the revival. I already knew Father Tony from back home. I also knew that he was a powerful, dynamic speaker and that his boisterous, Italian-American voice tended to carry throughout the church when he sang. But I soon learned something new about Father Tony. Before working in Kankakee, he had been here at Sacred Heart as its resident pastor. He hugged several people as he entered during the processional song, telling his former parishioners how good it felt to be back among family.

The revival included a shortened Catholic mass, but there was a more striking emphasis on singing and preaching. The music ran longer than usual because chorus leaders repeated hymn verses two or three times while people moved and clapped to the rhythm. You could hear Father Tony sing, but here he wasn't the only one. Every parishioner raised his or her voice too—just as loudly, just as lively, and at times, just as off key. One woman in particular took special delight in the evening. Before she got up to read from the Bible, Father Tony introduced her as Gertrude Higginbottom. I sat in my pew and watched her enthusiastic worship with curiosity. Ms. Higginbottom called us all her "children" and punctuated each paragraph with a "Thank You, Jesus."

It was a spiritual service, but Father Tony delivered a scientific homily. He told us first to consider Velcro, the scratchy material inspired by the painful burrs that stick to pant legs in the woods. Velcro has hooks and loops that cling together, but they must be ripped away before fastening to something else.

Alternatively, he said, take Polytetrafluoroethylene, or Teflon as it's otherwise known. Teflon was discovered accidentally when a chemist found that his high-pressure tank of gas had created a smooth, silky, slippery substance. People soon learned to put Teflon on cookware and machinery to ensure that things didn't stick.

Father Tony then spoke specifically to us teens. He told us that this week we must be like Teflon. Not Velcro. This week we should be ready for the unexpected. We could not cling to our existing understandings, or what we already thought to be real. We should be ready to let go. In order to symbolize what he hoped we would feel this week, Father Tony gave us each a small piece of smooth, silky ribbon. With these in hand, we could be ready for a Teflon moment.

* * *

Pembroke abuts the border between Illinois and Indiana, each state proudly celebrating its ties to the Great Emancipator, Abraham Lincoln. One can follow an Illinois vehicle with its Land of Lincoln license plate past a welcome sign that announces Indiana as Abe's boyhood home. These states clearly take pride in the leadership of President Lincoln that kept the Union intact and abolished slavery. Yet even while Lincoln grew up in the "free states" of Illinois and Indiana—jurisdictions in which the Northwest Ordinance of 1787 expressly prohibited slavery and involuntary servitude—thousands of black Americans there were encumbered by enforceable labor contracts that amounted to legally sanctioned bondage. In spite of these obstacles, a small number of predominantly black towns were established throughout Indiana and Illinois; however, even there, harmful vestiges of slavery impacted daily life.

Pembroke was one such town. Around the time President Lincoln left Illinois to move into the White House, Joseph "Pap" Tetter, his wife Mary Eliza Tetter, and their family arrived in Illinois by caravan from the Southeast and chose to build a community in a corner of the newly organized Kankakee County. Pembroke Township had not yet been dedicated, nor would it be for over a decade. Other families soon joined the Tetters, but these dark-skinned farmers were separated from the rest of the county by a chasm of ignorance and speculation. Tales from within Pembroke describe life as normal, with memories of one-room schoolhouses and box socials, but descriptions from outside reveal confusion and resentment toward the community. Against this historical backdrop of repression and isolation, Pembroke forged its identity.

Slavery came to the Midwest along with the earliest European settlements in the Ohio River Valley. After the expedition of Joliet and Marquette in 1673, French settlers established villages along the river and had African slaves assist them with subsistence farming and domestic tasks. As of 1750, over three hundred black slaves inhabited the lands that would become Illinois, and more slave owners from Virginia and other southern states continued to move into the Valley.[1]

The Northwest Territory was established in the summer of 1787 by the Continental Congress, which remained in session in New York even while the Constitutional Convention met in Philadelphia. On July 13 of that year, one day after convention leaders reached their three-fifths compromise that assigned fractional representation to enslaved black Americans, the Continental Congress passed the Northwest Ordinance.[2] The law defined boundaries of the Northwest Territory, provided a basic governance structure, set a procedural path to eventual statehood, and declared certain enumerated rights for the inhabitants of the territory. The most notable right was contained in Article VI and stated, "There shall be neither slavery nor involuntary servitude in the said territory. . . ."[3] Thus, despite the Founding Fathers' willingness to agree to a constitutional provision defining slaves as three-fifths of a person, they concurrently acted to contain the spread of slavery, at least in the Northern lands.

Shortly thereafter, inhabitants of the Indiana Territory (which was divided from the Northwest Territory in 1800 but still included modern Illinois) petitioned Congress to rescind or relax temporarily the prohibition of slavery in Article VI. In 1802 a convention led by then–territorial governor William Henry Harrison passed a petition to the U.S. Congress arguing that the slavery ban prevented growth in the territory by causing slave owners merely to pass through the crossroads of Indiana rather than settle there.[4] According to an official proclamation made by the Indiana Territorial Legislature in 1807,

> Slavery now exists in the United States and in this Territory. It was the crime of England, their misfortune. And it now becomes a question merely of policy in what way the slaves are to be disposed of, that they may be least dangerous to the community, most useful to the proprietors, and by which their situations may be most ameliorated.[5]

When Congress repeatedly refused to alter Article VI, territorial leaders developed other means to circumvent it, in one instance by offering a legal interpretation that the Northwest Ordinance had no effect on slaves living in the Indiana Territory prior to passage of the ordinance in 1787. As such, these individuals remained slaves. Additionally, the territories instituted a *de facto* form of slavery through "Black Codes" that were just as restrictive as their counterparts in southern states. For example, in 1804 Indiana passed a law that permitted slave owners from other states to bring their slaves into the territory. The incoming slaves had to appear before a county official and give "free consent" to contracts of servitude that were specifically enforceable (a legal term meaning a party could sue to compel the other party to comply with the contractual terms rather than merely obtain monetary damages for any harm resulting from the breach). Duration of the contracts went as high as ninety years, and if any slave refused to consent, the master could make the slave return to the former state.[6]

Indiana lost many of its supporters of slavery in 1809 when it was divided, the western portion becoming the Illinois Territory. In Illinois, however, slavery nearly took permanent root. In addition to establishing a similarly harsh system of indentured servitude, Illinois passed its own Black Codes and banned free black people from migrating into the territory unless they already owned land or paid a $1,000 bond intended to show that the migrant would not become a drain on public resources.[7] When Illinois became a state in 1818, its constitution banned the further introduction of slaves but permitted existing slaves to remain. It also provided a specific exemption allowing slavery at the salt works in Shawneetown.[8]

By 1822 more opponents of slavery had moved into Illinois, and they narrowly elected as governor Edward Coles, a former slave owner turned abolitionist.[9] The pro-slavery forces subsequently initiated a campaign to call a new constitutional convention that would ensure protection of their "property rights." They argued that the Northwest Ordinance no longer applied to the sovereign state of Illinois, which could determine its own status as a free or slave state. Over the next two years, Illinoisans engaged in an intense—and at times violent—debate. Riots erupted on several occasions in front of Governor Coles's home in Vandalia. The people of Illinois ultimately rejected the permanent institution of slavery and voted to keep the original state constitution of 1818 by a vote of 6,640 to 4,952.[10]

Resistance to complete abolition continued in both states. Only after the Indiana Supreme Court held in 1820 that all slaves there were freed under the state's 1816 constitution did the number of slaves significantly decrease there. According to the census, the recorded number of black slaves and servants in Indiana dropped from 237 in 1810, to 190 in 1820, to 3 in 1830. In Illinois slavery was not actually outlawed until a new constitution was adopted in 1848. There the census reported that Illinois had 917 slaves and servants in 1820, dropping to 747 in 1830 and 331 in 1840.[11] Some white citizens nonetheless bucked the constitutional bans by keeping their servants in bondage through the Civil War, and the states' Black Codes were not repealed until the war's conclusion.[12] Although Illinois and Indiana were counted as "free states," such a label clearly requires a number of caveats.

Even with the heavily restrictive rules in place, including ones that banned migration of free black Americans into Illinois and Indiana, some skirted the laws or found loopholes allowing them to settle in these two states. Most were free people from slaveholding states like Virginia, North Carolina, and Kentucky, and many would have to trace their lineage back two or three generations to find someone who had been a slave. Despite these families' liberated status, their progress in the East was hindered.[13] Some had sufficient wealth to purchase a homestead, but land had become increasingly scarce, and even where it was available, white landowners often refused to deal with black buyers.[14] Further, a higher number of slave rebellions, like that of Nat Turner in 1831, generated an increasingly dangerous environment for black people—enslaved or free. So like most westward American travelers, they moved in order to expand and increase their holdings, but they also moved to escape hostility. When they did, they gravitated not to the larger cities but to remote, unsettled corners of the country. By 1860, nearly three-quarters of the sixty-four thousand African Americans in what used to be the Northwest Territory lived in unincorporated areas or villages with less than four thousand people.[15]

Two examples of black farming communities in Indiana were the towns of Beech and Roberts. Both preceded the first black settlements in Pembroke Township by thirty or forty years, but their histories likely bore similarities. According to oral accounts, a black family from North Carolina, the Waldens, left their home in the 1820s, and like the Tetters of Pembroke, traveled by caravan. Although the Waldens possessed the proper papers to prove their status as free people, they had heard tales of such papers being taken and destroyed while on the road. The settlers did indeed experience a tricky situation when several white men began to follow them. Rather than risk a return to slavery, Martha Walden, whose lighter skin could pass for white, pretended to be a supervisor of the others' transport, and the family was left unmolested. Eventually they arrived in Rush County, approximately fifty miles southeast of Indianapolis, and established a community that became known as Beech. News of the settlement spread, and a steady trickle of people continued to move there. Some, however, were not content to remain; in the late 1830s members of a family in Beech, the Roberts family, moved northwest to Hamilton County where they founded their eponymous town.[16]

In Beech and Roberts, the families purchased ample land from the federal government at low prices. According to historian Stephen Vincent, the cheap property "provided a livelihood as well as immunity from depredation. It gave them identity before the law and security in times of trouble." People there primarily made a living by farming, and those who did not own land could find work on others' farms. Relations with white neighbors remained strained, particularly as national and state politics became further embroiled in the issue of slavery. Indiana had technically outlawed slavery in 1816, but racist sentiments endured and resurfaced in 1851 when the state prohibited black Americans from entering the state and declared any contracts with a black person invalid. The laws stifled growth in Beech and Roberts. Although the towns survived through the Civil War, they were practically uninhabited before the end of the century as people moved toward economic opportunities in the factories of larger cities.[17]

Illinois had its own early black farming settlement: New Philadelphia. "Free" Frank McWorter was born a slave in South Carolina in the late eighteenth century. His master (who was believed to be his father) took McWorter to Kentucky, where he was able to illegally hire out his spare time for wages and operate a profitable but likewise illicit saltpeter business at night. McWorter bought his wife's freedom in 1817, his own in 1819, and eventually that of fourteen children and grandchildren. He purchased land from an Illinois physician, thereby exempting himself from the state's prohibition against black migration into Illinois.[18] In 1830 McWorter moved to western Illinois where he platted the town of New Philadelphia in 1836, making it the first community in the nation founded by a black American. Though often described as a black community, New Philadelphia could more accurately be described as "integrated." At its peak population in 1860, only 48 of the town's 160 inhabitants were black; the rest were white or Native American.[19] Some segregated conventions endured, like separate cemeteries for separate races, but others were ignored. For example, the children of New Philadelphia learned in an integrated schoolhouse.[20] By the beginning of the twentieth century, the town's population, like that of Beech and Roberts, moved to larger cities or towns with more economic options, leaving New Philadelphia in decline.[21]

Other black settlements were established close to the primary commercial conduits of nineteenth-century Illinois, the Ohio and Mississippi Rivers. These locations included Massac, Pulaski, Alexander, St. Clair, and Madison counties.[22] In 1819, a few years before his successful campaign for governor on an antislavery platform, Edward Coles freed the seventeen slaves he had inherited and used his position as register of the federal land office to help each family secure 160 acres near Edwardsville to build what was known as a "manumission colony." There newly freed people were encouraged to develop skills of self-sufficiency. While the settlement ultimately disbanded as people assimilated into various communities of the region, other nearby black towns like Brooklyn, Illinois, have been longer lasting.[23]

Brooklyn was established in the late 1820s by eleven black families who moved from Missouri to an undeveloped spot immediately across the Mississippi River from St. Louis. Several white families followed, but the community's racial majority remained black. In 1873 several of the white inhabitants officially incorporated Brooklyn as a village and elected a white mayor.[24] At that time, any free person could subdivide and plat a town that would remain subject to the county authority—as Free Frank McWorter did in New Philadelphia—but black citizens were not legally permitted to initiate the formal incorporation process and create a self-governing municipality.[25] Regardless, Brooklyn's black population continued to grow and mobilize politically. In 1886 Brooklyn likely became the nation's first town led by an African American when John Evans was elected mayor. Evans also helped to integrate Brooklyn's schools, but notably, a rival faction of black leadership assumed control of the school board in 1894 and (with white support) opted to resegregate their facilities. Historian Sundiata Keita Cha-Jua describes Brooklyn as an early manifestation of black nationalism where the community organized itself around issues of racial solidarity and empowerment to establish and control local governing institutions.[26] Comparable strands of this philosophy would later surface throughout Pembroke's history as well.

Although some people in these black settlements along Illinois' southern rivers began as farmers, the waterways provided access to jobs in the rapidly growing number of factories built close to the rivers.[27] Thus, while the industrial revolution of the late nineteenth century depleted the agrarian villages of Beech, Roberts, and New Philadelphia, black populations generally continued to grow in places like Brooklyn that were closely tied to an industrial base.

While many free black people came to the Midwest in search of economic freedom, a separate, more secretive movement came from the South during the mid-nineteenth century seeking their outright freedom. The famed Underground Railroad, an informal network of people who aided fugitive slaves to travel northward where they might leave slavery behind, operated in this area. Conductors included both white and black abolitionists who guided escapees from one station to the next. The railroad began in the early nineteenth century but reached its peak during the 1850s.

An estimated six thousand fugitive slaves traveled on the Underground Railroad in Illinois, which primarily operated along western routes that followed the Mississippi River through cities and towns like Chester, Alton, Quincy, Galesburg, and the Quad Cities—as well as New Philadelphia and Brooklyn—before turning east toward Chicago.[28] From there fugitives could continue to Canadian freedom by going east toward Detroit or north through Wisconsin and Minnesota. The Underground Railroad also had eastern routes in Illinois. It entered the southern portion of the state in Cairo or Chester, then traveled northeast through Decatur, Bloomington, Wilmington, and Joliet on its way to Chicago. Some maps extend the route as far east as the Illinois Central Railroad that runs through Kankakee County.[29]

Local legend marks Pembroke as a stop on the Underground Railroad. According to a 2009 article in the *Kankakee City News*, a newspaper serving the black community in the area, "The small population and isolation of Pembroke Township attracted runaway slaves as well as those freed by the

Emancipation Proclamation in 1863 and is believed to have been a major hub in the Underground Railroad."[30] Hopkins Park resident Basu has argued that the existing network of trails blazed by the Potawatomi were used by fugitive slaves.[31] Merlin Karlock, a white man who lived in Pembroke during the 1930s and who would play a significant role in the community's later development, recalled that Pap and Mary Tetter's son, Richard, referenced stories about "underground people" coming into the community years ago. According to Karlock, the Tetters provided lodging, but typically for no more than a night before the migrants were back on their way.[32]

Certain evidence reduces the likelihood that Pembroke was a prime stop for fugitive slaves. Even the earliest accounts of Pap and Mary Tetter's arrival put them in Pembroke around 1862, when Underground Railroad operations were winding down.[33] The Tetters were the first black people to settle that section of Kankakee County, and it is questionable that the few farmers and fur trappers there prior to the Tetters would have shown much hospitality to black refugees. Moreover, many historians believe that the western route of the railroad was the more frequently used path in Illinois, and the easternmost routes on their maps only run through Dwight or Wilmington, which are still over forty-five miles away from Pembroke.[34]

However, other evidence cuts against a categorical rejection of the local legend. For one, proof of Underground Railroad stops has been found in south Chicagoland suburbs like Crete, Illinois, and Dyer, Indiana, which are immediately north of Pembroke. Glennette Tilley Turner postulates that slave catchers regularly patrolled Chicago, leading conductors to bypass the city and guide the fugitives around suburbs along the south shore of Lake Michigan.[35] It may also be true that the easternmost routes of Illinois' Underground Railroad actually hugged the state border, thereby running through Pembroke. As Basu suggests, the Native American trails on the border, as well as those, like Hubbard's Trace, created by fur trappers are exactly the types of abandoned paths that fugitives would have traveled in secret.

Further, Pap and Mary Tetter may have been the first black family in what would become Pembroke Township, but they were not the first in the region. As early as 1852 there are records of black residents in Iroquois County just south of Pembroke, and Kankakee County had nineteen black residents by 1860.[36] When the Tetters arrived during the Civil War, the Underground Railroad may not have been fully operational, but a number of fugitive slaves or recently freed people still likely traveled northward. While the notion of Pembroke as a major hub of the Underground Railroad may be a stretch, it is certainly a possibility that some runaway slaves did journey through Pembroke or nearby territory.

According to relatively undisputed accounts, the Tetters came to Pembroke in covered wagons sometime between 1861 and 1864. They traveled with Pap's brother John Morgan and sister Sarah Morgan.[37] The Tetters also had a total of eighteen children, but seven would die at an early age from diphtheria.[38] After arriving in Pembroke, the Tetters and their family settled on a tract of land very close to the area now known as Old Hopkins Park where Sacred Heart Mission is located. Land in the area was cheap due to its remote location and poor soil quality, but the Tetters may have acquired their land through adverse possession, otherwise known as squatters' rights. According to records dated 1900, the Tetters ultimately took title to the land.[39] Other black families followed the Tetters' lead. Children of the Morgans established themselves there, and the Greenley family, one of the first black families to move to Iroquois County, also relocated to Pembroke after Sadie Greenley married Pap and Mary Tetter's son Richard in 1902.[40]

Additionally, multiple theories imbued with their own historical assumptions try to explain who the Tetters were and why they settled in a remote corner of the country. One origin story resembles that of the manumission colony near Edwardsville. According to Merlin Karlock, Pap Tetter used to be a slave of John Hopkins, for whom Hopkins Park was eventually named. Hopkins intended that his former slaves would have a fresh start in the area, and they traveled together in caravan from North Carolina. The new community was to be "a safe haven with no reason for commotion," said Karlock. Hopkins wanted seclusion so that he and his former slaves could isolate themselves from the turmoil that had overtaken and divided the country. According to Karlock, Hopkins was remembered in Pembroke for the respect he showed Tetter and his former slaves.

Dr. Jihad Muhammad of the African Scientific Research Institute (ASRI) posited a strikingly different theory. He suggested that Pap Tetter was born a slave but escaped to Illinois, where he acquired forty-two acres in the sparsely populated area. He then subdivided the land and sold the lots, using the money to assist families traveling on the Underground Railroad. When some of the refugees saw the Pembroke savanna, it reminded them of land in Africa or the American South, and many opted to stay with Tetter.[41] In 2005 Muhammad and the ASRI proposed launching an archeological excavation to find and examine the remains of Tetter's settlement,[42] believing the artifacts would tell "a chronicle of racial [uplift that] centers on the success of an African-American family and the ability to survive and prosper in a racist society of that era."[43]

Several descendants of Pap and Mary Tetter have told a third story, disagreeing not only with Muhammad's origin theory but also with the plans for excavating the old Tetter homestead. Soon after the ASRI announced the Hopkins Park project, certain family members publicly expressed their dissatisfaction. Rose Merrill, the last surviving grandchild of Pap and Mary Tetter, threatened legal action if the ancestral gravesite, which was located on the homestead, was disturbed. Merrill and her relative Vivian Lee also disagreed with accounts that Pap Tetter had ever been a slave. According to Lee, "I traced back as far as I could. If anyone else found anything about him being a slave, I don't know it."[44] Their understanding was that Tetter left North Carolina of his own accord and sought more land on which to grow crops and establish his family—much like the first residents of Beech and Roberts in Indiana and Brooklyn in Illinois.[45]

Tetter descendants also have their own understanding of Pap's and Mary's race. Their great-great-granddaughter Lana Higginbottom asserted that Pap was part French and that his descendants came from New Orleans.[46] Rose Merrill agreed: "I know what he was. That's my grandfather. He wasn't no slave. He was a Frenchman."[47] Records support the fact that Tetter was not 100 percent African American. Although the 1870 Kankakee County census lists Tetter as black, others list him as mulatto. Records also indicate that Mary Tetter was part Potawatomi.[48]

Thus, much like Free Frank McWorter's New Philadelphia, Pembroke was built from multiracial stock and operated according to a different set of racial rules than the rest of society. Some settlers sought to escape the burden of the traditional racial code, particularly those whose dark skin relegated them to second-class status elsewhere. Although the Tetters, Morgans, and Greenleys likely had some white relatives, even a fraction of black or Native American heritage would have set them apart from the contemporary white society in Kankakee County.

Yet it is also clear that some people deliberately sought to leave the white side of the color line. Around the turn of the twentieth century, one of Pap and Mary Tetter's sons, William, married a white woman named Ellen Collins. Her nephew, Arthur Collins, was born in Green Bay, Wisconsin, in 1917, and Arthur lived with his father and brother there until approximately 1927 when he moved to Kankakee County. "Dad brought us out from Green Bay in our old Hoynes car," he said. "I lived in St. Anne for five years. Then, I moved onto the eighty acres of Bill Tetter and Aunt Ellen."[49] Collins came to know new family, none of which was connected to him by blood. He eventually left the farm for the woods where he lived by himself without running water or electricity. Even after his aunt passed away, he still went to holiday meals with the extended Tetter family. Lana Higginbottom recalled childhood Thanksgivings and New Year's days spent with Collins. According to Higginbottom, "Art is white, but he'd say that he was black." Collins passed away in August 2013 at the age of ninety-six.[50]

Racial integration infiltrated certain aspects of daily life in Pembroke during the late nineteenth and early twentieth centuries. Like New Philadelphia and Brooklyn for a time, certain schools in the township had a racially mixed enrollment.[51] Black and white farmers sold supplies to and harvested crops with each other as needed.[52] Yet even within this diverse community, the racial divisions certainly did not disappear. Apparently threatened by the growing nonwhite population in Pembroke, white families often banded together and refused to sell their land to black farmers. Elvia Steward, who was born in 1916, recalled that her in-laws were only able to purchase their land from the Templetons, a white family, because Mr. Templeton became sick and needed money for his health care. According to Steward, the other white families ostracized him for the sale: "Before Mr. Templeton passed, they never went to see him while he was sick or anything."[53]

White and black families separated themselves in social settings as well. For example, like most small communities of the time, Pembroke residents sometimes gathered on weekend nights for "box socials." According to Rose Covington, women would make a dinner for two and put it into a box. Then the men would bid on the box and sit for a meal with its cook.[54] Merlin Karlock noted that men placed bids strategically "knowing either that Mrs. X made delicious pies or that Miss Y was the best looking gal." Although Covington and Karlock largely describe the same event, they never would have seen each other at a box social. Covington would have attended the black version, while Karlock would have been at the white counterpart.

The color line also manifested itself within interracial families, as differences in physical traits, even among siblings, caused division. Sara Tetter Schwartz described her family: "Some descendants show the Negro, some show the blend, and some cannot be distinguished from white."[55] Lana Higginbottom noted how skin hue affected which part of the family they identified with. Her mother Gertrude, née Tetter, had the darkest skin of her siblings. According to Lana, "We wouldn't even know we were related to some of the Tetters. . . . We were always the darkest family, so we didn't associate. Instead, we hung around more with the Higginbottom side of the family."

Race created some barriers within the early community of Pembroke, but these barriers were comparatively thin. Black and white residents were actually in contact and communication with one another, necessitating a different ethic and worldview than that of its neighbors. Because of this interaction, the rest of Kankakee County viewed Pembroke as distant, strange, and wrong. To them, it was a Dark Continent in the Midwest.

Though only twenty miles away, Kankakee residents did not and could not relate to Pembroke, and to a great degree, they ignored it. During the 1930s one of the local papers, the *Kankakee Daily Republican*, carried short columns about quotidian life in communities throughout the paper's circulating area. The paper reported on first communions and bake sales in tiny crossroads settlements like Cabery, Kempton, L'Erable, and even Tallmadge (a primarily white hamlet in northern Pembroke Township), but it did not mention the box socials in Hopkins Park.

The limited accounts of news in Pembroke consisted of eerie tales of criminal activity. An article in the *Kankakee Republican* from June 24, 1931, described "Fred and Elizabeth Estes, colored," who lived on a farm near Hopkins Park. The county sheriff was holding the couple as accomplices of an unknown, at-large white man who robbed another white man, F. O. Bicknell, at gunpoint. According to the report, the Esteses went to Bicknell's home, as they had done several times in the past, to discuss a sale of cattle. But when they entered, the assailant was behind them with a gun demanding money from Bicknell and the Esteses. Fred Estes turned over the only dollar he had, and he urged Bicknell to give all the cattle money as well. Papers from the subsequent weeks contained no follow-up of the encounter.[56]

Another *Kankakee Republican* piece from the mid-1930s was far more explicit in its characterization of Pembroke as bizarre and uncivilized. The article was entitled "Hopkins Park—A Bit of the Tennessee Hills" and confirmed rumors of "inter-marriages between Negros and whites, and of people who live like mountaineers and backwoodsmen of Tennessee." It continued, "There seems to be little respect for marriage laws in Hopkins Park. People live together frequently without the ceremony, and as one girl, eldest of four, put it, 'I don't know why mother and father haven't married. They just didn't, I guess.'" The race of people found in Pembroke also shocked the author, who wrote, "A strange mixture of blond hair and freckles is noticeable among dark skinned people, and one informant states that there is no child in school without some negro blood in his veins."[57]

Pembroke's isolation was not only racial, but economic. Development efforts either halted quickly or avoided the town altogether. On April 18, 1931, the *Daily Republican* ran a headline, "New Oil Well Seen at Pembroke." The article referenced the hope of the project's geologist and a rumor that oil once spouted from the ground during the laying of water pipes.[58] Not even a month later, however, both oil and optimism ran dry, and the paper reported, "Pembroke Oil Well Project Abandoned" after prospectors pulled their funding.[59]

When the advent of natural gas technology promised a cheaper, cleaner form of energy, a $75 million pipeline from the Texas panhandle was connected to Kankakee County. Extensions hooked the main line to Kankakee, Momence, and St. Anne. Despite the apparent proximity of Pembroke to any geometric line that would connect these three cities, it was not a recipient of this initial outlay of infrastructure.[60] To this day, Pembroke residents are not connected to a natural gas line.

Even though Pembroke's isolation made it less dependent on the national economy than other places, the *Kankakee Republican* article reported that the Great Depression still hit Pembroke hard. When the author interviewed a group congregating outside a general store, most demonstrated a "reluctance to speak of personal conditions."[61] One man stated that he was a member of a Kankakee labor union, but that he had not worked for nearly a year. He explained, "I'm not married, you see, and no single man has a chance of getting on the WPA [Works Progress Administration] around here. . . . Hopkins Park has no industries, no available jobs of any kind." The author also reported that the average income for a family of nine was $44 per month or $528 per year.

The Tetters and other early inhabitants of Pembroke, like people in other black towns in Indiana and Illinois, undertook an ambitious experiment by creating a new community. They constantly felt the effects of an institutionalized form of slavery in everything but name, yet they crafted a free way of life rooted in unorthodox constructs of race and culture. It was not, however, just these ideas about race that baffled people outside of Pembroke. The surprised Kankakee journalist also noted, "Though their living conditions are far below the average, reports state that they are content."

3

The Second Migration

Monday morning. 7:10 A.M. None of the others in the church base-
ment were awake, and no one would need to be up for another hour
or so. But I couldn't sleep. In fact, I had not been able to sleep much
at all last night. I should've known. Every time I slept somewhere
new, away from my normal bed back home, I didn't get any rest the
first night. This was no different.

Finally I got out of my bed, tiptoed through the maze of inflat-
able mattresses, and brushed my teeth. Although the basement had
working sinks, there were concerns about the well water quality out
here, so we were told to make use of the huge supply of bottled water
that we imported.

I decided to go for a run. I was on my own, but even at this early
hour, there were a few people on the roads. Some drove cars, tractors,
and ATVs while others walked. I would later write in my journal,
"Despite what people have said, this place seems safe. Friendly peo-
ple on all the roads. Waved to by almost everyone." When I returned
to Sacred Heart, people were moving about. The girls were gradually
coming over from the rectory where they were staying because Father
Tony was going to lead us on a tour of the blocks around Sacred
Heart, or what he called Old Hopkins Park.

The group met outside the front steps of the church. I stood and
chatted with some friends whom I had known for years. On the
other side of the gathering, I saw people like Adam, who was only

a sophomore but already on the varsity basketball team. He stood next to his older sister Angela, a senior and the unofficial leader of the youth group whose example we all watched and followed. I wondered if we would greet each other should we pass in the school hallways. Probably not.

Father Tony began the tour, strolling backward down the roughly paved street. He told us about Pap and Mary Tetter, the first black family in Pembroke who, almost a century and a half ago, settled very close to the spot where we stood now. Gertrude Higginbottom, who spoke the night before, was a great-granddaughter of the Tetters. Father Tony also told us that Pembroke grew when black people from farms in the southern United States decided they didn't like the city living of Chicago and moved here instead.

We passed a large blue shed, which Father Tony said was the Sacred Heart Re-sale Shop. He explained that the shop was established as a means to boost the local economy. The soil around Pembroke was too sandy for farming, which kept the land cheap enough for poor, black families to afford but offered little to improve their financial situation. The re-sale shop was a creative answer in a community that lacked a clothing, furniture, or appliance store. People donated or sold what they didn't need, and their neighbors bought what they did need at a low price. Somehow it worked.

We continued around the block, past a few small homes and a school. I walked and pondered what it would be like to be pushed out of the South then pushed out of Chicago. Even here residents were often separated from their neighbors by miles. What would it be like to live in that kind of isolation? Just then, I felt a hand slap my shoulder. I turned and saw Adam. "Hey, Dave. How's it going?" he said.

✴ ✴ ✴

Liberty entails the freedom to move, the ability to upend one's own life at will and seek a better one elsewhere. In 1863 Abraham Lincoln's Emancipation Proclamation freed slaves held in areas of the South that the Union did not control, and the remaining slaves received their freedom within a few months after the Civil War ended. By then most Northern states had also eliminated their restrictions on black migration into their territories, so black southerners technically had the freedom to relocate. Nonetheless, other constraints bound them to their longstanding homes. Moving required money and resources, and the prospect of leaving friends and family for an uncertain destination was daunting. The fundamental rule of inertia applied to humanity: people at rest tended to stay at rest, even when faced with scarcity and violence.

Yet at some point, the pressure to relocate reached critical levels. As with most mass migrations, it took a venturous few to leave before the reservoir crumbled and a torrent of people rushed forth. Between 1915 and 1970 approximately 6 million black Americans moved north of the Mason-Dixon Line.[1] One of the most significant movements was the initial wave that occurred between 1916 and 1919 when approximately five hundred thousand black Americans left their Southern homes. The Great Migration was the largest internal mass movement in the United States and forever changed the complexion of the country.[2]

Agnes Strong DeLacy took part in the mass exodus. She was born in 1905 in the small Mississippi Delta town of Shaw where she lived on a farm with her parents and ten siblings. Her great-grandmother had been a slave, and her family's economic standing in the South had not improved substantially since then. Strong DeLacy attended formal schooling until third grade, and at the age of fifteen she eloped with her first husband Dee Strong. In 1922 the newlyweds left Shaw and followed her relatives for the promise of industry and opportunity in Chicago.[3]

But for Strong DeLacy and many others, the journey did not end there. In the big city, her family found a different, more crowded version of scarcity and violence than existed in the rural South. Strong DeLacy, who ultimately had ten children, said that some landlords refused to rent to families with children, though she suspected this was merely subtext for excluding her family based on race. Her husband worked at the Chicago stockyards, but during the Depression, employment dried up. "Black people were losing their jobs, jumping out of windows," recalled Strong DeLacy.[4]

Her mind turned wistfully to the simpler life in Mississippi. She noted, "I was raised on a farm. I like farming and gardening. I had chickens, hogs, and horses. We couldn't do that in Chicago." She likely saw abundant real estate fliers and posters with pictures of wide-open spaces only an hour from Chicago. "Only $5 down and $50 per month after that; Call Moscickis Realty," read the ads. Once again she packed her life and exercised her freedom to move. In 1937 Strong DeLacy and her family left Chicago with another migrant named Carl Lee. They settled in a small part of the southern portion of Pembroke Township that came to be known as Leesville.[5]

Strong DeLacy knew immediately that life would not be easy. "There wasn't no brick roads so you'd get stuck in the mud. There wasn't no inside bathroom either." Yet she finally felt free. "When we moved out here, it was nice. . . . In Chicago, you were in apartments. Here, you get your own yard." After Dee passed away in 1969, Agnes married her second husband, James DeLacy, with whom she continued farming and gardening until she was eighty-eight years old.[6] According to a history of Kankakee County, Agnes Strong DeLacy, who passed away in 2010 at the age of 104, was part of a "great influx of blacks in the 1930s and 40s [when] families fled the social ills of the South, and then the urban life of Chicago."[7]

Pembroke's history traces not only the river of people flowing north, but a smaller creek that turned away from the river and flowed back south. During this second leg of the journey, Strong DeLacy and others like her could be more confident in their move, not only because of the shorter distance but also because they had uprooted their livelihoods once and were not afraid to do it again.

Conditions in the rural South had always been difficult for former slaves and their families, but in many ways those conditions began to worsen during the first decade of the twentieth century. Agrarian communities tied to a cotton economy began to stagnate. The boll weevil, a small beetle that feeds on the buds of cotton plants, entered the United States from Mexico in 1892.[8] It spread to Louisiana by 1903 and Mississippi by 1907. This insect, as well as a particularly high number of storms and floods, devastated entire crops, increasing the uncertainty in the market. Cotton could no longer be sold before harvest under a futures contract, and credit otherwise dried up as banks identified new risks.[9] Moreover, most black farmers operated as sharecroppers. Under these arrangements, the sharecropper, or tenant, would supply the landowner with a certain quota of the crop each year in order to continue residing on the land. Cotton produced above the quota could be sold for the tenant's profit. Landowners sometimes failed to keep their end of the bargain and demanded more than the agreed-upon terms, leaving less for the tenant to sell. The boll weevil infestation and inclement weather only exacerbated the issue.[10]

The flagging cotton economy hurt the entire South, but prevailing racial attitudes piled on the burdens for black southerners. Leaders passed laws that hopelessly complicated the right to vote and distributed state resources

unequally. The specter of violence also weighed heavily upon black southerners. Between 1910 and 1919, 620 lynchings occurred in the United States,
most of which took place in the Deep South.[11]

Strained eyes began to look elsewhere and soon settled on northern
cities. Unlike the agrarian economy of the South, the manufacturing industry ran strong. During the century's first decade, northern factories and
stockyards were staffed primarily by European immigrants, but World War
I led to federal policy changes that caused the number of people entering
the country to drop from 1.2 million in 1914 to 110,000 in 1918. The war
required increased domestic production, so northern companies turned to
other sources of labor. Some sent agents to small southern towns to recruit
low-wage workers with promises of good pay and lasting employment.[12]

Chicago was an attractive location for black southerners, particularly
those in Alabama, Mississippi, and Louisiana because the Illinois Central
Railroad connected the Mississippi Delta to Chicago. Like the Ohio and
Mississippi Rivers attracted people to southern Illinois during the mid- and
late-nineteenth century, the growing transcontinental network of railroads
increased Chicago's appeal.[13] By 1910 over one hundred thousand black
people worked for America's railroads, often as stewards and porters.[14]
They returned home to the South with accounts of economic opportunity
and integrated public accommodations in the North.[15] Another source of
inspiration to relocate was the *Chicago Defender*, founded in 1905 by Robert
Abbot, which was the most widely read newspaper among black southerners (and would later cover news and issues in Pembroke Township). In 1916
the paper's circulation was 33,000, but by 1919 it rose to 130,000. Readers,
most of whom were not from Chicago, could read about the city's successful black citizens, nightlife on State Street, and the city's renowned Negro
League baseball team—the Chicago American Giants—who played games
throughout the South for a week during the summer. The paper promoted
the potential for black people in Chicago and documented brutal injustices
occurring in the South.

Some, like Booker T. Washington, argued that the South was and should
remain home for black people. He stated that he had "never seen any part of
the world where it seemed to me the masses of the Negro people would be
better off than right here in these Southern states." But others were ready
to move on. Even the *Defender* initially advocated staying in the South but
changed its position in 1916 when employment became readily available in
the North. The *Defender* then encouraged black Southerners "to run any
risk to get where they might be freer."[16]

Certain patterns emerged as the growing movement northward reached a critical mass. The first migrants often served as scouts and sent information back to friends and families. Other black southerners wrote to established institutions in Chicago like the *Defender* or the Urban League to get more information and to ask if the promises were true.[17] Many formed their own migration clubs, often between ten and eighty people, who could travel together. Churches also provided a means for organizing. Some congregations left together from the South and established a northern branch of their church.[18] Much like the passengers on the Underground Railroad, migrants regarded their journey as a sacred, biblical path to the Promised Land. Some held ceremonies and sang gospel hymns while crossing the Ohio River; others moved from their black-only railcar into one of the integrated cars as a celebration of their new rights.[19]

For many, the excitement quickly transformed to shock and confusion when they arrived at Chicago's Central Station located at Michigan Avenue and Twelfth Street.[20] Many had never been to a city or seen buildings larger than barns, and few had experienced a northern climate. The immediate transition was so jarring that the Travelers Aid Society and Urban League hired a "Colored Assistant" in 1917 to greet newcomers at the train station and provide some bearings.[21] Other social welfare organizations—ones led by both black and white people—provided migrants with resources, such as transitional housing and training, but many were still quite lost in their new environment.

Other whites, however, provided no hospitality to the new black residents. Racism in the North was subtler than its southern counterpart, but it was real. Historian Allan Spear described the difference:

> To compare the evolution of the Negro's status in Chicago with the crystallization of the caste system in the South during the same period was an exaggeration. Discrimination in Chicago remained unofficial, informal, and uncertain; the Negro's status did not become fixed. Nevertheless, as Negroes became more numerous and conspicuous, white hostility increased and Negroes encountered an ever more pervasive pattern of exclusion.[22]

Tensions were particularly notable between black migrants and white union members, many of whom were Catholic, European immigrants. Chicago's organized labor force was keenly aware that black replacement workers had been used during the strikes of Illinois coal workers in the 1890s, tradesmen in 1900, teamsters in 1905, and newsboys in 1912. Resentment of the "scab race" grew as its population increased.[23]

Some white Chicagoans may have been willing to sit next to a black person on a bus, but fewer were willing to live next to a black family. In 1909 the Hyde Park Improvement Protective Club released a statement arguing that black families should reside only in particular districts and that real estate agents should refuse sale of property to black people outside of these districts. Agents and developers refusing to comply faced boycotts. The club also created a committee that bought land from black homeowners already living in white areas or gave bonuses to black tenants that agreed to terminate their leases. According to Francis Harper, a prominent attorney and leader of the club, "The districts which are now white must remain white. There will be no compromise."[24]

The black migrants found themselves pushed into a limited number of neighborhoods in the city's West and South Sides, which included a strip of territory along South State Street known as the "Black Belt." In 1898 only 27.9 percent of the black population resided in predominantly black neighborhoods, but by 1920 the figure increased to 50.5 percent and continued upward in subsequent decades. Although housing in this limited territory was finite, its demand continued to increase as more migrants arrived. Unlike white flight purportedly caused by dropping property values, transitioning neighborhoods often saw increases in value. High demand regularly forced black buyers to pay a price much higher than previous white owners.[25]

Eventually the tensions erupted into the sort of violence that first prompted the Great Migration. When a black family refused to move from their home on Hyde Park's Greenwood Avenue, vandals broke into the home at night to encourage their reconsideration.[26] Between 1917 and 1921 black homes east of Cottage Grove Avenue were bombed fifty-eight times.[27] Some of Chicago's worst race riots occurred over seven days in the summer of 1919, the blame for which several white officials largely laid on the black community. Although the riots led to 28 black deaths versus 15 white deaths and 342 black injuries versus 195 white injuries, the first 34 people charged for riot activities by the state's attorney were all black.[28]

Johnny Murrell and his family moved to Chicago from Tampa in 1932. As the second black family in his neighborhood, he was threatened often: "They had gangs, white gangs and colored. They would fight. They would throw bricks through your windows. . . . You couldn't walk down the street lessen somebody would strong-armed you."[29]

Even before the initial waves of the Great Migration, the northern, black, farming communities of Beech, Roberts, and New Philadelphia were all deserted. People in these communities, like the migrants from the South, left to take advantage of economic opportunities in the larger cities and their immediately surrounding areas. This is why the populations of places like Brooklyn, Illinois, located close to St. Louis, expanded during the late-nineteenth century. But as Sundiata Keita Cha-Jua also notes, this rendered the community more dependent on the industrial economy of the region.[30] When the economy nearly collapsed on a global scale during the 1930s, there were even fewer jobs, homes, and resources available for black urbanites.

During and following the Great Depression, residential options in Chicago remained constrained by white resistance even though southern migrants continued moving to the city. Families adapted in a number of ways—for example, some divided small apartments into even smaller ones that unfortunately bred unhealthy, disease-ridden conditions. As sociologist Mary Pattillo-McCoy wrote, "Figuratively, the Black Belt fastened around an obese black community." Some were able to loosen the pressure by relocating to the immediate periphery of the Black Belt—whether in previously white neighborhoods or suburbs close to Chicago.[31] But an even smaller number looked far beyond city limits, turning their eyes to open fields. Notions of another Promised Land would attract them to one of the few rural, black communities left in the North.

According to an article in the *(Kankakee) Daily Journal*,

> Numerous Negro families who had moved from the south to Chicago soon found that the Negro ghettos in the Windy City were worse than the segregation of Mississippi and Alabama. So, they moved out of the city, into the country where there was plenty of fresh air and elbow room.[32]

Johnny Murrell was one such individual, as he eventually tired of conditions in Chicago. Seven years after moving north from Tampa he moved again to Pembroke. In Murrell's words, "We went out to the country for a better life, a better place to raise kids." He found Pembroke through a real estate firm based out of California with offices in Chicago. For a total of $695 he purchased five acres that abutted the Illinois-Indiana state line. Unlike many black migrants, Murrell had never lived on a farm, but he quickly took to agrarian life by raising chickens, hogs, and cattle. He also accustomed himself to the lack of local amenities. "Things were rough then ... I didn't think that I would ever see lights out there. I didn't think we'd ever have running water ... or sewers. We had an outhouse until '52." Yet on these five acres Murrell found some satisfaction: "It was much better than in Chicago."[33]

This second migration began during the 1940s when black relocation to Pembroke increased 72 percent from the decade before.[34] Whereas northern companies seeking inexpensive labor and institutions like the *Chicago Defender* seeking racial uplift promoted the Great Migration north, the external drivers of the Pembroke influx were real estate agents and developers. Several individuals and firms purchased land in Pembroke and advertised heavily in Chicago's Black Belt, offering the prospect of what had been unavailable both in the South and Chicago: land ownership.

Two of the individuals behind Pembroke's midcentury growth were Merlin Karlock and Frank Moscickis. Born in 1930, Karlock lived in Pembroke Township for the first twenty-nine years of his life. His was one of the white families in Pembroke at the time, but like most families there, regardless of race, the Karlocks were not wealthy. Indeed, they were evicted by a Momence bank when young Karlock was two years old. His entrepreneurial drive surfaced shortly thereafter. At age ten Karlock's grandfather said they could not store any more of their harvested hay, so he suggested that young Merlin take and sell the rest. Merlin filled his wagon with the hay, pulled it to a prime location on the Blacktop, and sold it for fifty cents per bale. Karlock came to know his black neighbors well through the nascent business. His endeavors grew, and he eventually opened the first of many banks very close to the one that had evicted his family decades earlier.[35]

Frank Moscickis was a member of a Greek immigrant family in Chicago and had no education beyond the sixth grade. His father sold properties in the city and first purchased land in Pembroke in 1926.[36] Although Moscickis did not initially want to join the family business, he convinced his father to subdivide and sell a particular tract in Pembroke. It sold quickly, and Frank soon expanded his involvement in the real estate operation.

Karlock and Moscickis met in the late 1940s when a local Pembroke school district listed a parcel for sale. The two men were the only individuals to bid on the property. Before determining a winner, the auctioneer called a recess. Karlock approached Moscickis and initiated a conversation. They decided to buy the lot together and split it in half. When the auction resumed, they placed one more joint bid at one dollar above the previous bid. A few days later the men could not decide who would get which portion of the parcel, so they became partners instead.

Through their association, the men purchased and subdivided a great deal of land in Pembroke. Karlock oversaw the legal work, and Moscickis led the sales efforts. According to one Moscickis brochure, the new subdivision of Willow Estates offered "the ultimate in tranquility, serenity, dignity, and security."[37] Another advertisement described "Choice Blacktop Homesites on Hopkins Park Road" available for forty-eight dollars per month.[38]

The Moscickis offices were located around Chicago's crowded South Side neighborhoods from which he hired black salespeople to promote the properties. Moscickis brought potential buyers down to Pembroke for weekend treks during which he showed the land.[39] Upon arrival, Chicagoans inevitably saw numerous red, white, and blue realty signs that read, for instance, "Moscickis Realty welcomes you to a growing community where people buy land and own part of 'America' forever."[40]

Moscickis and other developers sold the land using installment contracts, according to which a buyer made a small down payment and followed with regular monthly payments for a specified term. Reverend Louis Barnes, for example, signed a contract in 1958, put five dollars down, and made monthly payments of forty-five dollars for the next several years.[41] According to a 1966 survey of 242 Pembroke residents, 74 percent bought their land on contract, 21 percent paid cash, and only 5 percent financed their land with a mortgage.[42]

Unlike a mortgage, the deed to land sold under an installment contract did not pass to the buyer until all payments were made. Parties could agree in advance to a remedy of forfeiture so that if the buyer missed or was late with a payment, the seller could reclaim possession of the land without the need to institute costly foreclosure proceedings in court.[43] Installment contracts and forfeiture clauses permitted lower closing costs and down payments for individuals with poor or no credit. However, in practice, they could also lead to harsh results. Buyers gained no equity in their investments. They might make payments for several years only to lose the land toward the very end of the agreement for missing one payment. Moreover, defaulters on installment contracts received none of the benefits of foreclosure proceedings, including a redemption period of several months when the buyer could pay the default amount and still keep the property. Failing this, foreclosure laws required the court to hold a judicial sale to pay the debt so that a defaulter received at least a portion of his or her investment.[44]

In many ways, installment contracts were like a lease with monthly rent payments. In fact, a Moscickis ad once touted an installment contract with payments as "low as $48.00 per month like rent."[45] Despite the similarities, a buyer did not receive the guaranteed benefits of a lease, which include an implied warranty of inhabitability. This legal protection requires a landlord to keep premises in good, livable condition even if it was not included in the exact terms of the lease agreement.[46]

The Illinois Supreme Court held installment contracts and forfeiture clauses to be enforceable as early as 1927,[47] but over time courts chipped away at the forfeiture remedy and found more reasons to refuse enforcement. Such reasons included

> the prior acceptance of late payments and whether the buyer has been given a reasonable warning that the seller will insist on prompt payment in the future; the length of time involved in the delay and whether the default has been repeated; whether substantial payment has been made on the whole contract; whether the purchaser has substantially improved the property; and whether there has been a mere delay rather than a suspension of the payments.[48]

By the late 1970s an "equitable mortgage" doctrine—that treated almost all installment contracts as mortgages—became well established. According to one judicial opinion, "Courts of equity abhor forfeitures and will enforce them only where the right to forfeiture is clearly and unequivocally shown and injustice will not result."[49]

In 1986 the Illinois General Assembly mooted the courts' subjective equitable mortgage doctrine by passing a statute that required foreclosure proceedings on any installment contract for residential real estate with a term longer than five years where the amount unpaid was less than 80 percent of the original purchase price.[50] Therefore, if a buyer made one-fifth of the total installment payments, he or she received the protections of a mortgage. Even after the establishment of these judicial and legislative solutions to prevent particularly harsh forfeitures, people of little means still would have difficulty paying an attorney to enforce those rights. Developers in Pembroke were sometimes willing to renegotiate an installment contract or provide a defaulter with leeway, but it appears that a good number of individuals had their land repossessed.

Another peculiarity about Pembroke's development was the long, narrow shape into which the lots were subdivided, which resulted from loopholes created by Illinois' land use laws and enabled developers to avoid certain basic improvements to the area's infrastructure. During the early twentieth century the Illinois Plat Act required that, if the subdivision was "for the purpose of laying out a town," a developer must prepare a land survey and plat for the subdivision and register it with the county. However, by simply claiming the subdivision was not for that purpose, the developer did not need to hire an official surveyor to carefully measure the land or make capital investments for new streets, alleys, parks, playgrounds, and other basic infrastructure.[51]

In 1955 the legislature amended the Plat Act and replaced the purpose language with a new exemption for property that was subdivided into parcels larger than five acres and that did not require the creation of any new streets or easements in order to access each parcel.[52] Developers therefore could build free of the expensive plat requirements if they subdivided the land into long, thin strips with at least one of the narrow ends fronting an existing roadway where the owner could enter. These strangely shaped lots, however, would not connect to sewer, water, or electricity lines unless they were close to existing lines along the Blacktop. The Plat Act also permitted county and municipal governments to pass more stringent subdivision controls. Kankakee County ultimately did impose tighter restrictions, but they reportedly were not always followed or enforced. These practices led to the odd look of Pembroke's property map, which even today resembles a Venetian blind.[53]

The developers have faced criticism for their methods in Pembroke. According to a report commissioned through the Kankakeeland Community Action Program (KCAP) in 1966,

> During the decade or so after World War II, Pembroke Township saw the greatest increase in population. At this time, many families throughout the nation were looking for new housing. Much exploitation by real estate agents occurred in changing neighborhoods within [Chicago] to meet this demand for housing on the part of minority groups who usually had to purchase on contract. It is interesting to note that the first widespread selling of lots in Pembroke Township was also made by several of the same real estate agents who had profited from changing neighborhoods in Chicago.[54]

The report described problems caused by the lack of infrastructure permitted by the purposefully narrow shape of the lots. Even where plats were recorded depicting a good distribution of roads, they "turned out to be very disappointing when the subdivision itself was visited, as the roads depicted on the plat were either non-existent or confined to sand ruts winding in and out among the trees."[55] In 1974 Barbara Harris discussed her experience in Willow Estates: "When Moscickis Realty brought us out there, you could really see the future. The way they talked to us, it would really be a residential area with roads that would be fixed." Harris's hopes were not met:

"You can't open your windows because of the sand and gravel from the roads. You just feel the grit on your floors. If it is residential, how come we don't have zoning and speed laws out here?" She added, "They say they've tested our water and its good, but sometimes the drinking water gives me the cramps."[56]

Others questioned a practice of repeatedly flipping the land upon default of the installment contracts. According to Elisah Berrin of Leesville, "I'm trying to buy 10 acres from Moscickis Realty to start a hog farm. I'm the fifth guy to buy it. All the others either pulled out or fell behind on the payments and was repossessed. Ya got to live here by the sweat of your brow."[57] Former township supervisor Larry Gibbs stated, "That was their game. They bought up a certain amount of land, sold it, re-sold it, and re-sold it again, making money off the people of this area."[58]

No easy answer explains how Pembroke became and remained poor. No single person, group, or institution is the antagonist in the story. Somewhere there certainly exists a line between reasonable enterprise and exploitation in the pursuit of economic development. Unfortunately, the exact profit margin at which that line sits is nearly impossible to determine, let alone agree upon.

Arguments on one side of that line contend that developers took deliberate steps to avoid investment in the land. They purchased cheap, infertile property and carved it up to avoid the expenses of infrastructure and service connections. They pushed sales to individuals with limited education and resources, using a financing mechanism with almost no risk to themselves. Upon default, they took the property back and sold it again. And they ultimately made more money than they spent.

Per arguments on other side, the exceedingly low financing costs enabled a voluntary exodus from highly undesirable conditions in Chicago. Even the otherwise critical KCAP report conceded that the developers' installment contracts "resulted in many low income families acquiring for themselves a house and lot who otherwise would not be able to do so."[59] According to that report, 79 percent of those surveyed in 1966 did not owe anything on their property.[60] The developers identified and served a legitimate need for housing stock in Chicago's growing black community. Moscickis may have been one of the individuals who profited from transitioning neighborhoods in Chicago, but he would have done so in the face of boycotts and threats from white groups like the Hyde Park Improvement Protective Club.

Reggie Stewart bought his land in Pembroke from Moscickis and turned it into a ranch for inner-city children to visit during the summer. Stewart readily admits that he likely could not have purchased the land and launched his business without using an installment contract. He described his relationship with the developer: "I look at him for who he was—a businessman. When we talked to him, he never said he was a priest or a compassionate guy. He said he was in real estate."[61]

One's perspective on the line between enterprise and exploitation may hinge on a matter of personal philosophy that separates those who work the land with promotional trips, advertisements, and financing from those who work it with hoes, shovels, and tractors. It was out of respect for the earth that many members of the latter group packed up their lives in Chicago and moved back to the country. But it is unlikely that this second migration could have occurred without the former group. In years ahead, conflict over the proper role, direction, and pace of economic development on Pembroke's land would return.

4

Welcome to Lamplight City

It was time to get down to it. After our tour of Old Hopkins Park, we had the remainder of the morning to begin work on our first projects. Michelle had mentioned I would start with Project Black Gold, but the new soil she and Ken ordered had not arrived yet. So Michelle assigned me to another project, adding that I should be sure to wear long sleeves and pants. This project, called "The Jungle," would clear an unkempt wilderness of grasses, shrubs, and saplings that had taken over the outdoor space immediately behind the Sacred Heart rectory.

No ordinary lawnmower could have handled the overgrowth; instead, using lawn scissors and a chainsaw, we hacked away with an excited intensity. There were five of us from the youth group, but some Pembroke residents also joined us. One of them was a young boy named Duke. I recalled seeing him the day before, watching intently as we arrived at Sacred Heart. Duke wasn't allowed to use the chainsaw (none of the teens were), so he helped by removing the fallen branches.

An older, bald man from Pembroke with chestnut skin, freckles, and a dark gray mustache assisted us as well. He and Ken took turns operating the chainsaw, and he would talk to me between the loud roars of the machine. He asked about my life back in Kankakee and what I thought of Pembroke so far. I muddled through a few respons-es, feeling pretty awkward. I mean, we probably had little in common, so I wasn't quite sure what to say or ask. He persisted and told me about the nuns who used to live in the rectory and how they used to prepare campfires in the space we were clearing. I figured that this man, whom I heard Ken call Robert, was a Sacred Heart parishioner. I was actually glad that the chainsaw filled in what surely would have been gaps of silence. We all worked up a dripping sweat, but by the time we stopped for lunch, our efforts had only seemed to push back the leafy boundary three or four feet.

I walked back to the church and descended the stairs into the basement, where I was surprised to see my mom behind a stack of bottled water and a tray of lasagna. Our parents had volunteered to feed us during our week in Pembroke and divided the meals among themselves. She asked about the trip so far. It actually felt like I had been in Hopkins Park for almost a week already, but I responded, "Well, it hasn't even been half a day." She eventually pried more details from me. I told her about my run, Father Tony's tour, and how we were now cutting our way through some weeds. I pointed to the people I had worked with. When I got to the older parishioner, Mom said, "You know who that is, don't you? That's Mr. Hayes. Joey's grandpa." Joey Hayes had been my best friend during preschool. We saw each other less now, but I still remembered some of our jokes and games. I had no clue he was connected to Pembroke, and I began picturing Joey with a mustache.

✳ ✳ ✳

As Pembroke's dusty roads blew in the wind, the rest of America constructed a vast network of new, solid, asphalt highways during the 1950s. Other than stopping for gas, one could drive across the country without even pausing for traffic lights. But what more greatly impacted daily American life was the fact that one could *leave* a city without slowing for the lights. President Dwight Eisenhower's interstate highways permitted people to live one place and work in another. And many in Chicago chose to do so, leaving the city for newly incorporated municipalities like Park Forest, Rosemont, Long Grove, or Burr Ridge.

With some exceptions, the explosion of American suburbs was mostly a white phenomenon. Some people left the cities because racially restrictive housing covenants and other means of exclusion had failed. Old neighborhoods no longer bore the complexion inhabitants once knew, so they created new, gated ones. Nonetheless, others moved for the same reasons that black Chicagoans moved sixty-five miles south to Pembroke: more space, less crime, the opportunity to build and own a new home, and a chance at the American Dream.

Jim Piekarczyk, who became Kankakee County's chief engineer, grew up just outside of Momence and witnessed the "suburbanization" of Pembroke. His father owned the Concrete Block and Supply Company, which he described as a "grocery store for building materials." Piekarczyk worked for his father as a teenager, and his weekends were busy. Starting on Friday afternoon, black Chicagoans came in the store and used their paychecks to buy supplies for their new lots, sometimes taking no more than ten concrete blocks at a time. According to Piekarczyk, "the families then built during the day and camped on their property at night."[1] Angeline Hughes bought fifteen acres in 1951 and followed this pattern to build her home over the next several years. "You could bring it out here Friday evening and leave it [on Sunday] and go back home and work," said Hughes. "And nobody never would bother your land, your lumber, or nothing."[2]

Incomplete foundations and walls of homes in progress stood throughout the township—some of which remained permanently unfinished. "They were abandoned dreams," said Piekarczyk. The *Chicago Defender* concurred in a 1963 article about Leesville, a settlement in extreme southeastern Pembroke Township described as "a village of many delayed dreams. It was dotted with half-finished houses started by people who wanted to get away from the big cities, but found themselves without enough capital to finish their dream homes."[3]

Other homes, however, eventually reached completion. The population grew as people added to the land brick by brick. Communal life in this rural, black town developed further as individual leaders emerged at the head of an uncommon, pragmatic brand of political engagement. In 1970 several residents of the township decided to incorporate themselves into a municipality. The official name was the Village of Pembroke, although it would later be renamed Hopkins Park.[4]

Larry Barnes, however, had a different name for his town. After a Chicago gang attempted to recruit him at the age of thirteen, Barnes's parents moved him out to Pembroke. There he attended the local public school, St. Anne Community High School, and he remembered driving home with friends after Friday night football games. Even from miles away he could see tiny pinpoints of light coming from the houses. He knew that some had electricity, but many had to use gas to light their residences, so he crafted his own suburban-sounding name for the village. Welcome to Lamplight City.[5]

According to U.S. Census figures, Pembroke Township was home to only 678 people in 1940. The number grew to 1,173 in 1950, then rose dramatically to 2,871 in 1960 and 4,351 in 1970 before slowing a bit with 4,693 in 1980.[6] According to most descriptions from nonresidents, living conditions throughout the township were bleak and primitive. In 1966 the *(Kankakee) Daily Journal* ran an article titled "Pembroke Revisited: Beyond a Road Sign, A Mystery to Most Kankakeeans," the subtitle referring to the green sign on Route 17 pointing to Hopkins Park. "If [visitors] did drive a few miles down the Hopkins Park blacktop they would find a predominantly Negro community with widespread poverty, bad roads, few productive farms, poor fire protection, limited law enforcement, and, in many areas, an attitude of despair nurtured by generations of shattered dreams."[7] A Kiwanis Club survey stated that in Pembroke they found crude huts and cabins where inhabitants ate "by picking berries and hunting wild game."[8] A planner with the Kankakee Community Action Program once stated simply, "Pembroke is a rural ghetto of Chicago."[9]

Descriptions by Pembroke residents were much less dire, but they readily note that life was difficult and often required creative resourcefulness. In addition to homes made of concrete block or wood, many in Pembroke lived in mobile homes. Bertha Tetter notes that her aunt converted an old Greyhound bus into a bedroom and kitchen.[10] Eva Grant's childhood home during the mid-twentieth century had "no lights, no electricity, only lamps." Grant's family also had no running water, but they drew it from a hand pump and carried buckets back to their home. During winters they kept the home warm by burning coal and wood in a black stove.[11]

Without much of a fire department, small accidents often led to complete destruction. Three years after Angeline Hughes first began constructing her home, it was hit by lightning and burned down. "I wasn't able to save anything but the washing machine," she recalled. "And I said, the Lord giveth and the Lord taketh away, blessed be His name. . . . So then I went on back and went on to work and got started again."[12]

The roads of Pembroke were also notoriously bad. People started referring to Pembroke's primary artery as the Blacktop because for a time, no other roads in Pembroke were paved. The rest were gravel or dirt, which put significant strain on vehicles and caused them to break down more often. Moreover, roads became a treacherous, muddy mess after rain. Indeed,

Howard Jones explained that in order to leave his house, he sometimes needed to drive through the woods to find a usable road.[13]

According to one estimate from 1977, the per capita income of $2,467 was only 39 percent of the state average, and unemployment around that time exceeded 50 percent.[14] Jobs within Pembroke were difficult to secure as manufacturing positions were limited and intermittent. Around this time, the Bronough Casket Company employed between sixteen and twenty-two people, and although they wanted to expand, they were unable to secure adequate financing and eventually closed.[15] Another company, American Pouch Foods, operated in Hopkins Park and supplied military field rations to the U.S. Defense Department, but the facility also closed in 1980 when the company lost its $27 million government contract.[16] Pembroke residents found a small number of jobs at restaurants, service stations, or mechanic shops, and others, like Arthur Collins, found miscellaneous demands to meet. Collins said he never had a steady, full-time job, but did woodcutting from time to time. "We'd chop it then sell it to anybody right away. Did it for farmers, the railroad, the Kankakee Farm Bureau."[17]

Despite the poor soil quality, some tried their hand at farming. Most growers in Pembroke did not have the equipment or acreage to raise large amounts of corn and soybeans like commercial farms in the area. Instead, they cultivated a wider selection of fruits and vegetables in large gardens or raised various types of animals. Eva Grant's father grew cabbage, greens, corn, carrots, radishes, and bell peppers, and they kept chickens, goats, ducks, geese, and pigs on their land. Louise Howard made money by canning her own produce, as well as produce supplied by other locals. In her first year she sold eight hundred dollars' worth of her pickled fruits and vegetables.[18] Although some, like Howard, sold goods for profit, most growers merely ate what they cultivated.[19]

Much like a suburb, though, most of the employed residing in Pembroke commuted elsewhere to work. Of those surveyed in the 1966 report by the Kankakeeland Community Action Program (KCAP), only 21 percent worked in Pembroke Township. It also stated that 19 percent worked in Kankakee, 12 percent in Momence, and 3 percent in St. Anne. Another sizeable block—over a third according to the KCAP report—commuted up to Chicago or its nearby suburbs. In one case, a husband and wife who lived in Pembroke had to drive two hours one way in good weather to get to the factory near O'Hare Airport where they worked.[20] Pembroke's terrible roads further exacerbated difficulties for those with extensive commutes, since tardiness from getting stuck in the mud could quickly lead to termination.

Conditions in Pembroke were undoubtedly substandard in many respects, but the accounts from outsiders that focused on the community as a pit of broken dreams failed to grasp an essential element captured by the authors of the 1966 KCAP Report:

> The paradox of the situation in Pembroke Township is immediately apparent. Although many of the homes look like something out of the poverty of the Mississippi Delta, the owners' attitude toward their properties can be detected by noting the names given to their holdings. The fact that an extremely modest house and lot along the road is named "the Ponderosa" by its proud owner, indicates that he has escaped from the crowded slums of the city and found his idea of a better place for his family in Pembroke Township.[21]

Another landowner contradicted the notions of despair by naming his homestead "Shangri La," meaning "land of hope."[22] In spite of their difficulties, Pembroke residents understood that they had found something worthwhile and worth improving. Like Pap and Mary Tetter who ventured boldly to start this community in the mid-nineteenth century, new leaders recognized the importance of continuing the progress of their town.

Lorenzo R. Smith was one such individual. Smith grew up in the southernmost reaches of Illinois in the town of Metropolis. The burly, muscular athlete set numerous records in high school and received a football scholarship and two-year degree from Western Kentucky State College, a vocational school with similarities to Booker T. Washington's Tuskegee Institute. At his football coach's urging, Smith enrolled at Kentucky State College where he received a bachelor's degree in education. Shortly after the attack on Pearl Harbor, Smith volunteered with the armed forces and served for several years in the South Pacific. In 1945 Smith moved to Pembroke and became one of the township's first black teachers.[23] According to Sister Mary Cecelia, a nun living at Sacred Heart Catholic Church, Smith began teaching when there was only "a smattering of one room schools manned in part by unqualified teachers. He worked long and hard, against terrible odds and unjust criticism until the present school system was organized and three beautiful, modern and adequately equipped buildings were established."[24] When Pembroke's elementary schools were consolidated into a single district, Smith became its first superintendent.[25]

Those who knew Smith stressed the value he placed on personal respect and discipline, not just within his schools but among the parents as well. According to Merlin Karlock, Smith used to tell his students' fathers personally that he wanted the children in class every day. If a student was chronically absent, Smith paid a visit to the parents' home. "When he stopped at your place, you usually ended up with your back against a wall," said Karlock. Smith faced his share of criticism as well, including from Gertrude Higginbottom who thought he was too strict on the children. This was one reason she sent her children to Catholic school in Momence.[26] Eva Grant, one of Smith's former students, affirmed his reputation as a disciplinarian. She said Smith could be nice, but when needed, he became a "mean man [that] did not take crap from anyone. You didn't get away with jack."[27] Most in the community, however, respected the man and his work, and they eventually renamed the largest elementary school in the consolidated district in his honor.[28]

Hollie McKee was another community leader who broke numerous barriers in Pembroke Township and Kankakee County. McKee was born in Troy, Alabama, in 1912. Two years later his family caught one of the initial waves of the Great Migration and moved to Chicago. McKee became a union bricklayer and married T. Iris DeLacy in 1934. McKee moved to Pembroke in 1943 where he employed his craftsmanship to build his own home. For the first eight years he lived there, McKee commuted daily to his job in Chicago, but in 1951 he found similar work closer to home and became the first black man to join the Kankakee Bricklayers Union.[29]

McKee first involved himself in politics in 1951 when he unsuccessfully ran for Pembroke Township's chief executive, a position known as township supervisor. Despite his ties to organized labor, a traditionally Democratic institution, McKee became a Republican precinct committeeman in 1956, and eventually the first black member of the county board. Much like the black town of Brooklyn, Illinois, in the late-nineteenth century, Pembroke had always been governed by white leaders.[30] McKee lost a second bid for supervisor in 1967 against incumbent Maggie Walker. Four years later he finally succeeded in becoming Pembroke Township's first black supervisor.[31]

Each county in Illinois has the right to decide whether to divide its territory into townships.[32] This level of government is responsible for filling the cracks that are overlooked by the county and state, including by providing short-term assistance to those in need, conducting property tax assessments, and maintaining nonstate and noncounty roads.[33] As the leader of this authority, Hollie McKee sought to address the township's sewage, draining, flooding, and other infrastructure problems.[34]

In 1974 McKee pushed an ordinance to ban mobile homes, which were quicker to fall into disrepair than permanent ones and provided far less tax revenue to the township.[35] According to McKee, "There's no real estate taxes on trailers, so they don't help support the schools they're dumping all their children into." Of those who sold the mobile homes, he stated, "These land sharks are taking everything out of here and putting nothing back in . . . no drain system or sewers or nothing."[36]

One mobile home owner, Lee Gray, decided to stop McKee's efforts permanently and contacted Stanley Russell of Chicago's Austin neighborhood to assist.[37] Russell and Gray telephoned McKee asking for a bottled gas delivery, which McKee sold to make money outside of his public duties. When McKee arrived, the two men pulled a gun and ordered McKee to drive to a remote location where they shot him. After lying in a coma for five days, McKee died on December 11, 1974.[38] The community mourned the loss of a man who had become known throughout Kankakee County as "Mr. Pembroke."[39]

Although Illinois townships can appropriate certain funds, they cannot pass ordinances or issue licenses and permits, which are powers that remain with the county government. For much of its history the community of Pembroke—particularly its black members—had little input to the county board. In August 1970 several members of the community decided to exercise the separate legal mechanism of self-governance by voting to incorporate as a municipality. Illinois defines municipalities to include both cities and villages. The two forms differ in size, organization, and certain aspects of legislative authority, but both are able to levy their own sales tax, pass their own zoning ordinances, and issue their own liquor licenses, thereby superseding county decisions.[40]

The newly incorporated municipality, the Village of Pembroke, was centered on the Blacktop intersection of 13000 East Road and 4000 South Road, over three miles west of Pap and Mary Tetter's homestead near Old Hopkins Park.[41] At this intersection a village hall was constructed and dedicated in 1973.[42] Although village president is the official title for the community's chief executive, Illinois law also permits the title of mayor for this position.[43] Most leaders in Pembroke have utilized this second, somewhat heftier term. Voters proved not easily satisfied: when Alex Jones, a former Pullman car conductor, became the village's first mayor in 1970, he was defeated only months later in spring of 1971 by Revered A. Austin Timms, who was subsequently defeated by Clarence Taylor in 1975.

In addition to frequent electoral turnover—a pattern that generally would repeat itself in Pembroke politics—the village's first few years were beset with volatility and controversy between the village board and mayor. Critics attacked Mayor Taylor for holding "secret meetings," and the mayor responded by accusing board members of failing their constituents. "When they walk into that room, everyone is telling the mayor how to do his job," Taylor said. "But when I assign someone to a job no one ever wants to complete it." At least once, citizens circulated a petition to un-incorporate the village.[44] Yet after its first, and somewhat rocky, decade of existence, the municipality was renamed the Village of Hopkins Park and has survived to this day.[45]

Hopkins Park, however, was not Pembroke Township's first foray into municipal self-governance. The short-lived Village of Leesville purportedly existed between 1954 and 1963, but controversy clouds whether the incorporation was actually valid. Leesville sits nearly three miles south and east of the Blacktop—placing it at the very edge of the township, county, and state. After the location's namesake, Carl Lee, moved there from Chicago in 1937, Leesville became known as the rougher and wilder portion of the already rough and wild Pembroke Township.[46] According to one account in the *Daily Journal*, "Leesville is a long way from the law. Even if a deputy happens by, he's not real likely to take a tour down the snow-clogged, frozen-sand that serves as a roadway here."[47]

In 1954 a Leesville village charter was signed, but Kankakee County officials refused to recognize the incorporation, claiming that the community failed to meet the legal prerequisites—which included, among other procedural requirements, a minimum of one hundred inhabitants within the proposed village boundaries.[48] But according to Carlos Lindsey, the purported mayor of Leesville, the county rejected the petition in order to keep collecting taxes from Leesville. The *Chicago Defender* reported that Lindsey's administration collected enough funds to employ a police force and planned to construct a municipal building and a much-needed seventy-bed hospital within the village.[49]

Leesville's ambiguous status led to difficulties in 1962. The Chicago Police Department raided a Leesville "police training academy" being held in the South Side of Chicago after an individual claiming to be a Leesville deputy sheriff purportedly tried to arrest an off-duty Chicago officer the night before, using a stolen Chicago police badge to do so.[50] The following year, eleven more men claiming to be Leesville police trainees were arrested during another academy session in Chicago's Cabrini Green projects.[51]

These incidents, as well as concerns about the village's legitimacy, led residents to question the value of being a municipality altogether, and they voted to un-incorporate in 1963. Subsequent efforts to reincorporate Leesville failed in 1970, 1971, 1974, and 1993.[52]

Conditions for African Americans during the mid-twentieth century were difficult in more urban centers than just Chicago, yet sizeable outward migration to rural, black-majority communities generally did not occur. A limited number of black suburbs like Robbins, Illinois, were established, but even these communities were in close proximity to the city.[53] In this sense Pembroke deviated from urban, black America.

Pembroke also differed in its political identity. While black voters across America moved solidly into the Democratic Party after Franklin Roosevelt's New Deal and Harry Truman's inclusion of civil rights in the party platform, black voters in Pembroke were more reluctant. Well into the 1980s Pembroke split its vote between the Democratic and Republican parties of Kankakee County, both of which sought to attract Pembroke voters through aggressive means.

For decades after the Civil War, African Americans felt a strong affinity for the Party of Lincoln and overwhelmingly identified with and voted for Republicans. During that time much of the Democratic Party—particularly in the American South—was openly hostile to black interests. Individuals moving northward during the Great Migration were more likely to be Republican and to espouse the conservative "pull yourself up by the bootstraps" philosophy of Booker T. Washington. A divide emerged in cities like Chicago between the southern migrants and the native black residents who more closely followed the ideology of W. E. B. DuBois, whose "Talented Tenth" philosophy placed far greater emphasis on racial uplift through formal education and the promotion of social equality and integration.[54] Alternatively, Washington accepted certain forms of segregation, once stating, "In all things purely social, we can be as separate as the fingers, yet one as the hand in all things essential to mutual progress."[55]

Black discontent with the GOP nonetheless percolated, eventually surfacing in Chicago as well as in Illinois' smaller communities. Black voters in downstate Decatur openly criticized and threatened to withhold support of two Republican officeholders for failing to prevent or adequately respond to the lynching of Samuel Bush by a white mob in 1893.[56] Additionally, after Brooklyn's John Evans—who was likely America's first black mayor—failed to win the Republican nomination for state representative in 1906, he continued his campaign as an independent candidate in part to show that his party could not assume unflinching black support.[57]

Following the 1932 election, Franklin Roosevelt embraced this political opportunity by enlarging the definition of the middle class to include black families. Subsequently, he actively sought black support for his New Deal agenda. Since then the largest share of the black vote garnered by a GOP presidential candidate was Dwight Eisenhower in 1956 with 39 percent. The figure has not risen above 17 percent in the past four decades.[58] Chicago followed this national trend starting in 1931 when Democrat Anton Cermak defeated Republican mayor "Big Bill" Thompson by constructing an electoral coalition of many ethnic groups that included African Americans.[59] Support for Democrats continued to grow within the black community of Chicago.

In Pembroke, however, a black Republican Party endured much longer than other places in the United States. Many of those who moved from the South to Pembroke via Chicago had long identified as Republicans. Moreover, the self-help ideas of Booker T. Washington aligned well with the prospect of building a new, primarily black agrarian community outside of Chicago. Lorenzo Smith, having been taught in a Washingtonian college, brought a related philosophy with him to Pembroke, and Hollie McKee was elected to the county board as a Republican.

Pembroke's population was not exclusively Republican by any means though. Accounts vary as to whether Pembroke was more red or blue during the mid-twentieth century. Interestingly, party adherents usually expressed that the other party had control. Ozroe Bentley was the founder and editor of Pembroke's only newspaper, the *Pembroke Herald-Eagle*, which ran from approximately 1960 to 1980. Bentley regularly encouraged readers to vote Republican. In one editorial published immediately before the 1970 midterm elections, he wrote: "From the very beginning of the founding of Kankakee County, it has been controlled by the Republican Party. . . . Of the seventeen townships within the County, only Pembroke Township has shown a desire to be a standoff and vote Democratic by a majority."[60]

Alternatively, Elvia Steward was a Democrat, eventually becoming a precinct committeewoman for her party, and her view of history differed from Bentley's. "At that time, politics was strictly Republican," said Steward. "There were very few Democrats because they'd said that if you didn't vote Republican, you couldn't get any of the benefits like getting a ton of coal or getting food stamps."[61] Regardless of whether Bentley's or Steward's impressions were more accurate, there was real competition in Pembroke between the two parties.

Pembroke Republicans saw their period of greatest influence during the 1970s. Ozroe Bentley was a clear leader in this movement. In addition to his role as editor of the *Herald-Eagle*, Bentley was a member of the school and township boards, the Illinois Department of Public Aid welfare service committee, and the Kankakeeland Community Action Program.[62] He continued his editorial by pleading with the Pembroke community to break from the past. After noting his perception of historical Democratic dominance, he wrote:

> What has it gotten you or those you want to help? In my honest opinion, it has ONLY gotten you a promise, this is not good enough where I'm concerned. So, I say to you my dear friends and readers, STOP thinking about what my father, grandfather, and others have said, "I'm a Democrat, and I'll be a Democrat as long as I live." . . . As a result of my observations plus findings, may I suggest to a majority of friends that they should not feel ashamed to cast a crossed ballot. Vote for whom ever you want, but include those whom I'm about to recommend.[63]

Not everyone was pleased with his involvement. According to Bentley, he once found himself with a gun pointed to his head after speaking out against raising a roads tax.[64]

Robert Hayes also handled the reigns of township government for several years. Hayes was born in Chicago in 1919. His mother, Harriet Tetter Hayes, a granddaughter of Pap and Mary Tetter, sent her son to visit her family in Pembroke during summers. In the late 1940s Hayes moved down to Pembroke where he met and married Lucille Greenley.[65] Hayes worked as a legal investigator for the Kankakee County state's attorney and as a part-time salesman for a car dealer in Momence. At the urging of Hollie McKee, Hayes became involved in area politics, serving as an elected county board member and one of the three Republican precinct committeemen in Pembroke.[66] In these roles Hayes developed relationships with local Republican power brokers, including fellow county board member George Ryan who would eventually become governor of Illinois.

When township supervisor McKee was killed in 1974, Hayes was appointed to succeed his political mentor. Upon taking office, Hayes said, "I will follow Hollie's interests in Pembroke as far as seeing it grow. My main objective will be to help the people."[67] His local connections resulted in his appointment to numerous positions in county government, serving on the planning commission, housing authority board, mental health board, and public health board. For a time Hayes was also Pembroke Township's fire chief and a truant officer for the Pembroke school district. With the backing of George Ryan, who rose to state representative in 1973, Hayes became co-chairman of the Kankakee County GOP in 1976.[68]

Hayes at times made statements seemingly compatible with Republican principles of self-sufficiency, once telling the *Chicago Tribune*,

> You can give a man a fish and he has a meal. But if you teach a man how to fish, you've taught him how to survive. To take an individual and simply give him food, clothing, and a salary, without the will to earn these things himself is genocide.[69]

When describing the General Assistance Fund available to township residents in need, Hayes made sure applicants knew it was "not a program of continuing welfare."[70]

However, people close to Hayes said that his party affiliation was more practical than ideological. When asked why he was a Republican, he told the *Daily Journal*'s Bob Themer, that it was the only way he could garner the connections and leverage needed to do anything for his community.[71] During his tenure as supervisor, Hayes brought a great deal of public money to Pembroke, including approximately $350,000 for jobs programs, $300,000 for rehabilitation programs, and $150,000 for road and home repairs, among other initiatives. He garnered funding to build a low-income senior citizens' center and purchase land that would become Martin Luther King Jr. Park.[72] Hayes was also very active in trying to recruit business and industry to Pembroke. After American Pouch Foods lost their government contract and left Pembroke in 1980, Hayes secured a $1.1 million grant to develop the facility as a cannery.[73]

Despite a few conservative tendencies, Hayes was nowhere close to a contemporary Tea Party Republican that would swear off all earmarks or outside funding. Indeed, Hayes regularly sought to boost public investment in private industry. Some of his initiatives (including the cannery which closed a few years later) fell short, but others promoted by Hayes (including the senior citizens' center and a community center) have become fixtures in Pembroke.[74] Hayes continued to try new ideas. He was a progressive Republican using his county- and statewide influence to push his self-ascribed motto that greatly resembled that of President Barack Obama's 2012 reelection campaign: "Moving Pembroke Forward."[75] Hayes was the township's longest-serving supervisor, filling the role for fifteen years in a community where incumbents were usually replaced after four. Hayes was defeated in 1989 by Barbara Smith-Jones.[76]

But when Smith-Jones later ran for county board in 1992, she did so as a Republican.[77]

The statements of Ozroe Bentley and Robert Hayes indicate that their Republicanism was not as much about ideology as it was about pragmatism. They both recognized that they were a long way from the Democratic Cook County machine and that in Kankakee County, the GOP ran the show. They mobilized much of Pembroke around this notion. During the midterm elections of 1978, Pembroke became a red township and cast a majority of its ballots for the Republican candidates for U.S. senator, congressman, governor, and state attorney general. One week later Bentley wrote the following editorial in the *Pembroke Herald-Eagle*:

> I must admit the voters made a liar out of my predictions of its outcome. It was pleasant though and I'm very glad those of you who voted made a liar out of me. Though I didn't publish anything or endorse any candidates, I did say verbally to a few people that NO republican candidate would beat any democratic candidate of the machine. . . . My reason for saying it was because I'd done research for many years back and knew that never, NEVER in the history of this publication and before had any Republican garnered any votes considered good enough to cause one to say "Ha the people of Pembroke are waking up at the ballot box by casting more votes for the GOP candidates."[78]

Not all in Pembroke agreed with either the principles or pragmatism behind support for the Republican Party. As indicated earlier, well before Pembroke's population boom in the 1950s, black America had already broken the color barrier into the Democratic Party and most labor unions. Many grew up supporting workers' rights to organize and collectively bargain. They came to view law and government as a means to promote a level playing field of opportunity for all people, and they saw liberal Democrats taking up the mantle of civil rights from liberal Republicans like President Lincoln and Congressman Thaddeus Stevens. When these Democratic-minded individuals arrived in Pembroke, they retained their party identity.

One such stalwart was Elvia Steward. Born into a Democratic household in 1917, Steward attended Howard University where she studied to become a nurse. There she met Lester Lee of Pembroke, and, as she recalled, "he convinced me that he wanted me as his wife and to come to Illinois." They soon married and moved to Pembroke in 1946.[79] According to Steward, "I didn't know who was running when I got here, just that I was a Democrat."

Steward worked as a nurse at the state hospital in Manteno, and she was a member of the American Federation of State, County, and Municipal Employees (AFSCME).[80] She took care of patients at the hospital as well as at home, as Lester Lee battled sickness for the last fifteen years of his life. After he passed away in 1970, Steward became more involved with her union.[81]

Steward once volunteered to attend a national AFSCME meeting in Detroit where she listened to Bill Lucy, the AFSCME secretary-treasurer, civil rights leader, and associate of Martin Luther King. Afterward Steward introduced herself to Lucy and told him, "I'm going back to Pembroke, and I'm going to put its name on the map." She soon began going to Kankakee County Democratic Central Committee meetings. According to Steward,

> I would sit there and listen. I noticed that every other village—Bourbonnais, Bradley, St. Anne, Manteno—every name was called, but Pembroke wasn't. We even had Pembroke Committeemen, but no one listened to them. I said, "What do you think Pembroke is? Chopped liver?" From then on, I was very vocal. I opened their eyes to Pembroke.

Steward became the party's precinct committeewoman, a position she would hold until 2008. She worked intently to get Democratic voters to the polls, but even more so, to get Democratic politicians to Pembroke. She said, "Everyone that was interested in being a leader got together and got behind me in Pembroke. I had rallies on my lawn with barbeques. You cook this. I'll cook that. Then, we all got together and went around." Candidates followed Steward to the churches, the homes, the taverns, the village hall, and the roads. In 1972 she sought to bring Democratic gubernatorial candidate Dan Walker to Pembroke. According to Steward,

> He didn't know whether to get to Pembroke or not, but finally, we got him out here. When he came to Pembroke, he said those were the worst roads he'd ever been on. He said he would go back to Springfield and let them know. After that, they finally put up a sign down on 7000 South leading from St. Anne to Pembroke.

In addition to her political involvement, Steward was also a member of Pembroke Community Reformed Church, president of its women's guild, treasurer of its choir, a Sunday school teacher, a board member for an adult training center, and bloodmobile volunteer.[82] She also led Pembroke toward the national political trend. Since the 1980s the township has become more solidly Democratic. Steward took pride in this fact, but she may have been even more proud of the installation of that green sign on 7000 South Road.

"I'm the cause of that sign being put up," she said. It was her tangible way of putting Pembroke on the map.

Steward also had her own response to those that argued Pembroke should vote according to its local, practical interests:

> Many people said they voted Republican because they had to in order to get anything . . . coal, food, you name it. They once told me, it's a pie. The money's all a pie. So many dollars go here. So many go there. I told them, I'll throw the pie in your face.

After full lives dedicated to numerous venues of public service, Ozroe Bentley, Robert Hayes, and Elvia Steward passed away—Bentley in 2004 at age eighty-eight, Hayes in 2011 at age ninety-two, and Steward in 2014 at age ninety-seven.[83] Despite the differences between their rhetoric and party affiliation, these leaders created a lively form of political engagement within their community. At least for a time, the Pembroke vote was competitive in both primary and general elections, which had both positive and negative effects. Party operatives were unabashed and aggressive in their attempts to persuade voters. According to some reports, both parties offered operatives in Pembroke one dollar for every voter they could get to vote their way. Parties also "hosted" campaign events in Pembroke taverns the night before an election, giving free alcohol and often cash in exchange for their vote the following day.

Yet simultaneously, the competitive nature of its partisan politics allowed Pembroke to wield influence in Kankakee County in selecting officeholders. According to Merlin Karlock, "It was the voters of Pembroke who would decide who the next country sheriff would be." Elvia Steward noted that election judges "had to wait for Pembroke to come out before declaring the winner." In this respect, Pembroke was like other "swing" suburbs of Chicagoland.

In his history of Brooklyn, Sundiata Keita Cha-Jua discusses a dichotomy between black suburbs and rural towns. The suburbs, which include places like Brooklyn and Robbins, formed along the "rings of industrial cities throughout the Midwest." They "were created by the newly dominant processes of industrial capitalism" that required a labor force nearby to staff their factories. Many such suburbs have survived to present day, albeit often in an underdeveloped state dependent on the urban economy. According to Cha-Jua, these suburbs differ from the "small, self-sufficient rural towns" that regarded land ownership and agriculture as essential means to independence and racial uplift. Such places, which include Beech, Roberts, and New Philadelphia, were nonetheless "doomed to failure" by the rapid urbanization and industrialization beginning in the late nineteenth century.[84]

Pembroke exists somewhere between these two classifications as an alternative version of black development. On one hand, it was and is still a suburb in many respects. A sizeable portion of Pembroke's population has always commuted to employment in Kankakee, Chicago, or elsewhere. Even though Pembroke remains underdeveloped like many black suburbs, its proximity to outside industry has also provided a degree of economic stability, particularly for vulnerable new residents during their first years after relocating there. On the other hand, Pembroke is an unmistakably rural outpost, geographically distant from an urban core and lacking the amenities available in most suburban villages. Barns and hedgerows greatly outnumber shopping malls and cul-de-sacs. Further, although Pembroke's economy continues to struggle, land ownership remains high.

Indeed, a more accurate classification of Pembroke would be that of a black "exurb." Columnist David Brooks once described exurbs as areas "that have broken free of the gravitational pull of the cities and now exist in their own world far beyond."[85] They are the periphery to the periphery where a town can grow without space constraints—a characteristic demonstrated by the Village of Hopkins Park's irregular, sprawling municipal boundaries. Unlike the deserted rural towns, Pembroke has been connected to nearby jobs and industry that have kept the community afloat, but it has not been a connection so entrenched or encompassing as to overtake Pembroke's agrarian qualities. Nor was the link so established as to immediately pull the Pembroke community in the same political direction as other black voters throughout the nation. Instead, the community fended for itself in Kankakee County during the mid-twentieth century by creating a political culture characterized by two-party competition and pragmatism.

Had a number of factors been different—for instance, if other racially integrated, rural settlements existed within driving distance to urban centers, or if more real estate agents had sought to solve the black housing crunch by looking farther outside city limits—then more communities like Pembroke may have developed. Today migration patterns are again shifting as gentrification and the demolition of high-rise housing projects push lower-income black households out of the city. Once again urban housing is scarce. Between 2000 and 2010 Chicago lost approximately 150,000 of its black citizens, many of whom moved to increasingly black suburbs and exurbs in the territory between Chicago and Pembroke, otherwise known as the Southland. Given current political demographics, a total Republican takeover seems unlikely, but similar patterns of community development, individual leadership, and political pragmatism may surface as black Chicagoland expands its geography.

5

"A Rip-Roarin' Time"

We worked hard during the day, but we also found plenty of time to engage in what had become the unofficial, unsanctioned pastime for our week in Pembroke. For ten or twenty minutes after breakfast or before the sun went down, a few of us would grab a soccer ball and gather in a circle near a wall. Someone would toss the ball up towards another. That player then had to keep the ball in the air without using his hands and pass it to someone else (or in soccer parlance, juggle the ball). If one of us allowed the ball to drop, he was assigned an "A." If the same player lost control of it again, he got an "S." The third time would warrant another "S," and a "trip to the wall."

Up to this point, the game was an exercise of finesse and coordination, but it quickly turned into a contest of brute force. The shamed individual would walk to the wall and, facing it, he would bend down and grab his ankles. Then, every other player would step back and take a shot at him from twelve yards away. Most of the inexperienced footballers kicked with their toe, mustering significant speed but usually sending the ball way off course. Those who knew what they were doing struck the ball on their laces, getting both the power and placement needed for a loud, satisfying smack.

The game was crude and painful. It went against plenty of the Christian virtues we promoted during our daily revival, likely made worse by the fact that we let ten-year-old Duke play. But during these moments of questionable judgment and competition, we talked, laughed, and enjoyed each other's company. Nobody had great foot skills, so every round was a mutual gamble. If someone had been hurt, we would have deserved the full and certain wrath of a displeased Michelle Barrie. But fortunately that didn't happen, and instead our risky game created camaraderie.

It was the afternoon of our third day in Pembroke, and we finally started on Project Black Gold. The topsoil we ordered had arrived earlier that day. We shoveled it into position and leveled it in front of the white cinder-block wall. The dark soil stood out against the lighter, sandy dirt around the rest of the church. We finished early, but I still felt energetic. I decided to forego a round of "ass-up" (which our game had surreptitiously been dubbed) for another run to the state line.

Heading east on the county road, I was surrounded by a wide-open blue sky. There was no one around me, and I felt as if I could run for hours, maybe days. I soon reached the Indiana line. On the Illinois side of the border, there was a small building seemingly abandoned for decades. Blue paint peeled from cement walls covered with encroaching weeds, and a broken beer sign hung above an entryway sprinkled with shattered bottles. This place looked much like the other buildings in Hopkins Park that I had seen the other day while driving out to Sacred Heart. The words "State Line Club" appeared in gold decals next to the rusty door, barely legible as they had peeled over time.

I turned around to head back. The sun was low in the western sky, so I heard an old pick-up truck coming toward me before I could actually see it. I moved to the right side of the road, and I put up my hand to wave as I had seen most other people in Pembroke do. But this time, the driver didn't wave back. He slowed down and looked at me with a suspicious, almost angry gaze, and for the first time in three days I felt like an outsider. As he passed me, I heard the truck speed up, which I also found myself doing on my way back to Sacred Heart.

* * *

Over the years, Pembroke developed quite a reputation. People from the outside knew very little about the place except what they heard regarding the wild and crazy things that went on there. Crime, violence, drugs, and prostitution—people knew little but rumors of moral depravity. While Pembroke has indeed been beset with illicit activity throughout its history, and vice is certainly part of Pembroke's narrative, it is not the entire narrative. Rather, it is an important chapter that explains the uncommon resilience that has become a virtue of the community.

Outsiders could view the problems from afar, but others grew up literally next door to them. Over fifty years ago Lana Higginbottom sat next to her mother Gertrude and her siblings in a pew of Sacred Heart Catholic Church. Lana, no more than six or seven years old, looked out the window. There she saw vivid, beautiful fabric hanging from the clothesline. Lana looked closer and realized that it was lingerie. "It was all ladies' underwear in bright, bright colors, all fancy styles. We said, 'Ooooh, that is so pretty.'" But her mother had a different idea, "Don't look at that," Gertrude said. "It's sin." Before Lana was ten years old, she knew exactly what went on in the establishment, known as a "doll house," next to her house of worship.[1]

As a teenager Lana also learned about the "Front," a stretch of 4500 South Road between what is known today as the 4-Way and Old Hopkins Park. Several bars used to line the Front, and from approximately 1950 to 1980 it was a lively, crowded place on Friday and Saturday nights. At first Lana's parents kept her from the Front. "I was the oldest, so my Mom and Dad wouldn't let me go out," Lana said. "Orland, the oldest boy, he was just younger than me, but he would go to the Front. He'd say 'You can't go, sis. It's not the right crowd.'" Although she was forbidden from visiting, Lana knew what the Front was all about. "That place was boppin'. It was a rip-roarin' time."

People who visited the bars on the Front were not exclusively from Pembroke. "Folks came in from all around," Lana said. Indeed, much of Pembroke's questionable activity did not originate within the township, but was imported from Kankakee, Chicago, and elsewhere. Not only did outsiders party in Pembroke, they used Pembroke as a vice den where they could hide from the police, produce and sell illicit substances, and illegally dump unwanted materials without significant risk of repercussion. While some avoided Pembroke because it was known to be a place where anything goes, others were attracted because of it.

Pembroke first became acquainted with vice well before the turn of the twentieth century. As other parts of Illinois were settled and civil order was established, the Grand Kankakee Marsh remained practically untouched by the law. According to Earl Reed's early account of the swampland, at that time the area was home to trappers, horse thieves, counterfeiters, and moonshiners.[2] Before the bars along the Front opened, people could meet and drink at any one of the area's early taverns, including the one after which Pembroke Township was reputedly named.

The wealthy elite of Chicago took interest in Pembroke as a remote, undisturbed hunting ground, but these characteristics also appealed to another powerful faction from the city. The Chicago mob had numerous outposts in Pembroke where Al Capone and his lieutenants could "cool off" after committing some nefarious act.[3] The secluded territory also provided a place to dispose of the victims of those acts.

Capone controlled several illegal distilleries in the area from which he supplied a significant portion of the Midwest with liquor during Prohibition. Some production occurred in the basements and backrooms of taverns and homes, but most occurred in larger facilities. In fact, Pembroke housed one of Capone's largest distilleries to be discovered by federal authorities, a barn at the top of a hill near Old Hopkins Park.[4] When in operation, it produced 550 gallons of 188-proof liquor per day, and it contained nine vats each holding ten thousand gallons and two sixty-horsepower boilers. In order to avoid detection, the equipment had been brought to the barn piece by piece after having been previously taken apart and reassembled in eleven different locations.[5] The distillery supposedly sat above a series of tunnels that ran in all four directions for miles. Capone built them so that his associates could escape at the first sign of trouble from the G-Men.[6]

The secret distillery in Pembroke almost survived to the end of Prohibition. But at the same time that U.S. Treasury officials were building their case against Capone for income tax evasion, they also learned of his operations in Kankakee County. In September 1931 approximately one hundred agents raided thirty different establishments serving alcohol in the county.[7] Around that time, agents also shut down the Pembroke distillery and confiscated its equipment, but consumers throughout the country were likely served from the Pembroke supply until Prohibition ended in December 1933.[8]

Illegal alcohol production was not the only illicit industry to thrive in the backrooms of Pembroke taverns. As one article in the *Chicago Tribune* described, "In the lush farmland along the Kankakee river, less than 60 miles from Chicago, the saloons stay open all night, slot machines and pin ball games run night and day, and the doors of the brothels swing open before noon on Sunday." These were "the wide open rural vice dens."[9]

The *Tribune* article only counted five brothels in Pembroke Township, but others contend that a more accurate count was closer to twenty or thirty.[10] According to inhabitants, places like Red Boys, Bluebird Inn, the Do Drop Inn, and the Country Club were known houses of prostitution.[11] The "doll houses," as they were known, were not just restricted to bars but could also be found in homes, former schools, and, in one case, a trailer behind a barbeque stand.[12] Their proprietors were a similarly eclectic group. For example, one used to teach at a Hopkins Park elementary school, but she tired of her job. One day after school she walked into a doll house close to Sacred Heart and announced her intention to buy it. She soon became the house's madam and recruited women from across the state to work there.[13]

Pembroke's vice dens attracted most of their customers from out of town—many of whom drove the twenty-five miles from Kankakee. In this respect, Pembroke was similar to Brooklyn, Illinois, where customers from St. Louis crossed the Mississippi River to engage in illicit activities.[14] According to Merlin Karlock, it was not just the dregs of Kankakee County who visited Pembroke: "Our elite, our attorneys, our politicians made their way out there." Johnny Murrell of Pembroke noted that Kankakeeans "called [Pembroke] Sin City, but Kankakee was letting it go on. The Negro people weren't supporting those places. White people were. Cabs would come out there and bring those high guys, and they'd stay all night."[15] The reputation extended well outside of Kankakee County and throughout Illinois and Indiana. As Karlock noted, "Every Chicago taxi driver knew where Hopkins Park was." The *Tribune* once described the vice den patrons as "businessmen and salesmen from Chicago, laborers, steel workers, and farmhands from Indiana, car after car loaded with underage drinkers from Chicago and its suburbs."

According to several articles in the *Chicago Defender* during the late 1950s, Pembroke residents organized against the doll houses, their owners, and their patrons. A group known as the Pembroke Decent Citizens Committee particularly rallied around the charge that at least six of the establishments exploited young, black, local women, and only permitted white patrons inside their doors.[16] In an open letter to the women of Pembroke, Pearline Thomas wrote, "This is our town, and it is up to us to clean it up. . . . Low types of white men are using our neighborhood for their dirty work, then deny us the right to live in their neighborhoods."[17] According to Matthew Brandon, a retired Army officer and leader of the Decent Citizens Committee, the vice dens hurt everyone in Pembroke: "No longer is it safe for a Negro man, woman, boy or girl to walk the streets of Hopkins

Park, especially at night, without fear of being molested by white men."[18] Brandon received multiple threats for his activism from those connected to the vice industry, including one person that claimed certain county officials had already agreed not to prosecute him if he carried through on the threat against Brandon.[19]

Organized crime was present, but for the thirty years after Prohibition, the Chicago mob generally left Pembroke Township and Kankakee County alone.[20] "By tradition, the county rackets are conducted by local operators independent of the Chicago crime syndicate," stated one report. "The domain of the Chicago mob reportedly ends at the Kankakee county line."[21] However, in 1961 the mob sought to reassert its control. For several months, groups that included John "Jackie the Lackey" Cerone, Willie "Potatoes" Daddano, Sam "Mooney" Giancana, and James "Mugsy" Tortoriello intimidated Pembroke tavern owners with threats of violence. A police investigation revealed that on the morning of August 23, 1961, three individuals from the south suburb of Chicago Heights kidnapped Bud Greenley, owner of a tavern in Hopkins Park. The abductors took Greenley to Chicago Heights where they told him that if he didn't cede control of his bar, he would meet their bosses further north. Soon after the incident Greenley temporarily fled to California.[22]

Kankakee County state's attorney Edward Drolet resolved to address the vice dens in Pembroke—whether controlled by the local racket or the Chicago mob. Drolet first sought the assistance of County Sheriff Carl McNutt, who declined to pursue the issue. Around the same time, a cook discovered a paper bag containing eight thousand dollars in cash in the cupboard of the county jail.[23] When officers were counting the money, Sheriff McNutt's wife entered the room and claimed it belonged to her and her husband. According to Mrs. McNutt, the money had gone missing after a certain prisoner escaped.[24] Days later, William Crause, a deputy involved with the investigation of illicit activity in Pembroke and also one of the individuals present when the money was found, resigned from his position. He explained, "I could no longer work honestly as a policeman."[25]

Sheriff McNutt was subsequently indicted for the offense of failing to suppress vice, but he still refused to act against the racket in Pembroke. So in November 1961 State's Attorney Drolet sent a request to the superintendent of the Illinois State Police to assume complete control over regulating the county. In the past, county authorities had often asked the state force for assistance, but there had never been a request for the state police to supersede the sheriff entirely.[26] Drolet and the state police led several raids against Pembroke establishments and won several convictions that slowed illegal activity but failed to stop it entirely.[27] Matthew Brandon and the Decent Citizens Committee argued that many of the raids were half-hearted and ineffective because they focused on punishing the tavern operators and prostitutes rather than the white patrons of the establishments.[28]

The Front served as Pembroke's equivalent of Bourbon Street—the famously raucous corridor of New Orleans. According to one account printed in the *(Kankakee) Daily Journal*, "Things used to really jump out there. The nightlife was really something! Girls, booze, everything."[29] As Larry Barnes remembered, some of the establishments were "juke joints" that played live blues music, and others resembled "old-time speakeasies." He further recalled, "People used to party inside *and* outside the joints."[30] Crowds spilled out onto the roads, rendering them nearly impassable. Kankakee County engineer Jim Piekarczyk said that he once drove through Hopkins Park on a Friday afternoon, and even then the space between the Blue Bird Inn and a liquor store across the road was packed with people.

The State Line Club was located as far east as possible in Illinois. Though not technically on the Front, it was just as lively and stayed open for the late-night revelers after other places closed.[31] Patrons of the State Line Club heard everything from blues to karaoke, and its owner was known for accepting any dare given to him. He once rode his horse right onto the dance floor of the club. In the words of Lana Higginbottom, "There was some swing dingin' doodles in there."

The Front served as the focal point for nightlife in Pembroke starting in the late 1950s, but establishments began shutting down in the 1980s and 1990s. In 1992 the state revoked the liquor license of Bob Hall's Grocery and Tavern for failing to pay taxes.[32] Bob Hall's eventually reopened but closed again in 2001.[33] Others closed after county authorities discovered drugs being dealt out of the establishments.[34] Finally, in 2002 Curtis Butler decided to close Mr. Curt's Lounge, the last remaining bar on the Front. In addition to being a tavern proprietor, "Mr. Curt" was a township trustee for six years, and his wife, Cleatie Ivy, served on the school board for fifteen years. He said that the tavern was still busy on weekends and that he would gladly sell it. But no one with money or credit wanted to buy it, so the last tavern on the Front perished.[35]

Without any bars left on the Front, the young people of Pembroke had to find new places to congregate. Nightlife has since relocated to places like the Citgo gas station on the Blacktop. Although crowds may not be as large, similar activities take place. When Hopkins Park sought to hire a police chief in 2009, one of the first questions the village board asked prospective candidates was how they planned to patrol the Citgo station. Even more recently in 2015, a food pantry preferred to avoid building a permanent structure in that area because of concern that the location would keep people away, impeding the pantry's ability to serve the needy. According to Lillian Spencer, director of the Lord's Lambs Ministry which runs the pantry, "There is too much shooting down there. We spoke with the clients and we know the numbers [of food recipients] will go down if we move there."[36]

For many crimes, Pembroke merely played the role of host. When newspapers run accounts of criminal activities in Pembroke, at least one of the alleged perpetrators often hails from somewhere outside the township. For example:

- February 7, 1992: Two young men from Chicago shot while attempting to recruit younger residents to sell drugs in the area.[37]
- January 19, 1993: Three men from Chicago and one from Milwaukee arrested after reportedly breaking and entering into a Pembroke home.[38]
- August 10, 2009: After months of police investigation, man from the south suburbs of Chicago charged with running a dogfighting ring in Hopkins Park.[39]

Much like Al Capone, individuals with criminal intent sought out the territory for its remote and relatively lawless qualities. Underground markets like moonshining, prostitution, narcotics trafficking, and dogfighting developed from the opportunities made possible by a lack of oversight.[40] One resident, who noted that he began driving at age eleven, said that he believed the sheriff only sent one deputy—usually a terrified rookie—to Pembroke. "Nothing was enforced," said the resident. In this environment outsiders could enter Pembroke to commit deeds that they could not do elsewhere, and as the following bizarre stories demonstrate, many sought the isolation of Pembroke strictly for its ability to keep a secret.

The Disappearance of Stephen Small

The Small family was one of the most prominent and wealthy in Kankakee. Stephen's great-grandfather, Len Small, served as governor of Illinois during the 1920s, and until 1986 the Small family owned a multistate media company, of which Stephen had been an executive. The Smalls also owned the Bradley House, a beautiful, ornate home designed by Frank Lloyd Wright and located in Kankakee's Riverview neighborhood.[41]

On September 2, 1987, shortly after midnight, Stephen Small received a phone call reporting that someone was breaking into the Bradley House. When Small went to investigate, he was kidnapped. Three hours later, Small called his wife and told her what happened, saying that his assailants were demanding a million-dollar ransom. A second call provided details for a proposed exchange. Police eventually traced the calls to gas stations in nearby Aroma Park. A couple, Danny Edwards and his girlfriend Nancy Rish, had been seen there, and they were arrested two days after the kidnapping.[42]

Edwards led police to a remote field in Pembroke Township, where they found Small's body buried in a homemade wooden box six feet long and three feet wide. Edwards and Rish had intended to keep Small alive, placing water, candy bars, and a flashlight in the box with him. Tragically, Small died from asphyxiation because the pipe running from the box to the open air was too thin to provide adequate ventilation. Kankakee County Coroner James Orrison reported that Small could not have survived more than three or four hours in the box.[43] Orrison described the location where Small died: "It's a very isolated area out there, just woods and sand."[44] Edwards and Rish were both convicted of murder and sentenced to life imprisonment.[45]

21st Century VOTE Rally

The Gangster Disciples have been one of Chicago's largest street gangs, and most people have a general idea as to their inner-city operations. But less known were the gang's connections to political organizing efforts to shape the passage and enforcement of laws. They were affiliates of the political action group 21st Century VOTE, and on September 11, 1993, the organization held its annual rally on a private fifteen-acre field outside of Leesville in Pembroke Township.[46]

According to estimates, between seven and ten thousand people surged into Pembroke that day in hundreds of buses and cars.[47] An event flyer directed participants from Chicago to take the less populated back roads instead of Interstate 57.[48] Unsurprisingly, Pembroke's neighboring communities were unsettled upon learning of the gathering and its gang affiliation. Most gas stations and small businesses in Momence and other nearby towns closed early that Saturday afternoon.[49] Pembroke Township supervisor Barbara Smith-Jones also expressed reservations about the rally:

"We don't know anything about it. People asked, and I didn't know anything. . . . To come into the Township and not tell anyone about it—this is wrong." After the Chicago Police Department's Gang Crimes Unit alerted Kankakee County sheriff Bernie Thompson about the rally earlier that week, Thompson assigned all sworn personnel a full-day shift and activated his auxiliary deputies. He ordered the officers to create a perimeter around the field as a "passive" measure to ensure that traffic kept moving and that ambulances could enter as needed.[50]

One rally organizer, Tom Harris, stated that the local communities were overreacting to a picnic solely meant to mobilize political action surrounding upcoming elections of judges, aldermen, and state legislators. "Let's not assume that what you see is what it is because you really don't know," Harris said. Other reports suggested a clear presence of the Gangster Disciples. Various murals and signs displayed six pointed stars, pitchforks, and other affiliated symbols, as well as depictions of gang leaders. At one point a recorded greeting of "King" Larry Hoover, founder of the Gangster Disciples, was played to the assembly.[51]

According to the sheriff's police report, "sporadic gunfire" was heard throughout the day, but only one known injury—a woman struck in the head with a baseball bat—occurred, and she refused treatment.[52] James Taylor and his father attended the rally to report on it in their newspaper, the *Kankakee City News*. They stated that participants were reluctant to speak with them and only permitted a few photographs. Taylor also reported that event organizers had contacted a private ambulance crew from Chicago to be present, but the crew left after only an hour.[53]

The sheriff never felt the need to move in and break up the rally, which began to dissipate on its own around 7:00 P.M. when lightning and rain threatened. The sheriff also noted that participants were careful to clean the site of trash and other materials before departing.[54] This fact did not placate Bruce Huot, a county board member and owner of two gas stations in Momence that closed early that day. The following week Huot pushed for a stronger county ordinance to govern large gatherings.[55] According to Huot, "The eastern edge of the county was laid siege to by a bunch of thugs."[56]

Illegal Dumping

Pembroke Township has hosted a particularly unsanitary underground market, serving as the dumping ground for those looking to rid themselves of noxious, poisonous, or otherwise undesirable materials. Paying little regard to the natural habitat or the people in close proximity, outsiders travel to Pembroke—often during the middle of the night—to dispose of substances that licensed landfills refuse to accept. Authorities once discovered ninety-three rusting drums of suspected chemical waste in an open field behind an abandoned home on Old Spinning Wheel Road. The former owner of the land (who technically lost the property when he failed to make a payment on his land installment contract) struck an agreement with a junkyard operator in Indiana who said that the landowner could have the barrels if he got rid of whatever was inside them.[57]

In another example, huge piles of tires have often collected on Pembroke land, the largest of which contained approximately 1.5 million tires.[58] Whether they were dumped with permission or without, the tires posed a major health risk. Water collecting inside them served as a breeding ground for mosquitoes and other insects. Moreover, the tires often caught fire due to arson or natural causes, which released harmful gases and oil that could have seeped into the township's drinking water supply.[59] Even though the state spent millions to shred and discard the tires safely, the piles continued to reappear when authorities were not looking.[60]

One of the strangest examples of illegal dumping occurred on the land of Pembroke resident Willie Nettles Bey. She arranged to have a small amount of fish scraps delivered to her property that she could use as fertilizer, but the selling party used the opportunity to dump all of their unwanted refuse. One day Nettles Bey went to Chicago for a funeral and returned to find large piles of fish parts in her front yard. According to her, "Right out there from that mulberry tree, there was three piles—and I'm not exaggerating—almost as tall as me, running blood red, with fish heads, skins, and guts."[61] Nettles Bey then hired someone to spread the fish parts around her entire lawn, but the ordeal was not over:

> I went to sleep one night, and my grandson said, "Grandma, someone is in the back." Well, I go to bed at 8 o'clock. I didn't feel like getting up. I told him, "Maybe they're hunting." I don't approve of hunting on this place, but just let me sleep. He said, "Grandma, they still back there." So I got up, got dressed, and went back there. There was a 40-foot trailer with 162 55-gallon drums. . . . Fish heads and guts were everywhere.

Unable to spread any more of the fish parts on top of her lawn, Nettles Bey needed another solution. At times she used them for fuel. "It's amazing how much fat is on a catfish head. I know that from experience because I ran out of wood, and I went out there with my bucket, and I got a bunch of catfish heads, and I burned the catfish heads. They make excellent fires." Yet

Nettles Bey could not burn all of what was deposited on her land without alerting the fire department and eliciting a hefty fine. Instead, she gathered several volunteers from the community to dig a huge hole on her property. They put the fish parts in the hole and covered them with a thick layer of soil. Feeling there was no sense letting the fertilizer go to waste, Nettles Bey planted corn, beans, watermelons, and squash on the land. "Some of that corn is probably fifteen feet tall," she said.

Although Pembroke bears a reputation throughout Kankakee County for disproportionately high crime, analyzing actual crime statistics is not a straightforward process. Federal law requires law enforcement agencies to report certain "index crimes" to the FBI annually, but neither Pembroke Township nor the Village of Hopkins Park has maintained a police force to tally local offenses. The Kankakee County Sheriff's Office has regularly patrolled Pembroke, but it is not required to report crime statistics at the township level. The sheriff's office makes certain geographic data regarding six index crimes—homicide, robbery, aggravated assault and battery, burglary, theft, motor vehicle theft—publicly available online, and this information can be used to estimate crime figures in Pembroke. The data, however, reflect preliminary assessments of crimes soon after they occur, rather than the final dispositions of police investigations used in the FBI's Uniform Crime Reports. Further, these crime records are only available for complete years since 2011, so it is not possible to determine whether historical rumors of rampant crime during prior decades are grounded in reality or mere speculation.

In spite of these limitations, estimates indicate that Pembroke's incidences of illicit activity during recent years are relatively numerous. Table 5.1 generally compiles available data from 2011 through 2014 and depicts the average number of crimes per year in Pembroke Township, other nearby towns, and the county as a whole. The numbers are adjusted for population in table 5.2.

Any inferences from the tables must be tempered due to the small sample sizes of population and crimes—particularly with low-incidence crimes like homicide for which a single occurrence can considerably influence seeming trends. Nonetheless, with a few exceptions, rates for nearly all types of these index crimes during the last few years are higher in Pembroke than elsewhere in the county. Even next to statistics from the highly urban contexts of Chicago and Cook County, incidences of homicide, aggravated assault, and burglary in Pembroke are comparatively high (table 5.3).

Table 5.1. Average Annual Number of Crimes by Area, 2011–14

	Homicide	Robbery	Aggravated Assault/ Battery	Burglary	Theft	Motor Vehicle Theft
Pembroke Township	1.25	1.75	11.75	39.00	50.25	6.50
Village of St. Anne	0.25	0	0.50	6.50	23.75	0.25
City of Momence	0	1.25	5.50	15.50	32.25	1.25
Village of Grant Park	0	0.25	0.25	2.50	9.75	0.25
City of Kankakee	5.00	86.50	107.75	330.25	831.50	41.50
Kankakee County	7.25	102.75	194.00	627.50	2,213.25	83.75

Source: BAIR Analytics, *RAIDS Online: Regional Analysis and Information Sharing,* accessed January 23, 2016, http://www.raidsonline.com; Illinois State Police, *Uniform Crime Reports,* 2012–14, http://www.isp.state.il.us. Pembroke statistics reflect data from the Kankakee County Sheriff's Department as provided on the RAIDS platform. Statistics from St. Anne, Grant Park, City of Kankakee, and Kankakee County reflect UCR data. Statistics from Momence reflect UCR data for years 2011 through 2013 and RAIDS data for year 2014 (2014 data not reported in UCR).

Although much of this crime has been imported into Pembroke, authorities often have had the most difficulty dealing with homegrown problems. Many local residents have a deep distrust of police and a reluctance to say anything about the misdeeds of a neighbor. In one incident, two Hopkins Park residents called the sheriff's office to report that they were being followed and harassed by three others in a car. When a sergeant responded, the car sped away. The officer pursued and stopped the three to arrest them, but a crowd of more than thirty family members quickly gathered, intimidating and threatening the officer. Only after several other officers responded could arrests occur.[62]

When pushing for the creation of a neighborhood watch program in Hopkins Park, Sheriff Thompson addressed the issue. He recalled a shooting at a tavern along the Front:

**Table 5.2. Average Annual Number of Crimes per One Thousand
Persons by Area, 2011–14**

	Homicide	Robbery	Aggravated Assault/ Battery	Burglary	Theft	Motor Vehicle Theft
Pembroke Township (2010 pop.: 2,140)	0.58	0.82	5.49	18.22	23.48	3.04
Village of St. Anne (2014 pop.: 1,233)	0.20	0	0.41	5.27	19.26	0.20
City of Momence (2014 pop.: 3,246)	0	0.39	1.69	4.78	9.94	0.39
Village of Grant Park (2014 pop.: 1,311)	0	0.19	0.19	1.91	7.44	0.19
City of Kankakee (2014 pop.: 27,026)	0.19	3.20	3.99	12.22	30.77	1.54
Kankakee County (2014 pop.: 111,375)	0.07	0.92	1.74	5.63	19.87	0.75

Source: BAIR Analytics, *RAIDS Online: Regional Analysis and Information Sharing*, http://www.raidsonline.com; Illinois State Police, *Uniform Crime Reports*, 2012–14, http://www.isp.state.il.us; U.S. Census Bureau, *Twenty-Third Census of the United States, 2010 Census Summary File 1: Total Population*, http://factfinder2.census.gov.

50 or 60 people saw it, but only five of them came forward, and the ones that did were related to the victim. I understand their fear of retaliation. They're worried about themselves and their families, but we need the witnesses to make an arrest. People have to pull together and help.[63]

Barbara Bratton of Hopkins Park recognized, however, that the reluctance to inform originates from more than a fear of retaliation. After the remains of a local high school student were found four months after she went missing in 1978, Bratton wrote a column in the *Pembroke Herald-Eagle* and implored her neighbors to report what they knew:

This week, we all remain alarmed over the rash of crimes in our area. The break-in of the Alternative School, the disappearance of equipment at the Senior Citizens Building, [and] the body found in Strickland Park.

Table 5.3. Average Annual Number of Crimes per One Thousand
Persons in Pembroke and the Chicago Area, 2011–14

	Homicide	Robbery	Aggravated Assault/ Battery	Burglary	Theft	Motor Vehicle Theft
Pembroke Township (2010 pop.: 2,140)	0.58	0.82	5.49	18.22	23.48	3.04
City of Chicago (2014 pop.: 2,724,121)	0.16	4.50	4.72	7.49	24.81	5.39
Cook County (2014 pop.: 5,246,456)	0.10	2.75	2.89	5.87	20.75	3.39

Source: BAIR Analytics, *RAIDS Online: Regional Analysis and Information Sharing*,
http://www.raidsonline.com; Illinois State Police, *Uniform Crime Reports*, 2012–14,
http://www.isp.state.il.us; U.S. Census Bureau, *Twenty-Third Census of the United
States, 2010 Census Summary File 1: Total Population*, http://factfinder2.census.gov.
Chicago and Cook County statistics generally reflect UCR data.

. . . Most times, we know our neighbor's kids are involved in some petty
crime and we refused to report it because we know it will hurt the parent,
or if we tell the parent, the kids will say you don't like them and the parent
excepts [*sic*] what the child says. As much as we hate it, we are going to
have to stop protecting our criminals. It will be hard, but as Christians,
we are as guilty as they are when we buy stolen goods or protect them.[64]

Pembroke's refusal to report on itself may have perpetuated a destructive
system, but it is also indicative of a perspective held within the community.
To many, the fear of losing someone in the community to drugs or violent
crime exists alongside of the fear of losing someone else to prison. Losing
anyone is a severe loss in Pembroke where communal ties—formed during decades of isolation and struggle—are sacrosanct. The people that one
would turn over to the police are kin, whether they are related by blood or
not. As Larry Barnes described it, "It's hard to point a finger at who's who.
It's a close-knit community."

Glaciers flattened most of the midwestern terrain but left sand deposits in Pembroke that coalesced into tall dunes. Though not suited for commercial agriculture, these rolling savannas are home to several rare species like the black oak. *Photograph by author.*

Gertrude Higginbottom (*left*) was a great-granddaughter of Pembroke's first black settlers, Pap and Mary Tetter, who arrived in the 1860s. Arthur Collins (*right*) was a white man adopted into the growing black community after his aunt married one of the Tetters' sons. *Sacred Heart Mission Archives (reproduced with permission).*

After World War II, Chicago real estate firms offered installment contracts that allowed people with poor credit to buy property in Pembroke but permitted the firms to retake the land after one missed payment. *Wild Irish Rose Photography by Peggy Heck (reproduced with permission).*

After signing an installment contract, families would travel from Chicago to Pembroke on the weekends, using their paychecks to buy as few as ten concrete blocks to gradually build their country homes. Many were completed, but others were left as abandoned American dreams. *Wild Irish Rose Photography by Peggy Heck (reproduced with permission).*

In the 1930s and 1940s nuns from the order of the Sisters of the Sacred Heart of Mary rode Pembroke's dirt roads by horse-drawn buggy, looking to recruit Catholics. They helped build Sacred Heart Church, where a reverse evangelization also occurred as Catholic ritual was infused with black culture. *Sacred Heart Mission Archives (reproduced with permission).*

Barbara Bratton (*left*) wrote a weekly column in the *Pembroke Herald-Eagle* and founded a re-sale shop in 1962. The shop was a substitute for department stores, extending the lives of unwanted furniture, clothes, and appliances by supplying them cheaply to those in need. *Sacred Heart Mission Archives (reproduced with permission).*

Reverend Tony Taschetta (*left*) first visited Pembroke as a thirty-two-year-old priest in 1972, but once Barbara Bratton decided he should stay, she reached out to the area bishop. A few weeks later Father Tony became Sacred Heart's resident priest. *Sacred Heart Mission Archives (reproduced with permission).*

Ben and Bertha Koger built the Church of the Cross in 1989 with their personal savings. The interlocking Jesus sign is a familiar sight on the Blacktop, Pembroke's primary artery named when it was one of the few paved roads in the township. *Wild Irish Rose Photography by Peggy Heck (reproduced with permission).*

In 1999 Governor George Ryan announced that a $104 million women's prison, along with numerous economic benefits, was coming to Pembroke. Construction began but never finished, and the concrete structures meant to be the prison foundation now block the road leading to the site. *Wild Irish Rose Photography by Peggy Heck (reproduced with permission).*

Some have sought Pembroke for its isolation—not for tranquility's sake but to get away with something they could not elsewhere. Unfortunately, such illicit activity includes the dumping of cars, tires, chemicals, and more. *Wild Irish Rose Photography by Peggy Heck (reproduced with permission).*

Those who look only at the problems of Pembroke fail to grasp the pride and affection that many residents have for their hometown—powerful resources that have enabled the community to survive in the face of difficulties. *Wild Irish Rose Photography by Peggy Heck (reproduced with permission).*

The Nature Conservancy has established several preserves around Pembroke to protect the dunes from environmental threats. Many in the community support the goals of preservation, but they also worry about potentially losing control of their home. *Photograph by author.*

Pembroke's intersections become crowded during election season. Here, signs for state and local candidates in 2014 stand beside a poster for Basu Natural Farms, where the owners host an annual festival to commemorate the early twentieth-century black nationalist leader Marcus Garvey. *Photograph by author.*

Sharon White, Pembroke Township's supervisor since 2013, was trained as an electrical engineer. In 2003 she left her job as a voice-recognition software developer in Chicago's suburbs to grow organic vegetables on her farm in Pembroke and write grant applications for the community. *Photography by author.*

In Chicago, Johari Cole-Kweli was a biology researcher and her husband was an information-technology specialist, but they left for Pembroke, where they now teach computer classes and develop "green" methods to operate their farm sustainably, thereby incorporating twenty-first-century technology into rural life. *Photograph by author.*

The first Project Hearts of Hope team stands in front of the mural commemorating the group's experience in August 1999. On the right are the author and his friend Adam, who is perched on the author's shoulders. *Ken and Michelle Barrie (reproduced with permission)*

6

"In the Eyes of the Angels"

As part of our experience, Ken and Michelle had arranged for small groups of us to sit and meet with parishioners from Sacred Heart. Ken recommended that we prepare a few questions in advance for our interviews, so I wrote mine into my journal. When I returned from my run to the state line, I quickly cleaned up and prepared for my first interview of the trip.

We started off with the easy information. Name: Nancy Greenley Williams. Born: 1945 in Pembroke Township. Ms. Williams added that her parents and grandparents had also been born in Pembroke. She currently lived in Kankakee but continued to attend mass at Sacred Heart. When we asked why, Ms. Williams responded immediately: "I like the closeness and the sharing that we have." She emphasized that the connection within her community was not meant to exclude. "The love, the fellowship, we try to extend that to everyone," said Ms. Williams, and we agreed that we had felt that warmth inside the Sacred Heart walls during these past few days.

Ms. Williams continued and told us about a past ordeal through which she had come to feel such comfort in her church and faith. A few years before, her mother became ill. The doctors had located a tumor inside her brain, and they expected her to live only for a few more weeks. According to Ms. Williams, "It breaks your heart when you have to care for someone. When you know they're not going to get well. You see that person every day. Because you remember how the person was before."

Yet Ms. Williams found solace in her church. "Every day we had to constantly ask God for the strength to persevere," she said. When her mother could no longer attend weekly mass, Ms. Williams assumed her mother's responsibility of cleaning the building prior to services, a task Ms. Williams's grandfather had once performed as well. Despite the initial diagnosis, Ms. Williams's mother passed away a year after doctors first discovered the tumor. Ms. Williams continued to clean the church every week. She said it was her way of remembering her mother before her ailment.

Our forty-five-minute interview passed quickly, and we soon headed into the church for the Tuesday evening revival. But before we finished, Ms. Williams told us, "I think it's a wonderful thing that you're doing. I'm really proud of you. All of you."[1] We thanked her and walked into Sacred Heart together, extending the interview informally as we chatted along the way.

That night's revival was a full Catholic mass. The assembly sang all five verses of the entrance song, "We've Come This Far by Faith," and we listened as Mr. Hayes (the man I had met while cutting through weeds behind the rectory) delivered the first and second readings. After Father Tony's homily, we came to the Prayers of the Faithful. At my parish in Kankakee this portion of the mass consisted of five or six prayers, each no longer than a couple sentences read while the assembly remained standing. Near the end, the priest called for a moment of silence during which we quietly reflected upon our own intercessions. But here in Hopkins Park things were done differently.

As usual, Father Tony offered the first few prayers, after which he continued, "Now, we lay before You the prayers of those gathered here today." At that invitation all of the Sacred Heart parishioners sat down. When the teens realized it a few seconds later, we also sat. Then one at a time, the people of Sacred Heart stood and offered their prayers aloud. These intercessions usually started with a salutation to God, but it quickly became clear that the speakers weren't only directing their prayers upward, but outward to the other people there.

A woman began, *"I pray in gratitude and thanksgiving because Jesus is a friend. I just knew He would come through for me in His time. They've finally started work on my house." Another person reacted excitedly, "They did?" And another, "When they gonna be done, Betty?" The woman responded, "I don't know. They're just getting in on the electrical right now. But God is good." She spoke for a couple minutes about the refurbishments to her home that had been nearly destroyed by a fire several months ago, and the assembly answered back with words of encouragement and support. At the end she concluded, "We pray to the Lord," and all answered, "Lord, hear our prayer."*

The woman's prayer was a conversation—among herself, her parish community, and her God. Others stood up to discuss a son waging an ongoing war with alcoholism, a leaky roof and the hope for no rain during the upcoming week, and a cousin whose baby would turn two years old soon. In addition, they would reiterate the prayers of those people who had already spoken. "I want to pray for Betty, that her house gets fixed up soon," they would each say. "We are all so proud of her." Nancy Williams was the next to stand. "I want to say a prayer for my mother, who I miss each and every day," she said. The parishioners chimed in with words of concern, and a few minutes later, Ms. Williams ended her prayer, "For this community, where we can support each other."

At this point, I'm not entirely sure what went through my head, but I stood up. Maybe I considered Gertrude Higginbottom's words about letting go and letting the spirit out, or Father Tony's appeal for a Teflon moment. I may have thought how much easier it is to have a conversation than to speak publicly before a crowd, or maybe I considered a word I learned earlier that year in religion class— "agape." But for whatever reason, I stood up, and I offered my own intercession, praying for Ms. Williams's mother, my own mother, my father and sister, for our new friend Duke, for courage, for strength, and for this community. Looking out, I saw people from the teen group like Adam and Angela, as well as people from Pembroke like Ms. Williams, Mr. Hayes, and Ms. Higginbottom. All of them were nodding, smiling, and amen'ing back at me. I felt real, unconditional support. "We pray to the Lord," I said. The congregation answered back, "Lord, hear our prayer."

* * *

C hurch was and remains the hub for communal life in Pembroke. It has been a place for initial introduction into the community, a source of perpetual support during difficult times, a venue to mobilize and organize around important issues of the day, and a platform to worship in an open, expressive, genuine manner. On Saturday nights the party was once found in the taverns of the Front, but even decades after those taverns were shuttered, the Sunday morning celebrations in church halls across the township remain lively. Tellingly, during the high point of Pembroke's population in the 1970s, estimates put the number of bars at thirty, but the number of churches at eighty.[2]

Residents of Pembroke are predominantly Christian, but as Nancy Williams expressed, faith in Pembroke is not exclusionary.[3] The community has welcomed not only believers from outside the group, but beliefs outside the norm as well. When a Catholic priest and nun—both white French Canadians—came to Pembroke in the late 1930s, they arrived as missionaries to spread their catechism. Yet even though many in Pembroke converted to Catholicism, it became clear that a reverse evangelization also occurred. Catholic rituals became permeated with the spiritual virtues and richness of black culture. Faith in Pembroke offers a distinct model for the active and healthy interface of increasingly diverse religious communities.

Church was instrumental even during the early stages of Pembroke's settlement. At the beginning of the twentieth century, southern faith communities cultivated the growing momentum of the Great Migration by offering stability in the face of the journey's severe uncertainty. Hesitant travelers often found like-minded individuals at church, and they formed migration clubs so that they could encourage each other along the way. Would-be migrants wrote letters to churches in the North, inquiring not just about conditions for black people in Chicago but making sure they would have a place to worship.[4]

For many of the southern migrants, arrival in a large city allowed them for the first time to choose from a wide variety of Christian and non-Christian denominations. Some found a home in the South Side's established houses of prayer. Other migrants reconstituted their former churches from

Alabama and Mississippi in Chicago, using the same name, songs, and liturgy that they used before. Still others formed entirely new faith communities by associating themselves with the outreach efforts of northern (and traditionally white) denominations.

The origins of churches in Pembroke reflect a similar diversity. Much like the migration clubs in Mississippi and Alabama, individuals relocating from Chicago to Pembroke often planned and executed their journey together. In the early 1930s a group of families from the Morgan Park neighborhood of Chicago moved to Leesville where they sought to establish a Baptist church like their old one in the city. In 1934 they wrote to the leaders of their former congregation and asked them to send someone to Pembroke who could conduct services for them. The request was soon granted, permitting the new faith community to hold prayer meetings on Wednesday nights and services on Sunday mornings in various houses throughout the township. In 1939 the congregants requested a full-time pastor from Morgan Park, and Reverend William C. Dixon was sent to lead the newly named Greater St. Paul Baptist Church. Also that year the church purchased land in what is now Old Hopkins Park and on which they built a permanent home. As attendance grew, Greater St. Paul established a church board that oversaw numerous improvements to the building. Individuals from Pembroke were named deacons of the church, but the pastor usually commuted down from Morgan Park.[5]

Other residents created entirely new, independent churches. In 1971 Ben and Bertha Koger moved from Chicago to Hopkins Park to retire, but they remained incredibly busy. Bertha became a director for the Kankakee County Mental Health Center, state secretary for the Illinois Association of Senior Citizens, and an active member of the local Rotary Club and United Way.[6] Neighbors regularly called Ben "Dad," though he referred to himself merely as Bertha's driver.[7] For many years, the Kogers did not join a particular church in Pembroke, but tried several different ones. They eventually settled on Christian Hope Church, whose membership was outgrowing its facility. Bertha led a fundraising drive to build a new church and raised a considerable sum, but much of it ultimately was used to pay an outstanding debt on the old facility. Bertha had difficulty raising any more funds, so in 1989 she and Ben decided to build their own church. The Kogers used approximately $235,000 of their own money to construct the Church of the Cross. They wanted the 280-seat facility to be an active house of worship that would not only be used for liturgical services but also as a theatre, classroom, and banquet hall. The Kogers expressly dedicated the church as a nondenominational Christian community. "We all have the same God," they said. "This just gives [people] a chance to be a member of a place that practices that."[8] Reverend Jon Dyson, who would later serve as mayor of Hopkins Park, became the church's first pastor. Although Bertha died in 1994 from a brain tumor and Ben was killed eleven years later in a house fire, the church they founded to welcome all remains open.[9]

Still other faith communities developed as people from outside traditional African American churches established mission outposts in Pembroke. In 1949 Reverend James Lark, the first black Mennonite bishop, established the Rehoboth Mennonite Church in Pembroke. Rehoboth, which means "there is room," was opened to serve the Pembroke community and in turn to model and teach the Mennonite faith. Mark and Pauline Lehman, both white, came to town in 1955 as workers at Rehoboth, and Mark was soon named pastor. During their thirty-two years in Pembroke, Mark served as president of the local Habitat for Humanity chapter and a board member of the Pembroke Community Center.[10] According to an article in the *Pembroke Herald-Eagle*, Mark and Pauline "became well known and liked by many for the work and numerous services they rendered on behalf of those in need or otherwise."[11] After the Lehmans left Rehoboth in 1992 to pursue other ministries, Rose Covington, resident of Pembroke since she was two years old and township supervisor for several years, became pastor of the Mennonite church.[12] In no sense could Covington be deemed an interloper or outsider; her appointment demonstrated that, regardless of its origins, Rehoboth had become a Pembroke institution.

Groups of Methodists, Baptists, and Jehovah's Witnesses made similar outreach efforts in the impoverished community. Typically (and somewhat controversially), a mission of evangelization involves the efforts of an outsider to change the insider. But, as in the case of Rehoboth, the outsiders also changed. This pattern of mutual exchange is readily apparent in the history of Sacred Heart Mission, where two millennia of Catholic tradition found a new form of practice and expression.

Like many longstanding institutions in the United States, the American Catholic Church and particularly the Archdiocese of Chicago have at times struggled with racial prejudice. In the late nineteenth and early twentieth centuries, Chicago's Catholic community was composed primarily of white, ethnic immigrants who competed with the city's growing black population for jobs, housing, and political clout. Such tensions did not dissipate in Catholic pews and rectories. For instance, black Catholics were barred from clerical leadership in the United States until 1886 when the first African American priest, Father Augustus Tolton, was ordained. Even then some parishes would have refused to allow Father Tolton to celebrate mass. The priest instead helped to establish St. Monica's Catholic Church in 1893 in Chicago's South Side, which was formed after several black members of a predominantly white congregation asked for their own parish "where they might retain and build up their faith which was beginning to be greatly hampered by the growing prejudice in the white church."[13] Believing that separation would best allow the faith to prosper within a racially divided Chicago, Archbishop George Mundelein promised in 1917 that St. Monica's would stay "reserved entirely for the colored Catholics of Chicago."[14]

May Hogan, a Catholic, was a white realtor from Chicago who sold properties to black clients during the 1930s. Reviled by some within both the black and white communities, Hogan made a profit from her work, but she saw her efforts as a remedy to the ills of segregation in black urban neighborhoods. "The overcrowded conditions and restrictions in the City are appalling," Hogan once wrote.[15]

Hogan was committed to her church but found its treatment of black people equally as troubling. According to Hogan, "Our Catholic religion has opened its doors only partially to the colored people," noting that several parishes in Chicago still refused to accept black priests or nuns. She described her experience participating in mass at St. Elizabeth's, another predominantly black Catholic church located at Forty-First and Wabash Streets:

> It fills one with extreme piety to see those Negroes approaching and leaving the Communion's rail—[their] deep, sincere, devotion. They put whites to shame . . . for what is there to offer them when they can go only part way, and why? To me it seems so frightfully unjust.

Hogan, like Frank Moscickis and other realtors, believed Pembroke Township offered an opportunity for black Chicagoans to improve their situations. "My hope has been a colored Colony near to Chicago," she wrote in 1939. As she sold more land in Pembroke to black families, she became acquainted with the neighboring Catholic leaders.

Father Theodore Demarais was the pastor of St. Patrick's in Momence, and Sister Mary Adelaide Gagnon was a member of the Sisters of the Sacred Heart of Mary, a religious order of nuns that taught in St. Patrick's school. Father Demarais and Sister Adelaide knew of the overcrowded conditions in Chicago's black neighborhoods, but they also saw firsthand that rural life could be even more difficult in Pembroke where problems arose from an overabundance of space. Electricity and running water did not reach the remote homes of Pembroke at that time, and roads connecting the township became hazards after a light vernal rain. It took extra effort for community members separated by longer distances to meet, trade, celebrate, congregate, and worship together.[16]

Father Demarais and Sister Adelaide were compelled to help shorten those distances, and they reached out to people like May Hogan who might provide resources and ideas about how to serve the spiritual and material needs of people in Pembroke. In a letter dated July 25, 1939, Hogan wrote back to Father Demarais and related her experience helping Redeeming Christian Spiritualist Church, a black congregation in Chicago, purchase land in Pembroke for the construction of a satellite location. When promoting the land to Redeeming Christian, Hogan went into the homes of its members, attended their services, and met their pastor, a woman named Reverend I. Smith. Hogan had this to say:

> I've never mentioned my Catholic religion, nor they to me, but I suspect they know it. [I]t dawned on me all of a sudden, that these Spiritualist people are about 95 percent Catholic already. [Rev. Smith] only recently, said to me, "We are just the same as Catholics only our services are out loud while Catholics is silent."

Hogan felt that people in Pembroke would be receptive to the Catholic message of service and devotion. She also described the profound impact that this community had on her own faith, "No home in Chicago, regardless of creed is as demonstrative of Catholicity as [Rev. Smith's]. They observe Lent so strictly, I am ashamed."

Less than a month later, Father Demarais met with officials of the Archdiocese of Chicago to propose the foundation of a Catholic mission based out of Momence that would minister to the Pembroke community. On August 30, 1939, the archdiocese's vice chancellor responded, "I am writing to inform you that His Eminence gives you permission to open a Mission concerning which you spoke to me last week, provided it adds no greater burden to your parish and can be handled without too much difficulty."[17] The enterprise was named Sacred Heart Mission.

Sister Adelaide, along with other nuns of her order, immediately began the task of recruiting a membership. At the time, the number of Catholics in Pembroke was in the low single digits, and Arthur Collins was one of them. As he recalled, Sister Adelaide "found me while she was driving around, looking for Catholics."[18] When she could not use Father Demarais's car,

Sister Adelaide borrowed a horse and buggy from Collins's aunt and rode around the countryside wearing a black-and-white habit. She spoke with anyone willing to listen and offered catechetical instruction in the residents' homes.[19] But there was something missing—Sister Adelaide felt that their efforts would be futile until they offered a weekly mass. So like disciples of the early Catholic Church, Father Demarais, Sister Adelaide, and the first parishioners of Sacred Heart held liturgies in a makeshift tent that could not fit more than a dozen people. As attendance grew, they moved their services to a school basement.[20]

In early 1941 Father Demarais reported to the archdiocese on the mission and its growth. He noted that the sisters were "out in the woods again conducting their vacation school" where they taught not only religion, but basic academic skills as well. After specifically mentioning the growing activity and influence of other missionary groups in Pembroke, including the Nazarenes, Jehovah's Witnesses, and the "Holy Rollers" (a not-so-complimentary term for Protestant groups with active expressions of worship, sometimes including rolling on the ground), Father Demarais pointedly requested, "Perhaps His Excellency the Archbishop would feel that at this time it would be well to purchase property. . . . A chapel is needed and I feel certain it will crystallize our work."[21]

On June 30, 1941, the archdiocese granted Father Demarais permission to purchase land and promised to send the necessary funds for the property and building materials.[22] According to Father Demarais, the people of Pembroke and Momence donated over one thousand hours of labor to construct the chapel.[23] Long before the carpentry and woodworking were complete, weekly masses commenced for the eighty-five members of the new congregation. "We have no pews as yet," wrote Father Demarais. "They are using wooden folding chairs—which gives the Church the 'aspect of a mission.'"[24] On May 2, 1942, Samuel Cardinal Stritch, the new archbishop of Chicago, came to Pembroke and dedicated Sacred Heart Mission Chapel. Later that year Father Demarais sent a letter to the cardinal thanking him for his support and included a photograph of the finished chapel. Cardinal Stritch responded with pride, "This is one of the additions in the Archdiocese to which I can lay claim. It is not a great church but I am sure in the eyes of the angels it is a blessed spot of divine worship."[25]

Individuals like Father Demarais and Sister Adelaide came to Pembroke with an authentic willingness to serve, but they followed the community's lay leaders when identifying specifically how to do so. One such homegrown example was Barbara Bratton, who was born in 1902 in Duncan,

Mississippi, to the children of slaves. Before she turned ten, her family moved to Chicago where she lived for thirty-five years. There she worked at U.S. Tire and Rubber Company during the day and finished high school at night.[26] In 1945 a friend convinced her to spend a weekend away from the city so they could partake in one of Bratton's favorite hobbies—fishing. They traveled to the creeks of the Kankakee River, and with lines bobbing in the water, conversation turned to the topic of religion. Bratton was not Catholic, but she knew that her friend was, so she asked questions and listened intently to the description of the tiny new church in the country. Before the end of the weekend, Bratton attended mass at Sacred Heart with her friend and knew that she had found her version of the good life. Within a few years Bratton and her husband Carrol retired in Hopkins Park. She would later write, "What I wanted was a river to fish in and my church to pray in."[27]

Bratton quickly became active in the Pembroke and broader Kankakee County communities, serving on the boards of charities, social service agencies, and economic development organizations. She also wrote a regular column for Ozroe Bentley's *Pembroke Herald-Eagle* entitled "As I See It," which commented on everything from Christmas pageants at Sacred Heart to crime prevention within the community.[28] Although Bratton never had children, she helped raise hundreds, participating in numerous tutoring and literacy programs for young people and opening her home as a foster mother for approximately twenty neglected children of Pembroke.[29] Bratton's husband came to recognize a pattern that began upon meeting a disadvantaged child. He would say, "My wife is fixin' to give birth to another child. Her heart is pregnant."[30] According to another account, "In a crowd, no one would spot her as a leader. She was always clean, but disheveled. She would sit in a corner slouched over a cup of coffee with the ever present Salem [cigarette]."[31]

Bratton's contributions to Sacred Heart were numerous and substantial. In 1952 she helped to found the St. Martin de Porres Guild, an organization of parishioners dedicated to increasing membership, repairing the church, and hosting communal events like an annual fashion show.[32] The group also proposed and launched the Pembroke Alternative School, which partnered with the Kankakeeland Community Action Program and Diocese of Joliet (formed out of a portion of the Archdiocese of Chicago in 1948) to provide GED and job-training courses to people throughout the community.[33] St. Martin de Porres, who lived during the sixteenth and seventeenth centuries, had special significance to the Sacred Heart community because he was a person of mixed race remembered for his service on behalf of the poor. In spite of whatever indications may have existed to the contrary, St. Martin was a potent symbol that this predominantly black parish had a meaningful place within the Catholic Church.

During the late 1950s Bratton needed throat surgery that she could not afford, but Sacred Heart agreed to pay for her medical costs.[34] Her gratitude only increased when she learned that Sacred Heart itself was not financially self-sustaining. In order to repay the church, Bratton tried to find a way to ensure that Sacred Heart could pay its bills but continue to assist those in need.[35] She decided to open a store patterned on those of Catholic Charities, a social service agency that regularly opened establishments in low-income communities where people could donate or sell their unneeded clothes, appliances, and furniture, and others could purchase them as needed. After Bratton pitched her idea to parish leadership, Father Demarais sent her to Chicago for a week to study the methods of the Catholic Salvage Bureau. When she returned to Pembroke, she traveled throughout Kankakee County, speaking to regional women's clubs. Bratton's husband picked up donated goods once a week in his station wagon. "His pay?" Bratton would later write. "One 6-pack of beer for each day he worked. (smile.)" In 1962 Bratton herself paid the first two months' rent for a garage down the street from the church and opened the Sacred Heart Re-sale Shop.[36]

As manager of the re-sale shop, Bratton sought to turn out a competitive enterprise, ensuring a reasonable price for products that were always clean and clothes that were always pressed. Although the shop provided some revenue for Sacred Heart, it never refused anyone for inability to pay. It refurbished and restocked homes that were destroyed by fire.[37] In 1969 the shop itself burned to the ground, but volunteers rebuilt it twice as large and filled it with three times as much merchandise.[38]

Bratton passed away in 1990 from emphysema at the age of eighty-eight, but the re-sale shop continued to help those in need. A few years before her death, Bratton turned management of the store over to Louise Edwards, another Sacred Heart parishioner who upheld Bratton's philosophy. Edwards affirmed that it was her responsibility "to see that no one is in need."[39] Edwards's husband, Howard Jones, took over in 1995, and he welcomed an average of ten to fifteen people every day until poor health led him to retire in 2012.[40]

Due to people like Father Demarais, Sister Adelaide, and Barbara Bratton, Sacred Heart increased in numbers and presence within Pembroke Township. By the 1960s membership included an estimated three to four hundred people.[41] On June 16, 1968, Sacred Heart Mission was converted from a satellite mission of St. Patrick's in Momence to a freestanding parish known as Sacred Heart Catholic Church.

Father Joseph Butters became Sacred Heart's first resident priest. As a former assistant to Father Demarais at St. Patrick's, Father Butters was familiar with the community. He moved into the new church rectory that was donated by Pembroke resident Ellen Greenley.[42] Father Butters concerned himself not only with religious matters in the township but also the tangible problems affecting daily life. Along with other men of the community, Father Butters formed and served on a volunteer fire department.[43] He also worked alongside township supervisor Hollie McKee to advocate against the sale and placement of mobile-home trailers without ensuring they had proper drainage or septic systems—the very issue that spawned into an intra-village conflict leading to McKee's murder. One of the nuns at Sacred Heart recognized the leaders' courage in addressing the matter, although it is unlikely that she foresaw the tragic result: "Father realizes that this will bring on much adverse criticism against him and his co-workers, but neither he nor they will back down. They feel that the price of saving our people from the preying of these money-hungry men cannot come too high."[44]

Father Butters's eventual successor, Father Tony Taschetta, was a newly ordained, thirty-two-year-old priest when he first visited Pembroke in 1972. "My heart pounded as I got closer," he said. "I realized that I was in another world." Father Taschetta's first mass was Easter Sunday, and he recalled that everyone was dressed in his or her best, except Barbara Bratton. "She had on a pair of pants. I think I saw her wear a dress once in my life—and that was for the Bishop." After mass ended, Bratton went up to the young priest: "She looked me over, did everything but inspect my teeth, then turned to the congregation and announced, 'We'll take this one. He'll do just fine.'" Father Taschetta protested that he was still teaching at a seminary in the suburbs, but Bratton replied coolly, "We'll take care of that. Bishop Blanchette is a personal friend of mine. And I'm pretty close to God too." Two months and a petition drive later, Father Taschetta was assigned to Sacred Heart as an associate pastor.[45]

Father Taschetta, who was named pastor of Sacred Heart in 1976 and served in that role until 1982, brought his own cultural distinctiveness to Pembroke. Each January he commemorated the Italian Catholic holiday of the Epiphany by visiting as many homes as possible and extending the Christmas blessing of the Three Wise Men.[46] Even if he never led a mass by rolling on the church floor, Father Taschetta's active style and booming spirit mixed well with the vibrant Pembroke community. Indeed, Bratton would later write that he earned "the love and respect of Catholics *and* Protestants" in Pembroke.[47]

Sacred Heart received its first resident nuns in 1972 when Sister Mary Cecelia and Sister Ignatius Darch, both of the Sisters of the Sacred Heart of Mary order, moved to Pembroke. They cooked meals in exchange for lodging in a parishioner's home until the Martin de Porres Convent was built in 1978 on land purchased from Wesley Higginbottom, Gertrude's brother-in-law.[48] The nuns maintained Sister Adelaide's ministerial focus on education. They continued to hold supplemental lessons for Pembroke's youth, and at times they taught regular classes at the nearby public school. Lorenzo Smith, the local superintendent who was sometimes criticized for being an overly strict disciplinarian, found allies in the tough-minded sisters.[49] The following sentiment in the 1984 eulogy of Sister Darch reflects the attitude of every sister at Sacred Heart: She "had succeeded in something that many of us never realize. She knew that those whom she had come to serve had much to give her. She not only knew this but she also was ready and open to receive what they had to give."[50]

The church, in the spirit of its roots as a mission, has hosted a number of outside Catholic groups who travel to Pembroke for their own mission experience. As early as 1983, parish groups from the Chicago suburbs have given a week or as much as a month of service in exchange for the Sacred Heart experience.[51] In 1999 the Saints Patrick and Teresa Teen Group of Kankakee, led by Ken and Michelle Barrie, began their regular Hearts of Hope service trips. The latest iteration, Project Hearts of Hope 12, occurred during the summer of 2015. Various projects of past teen groups pepper the Sacred Heart property, including prayer gardens, signs, shelters, and murals.

The Sisters of the Sacred Heart of Mary have continued to send their members to live and work at Sacred Heart. However, as the number of available priests and Sacred Heart parishioners declined in the 1990s, the Diocese of Joliet determined not to assign a resident priest to the church. It has since reverted to its original status and name of Sacred Heart Mission.

Additionally, when Howard Jones retired from his position as manager of the re-sale shop in 2012, Sacred Heart also decided to close its doors. An aging membership and budgetary constraints cast perpetual doubt on Sacred Heart's future, but the parish has weathered such doubt before. A committed group of twenty to forty people continues to gather in the small church building on Sundays at noon and usually remains afterward for coffee and donuts in the church basement.

At its weekly mass, the Sacred Heart congregation unmistakably adheres to the official rite approved by the Catholic magisterium, but after years of practice, it has crafted its own form of worship. Sister Mary Beth Clements, one of the nuns currently living at Sacred Heart, arrives in the church before anyone else. No longer adorned in the formal black and white habit that Sister Adelaide once wore, Sister Clements stands near the front door in khakis and a navy blazer. She happily greets parishioners young and old by name. As people arrive, they pass images of a dark-skinned Holy Family and a statue of St. Martin de Porres on the way to their seats.

Mass generally begins a few minutes late as an electric organ and a choir of four or five elderly women lead a song from the *African American Heritage Hymnal* kept in every row. On special occasions a percussionist from the neighboring Protestant church adds to the music. The lector rises and recites the scriptural passage designated by the official liturgical calendar, but she includes a few extra words of color commentary to impress what she deems of prime importance. The insights of a visiting priest's homily are punctuated by exclamations of praise from people in the crowd. "Amen, Amen," they affirm.

At this point the pace of mass would allow it to finish within the unofficial Catholic time limit of one hour, but that schedule quickly derails. During the Prayers of the Faithful, any congregant (and usually every congregant) stands one at a time to offer their petitions before God and each other. After a minimum of fifteen minutes, the celebrant proceeds with the Eucharistic Prayer. Unlike many other Catholic assemblies where people avoid contact and awkwardly pretend to not notice their neighbors while reciting the Our Father, everyone at Sacred Heart joins hands. They create lines not only within their pews, but across and over the pews so that every person in the sanctuary is tangibly linked to each other.

The Sign of Peace lasts nearly as long as the intercessions because close friends and family members exchange stories instead of short handshakes and blessings. Following Holy Communion, parishioners make announcements about upcoming meetings or events not just planned at Sacred Heart but throughout Pembroke Township. They commemorate birthdays, anniversaries, and graduations and provide one final opportunity for any more Prayers of the Faithful that were missed earlier. Mass concludes with the recessional song, but conversation among the faithful continues for another half hour. Sacred Heart has developed an undeniably Catholic worship that connects the vibrancy of black culture with the intimacy of a small community.

Unfortunately, relations between African Americans and the American Catholic Church have been hindered by acts of inhospitality and intolerance that occurred in spite of the Church's official directive to spread love. As Sacred Heart parishioner and longtime township supervisor Robert Hayes once asked, "How many people went to communion to receive Christ, but hated their fellow man and fellow woman?"

Apart from the explicit exclusion of black people from certain parish memberships well into the twentieth century, a separate, unintentional form of exclusion may have kept many aspects of black culture away from Catholic communities even longer. An unyielding adherence to a practice of solemn processions, repeated chants, and particular music does not readily connect with a spirituality rooted in impromptu expressions of song and spirit. Even after the Second Vatican Council, when the Church opened itself up to a more congregation-driven form of worship and discontinued the use of Latin as the language spoken during mass, other barriers of translation likely served to keep the overall number of black Catholics low. Although African Americans make up 13.2 percent of all Americans, they represent only 3 percent of American Catholics.[52] Further, according to a collection of relatively recent estimates, there are approximately 41,500 priests and 60,000 sisters in the United States, of whom only 250 priests and 400 sisters are black.[53]

Nevertheless, this relatively small group has shown greater attachment to the Church than Catholics as a whole and particularly white Catholics. Dr. Darren Davis and Dr. Don Pope-Davis of the University of Notre Dame conducted the 2011 National Black Catholic Survey to analyze the religious engagement of African American Catholics. According to those sampled, 58.4 percent of African American Catholics, but only 40.3 percent of white Catholics, considered themselves spiritually engaged. This disparity is especially potent among younger Catholics aged eighteen to twenty-nine: 52.8 percent of young, African American Catholics said they were strongly engaged in their parish as opposed to 26.8 percent of young, white Catholics. When asked about why they would leave the church, 37 percent of the African American Catholics described a nonspecific, gradual drift away from their church, but 55.7 percent of white Catholics cite this drift.[54]

Other studies also indicate a declining adherence to Catholicism in the United States. According to the Pew Research Center, the Catholic share of the U.S. population dropped from 23.9 percent in 2007 to 20.8 percent in 2014. Of all people raised Catholic, 12.9 percent have left the Church. Although some people have converted to Catholicism, they represent a mere 2 percent of current Catholics.[55] Another study by Gallup reported in 2009 that since 1955 the percentage of Catholics attending weekly mass dropped from 75 percent to 45 percent, and among Catholics aged twenty-one to twenty-nine, it has dropped further from 73 percent to 30 percent.[56] These trends might be even more pronounced if not for the increasing number of Latino Catholics that have immigrated to the United States during the past half century.

While church engagement has waned in recent years among white Catholics, it remains comparatively strong among black Catholics. According to Father Cyprian Davis's *History of Black Catholics in the United States*, "The story of African American Catholicism is the story of a people who obstinately clung to a faith that gave them sustenance, even when it did not always make them feel welcome."[57] This experience offers promise to the American Catholic Church, which, as a perpetual institution, must continuously refresh and reinvigorate itself while holding on to its core elements.

Nationally, black Catholics continue to display high levels of engagement, but attendance at Sacred Heart has declined in recent years, coinciding with an aging and shrinking population throughout all of Pembroke. Nonetheless, the parish has found numerous ways during its seventy-five years to infuse Catholic tradition with an engaged black spirituality. The leaders of Sacred Heart have had enough faith in their own Catholicism that they could remain open to new forms of expression and service. Father Demarais and Sister Adelaide strove to spread Catholic teaching throughout the township, but it was their pastoral humility that permitted the teaching to take root and truly grow. They allowed individuals like Barbara Bratton to identify the needs of the parish and to respond with measures creatively and uniquely tailored to meet those needs. Father Butters understood that he must direct his energies beyond a simple stirring of spirits in the parish, to advancing the social needs of all in Pembroke. Finally, Father Taschetta unlocked the community's inherent curiosity by sharing his own cultural distinctiveness and traditions in a spirit of kinship. Each of these people helped to unleash the type of fervor, commitment, endurance, and hope that can benefit other Catholic communities.

Indeed, such efforts find support in the writings of St. Augustine, who argued that the Church fulfills its mission by embracing places like Pembroke. He stated in his seminal work, *City of God*:

The Church recruits her citizens from all nations, and in every language assembled her community of pilgrims on earth; she is not anxious about her diversities in customs, laws, institutions; she does not cut off or destroy any of them, but rather preserves and observes them. Even the differences in different nations she directs to the one common end of peace on earth.[58]

It may be difficult to label Sacred Heart or Pembroke as a city, but St. Augustine would likely bless both as small, rural communities of God.

7

Lunch Tables

By our fourth day in Pembroke, we did not have the same level of energy in the morning. Days of manual labor and nights of food fights in the church basement made the idea of another morning run to the state line less desirable. So I stayed back and wrote a few thoughts in my journal, including a quick note to Father Tony thanking him for leading our tour of Old Hopkins Park. The rest of the youth group was also slow to rise. When Ken and Michelle announced that we would take a break from our work projects that day in favor of some light recreation, they faced no objections.

We had come to know several people in the Pembroke community, including Gertrude Higginbottom, Robert Hayes, and Nancy Williams. But other than our young friend Duke, we had not met anyone closer to our age. That would change today, according to Ken and Michelle, because a large group of local kids, most of whom attended the nearby Lorenzo R. Smith Elementary School, was set to arrive at approximately 10 A.M. Then we would all travel to Ken and Michelle's home and spend a few hours together.

After the kids, including Duke, joined us, we climbed into several vans and departed Sacred Heart. Ken and Michelle lived only twenty minutes away in southern Kankakee County in a home surrounded by farmland. Members of the teen group knew the home well because Ken and Michelle often hosted events or led discussion groups there. In addition to an above-ground swimming pool and a batting cage in an old equipment shed, large, open fields that offered plenty of other opportunities for recreation surrounded the house.

We introduced ourselves to the kids from Pembroke as we played soccer, softball, volleyball, or dodgeball together, while others went swimming or played cards indoors. It was a great time, and we broke for lunch shortly after noon. After filling my plate, I found a seat in the kitchen next to a friend from high school, and soon a few other members of the teen group joined us.

When I stood to refill my drink, I saw a small group of the kids from Pembroke eating at a table on the back porch. They were a few years younger than we were, but age was not the only visible distinction between my table and theirs. I looked around, and despite a morning of shared amusement, the black youth and white youth overwhelmingly ate separately. Frankly it was not an unfamiliar sight to me. At my high school in Kankakee the lunchtime cafeteria had its own share of racially distinct tables. Sometimes I'd leave my predominantly white table to talk with friends at a black table or a Latino table, but usually it was just simpler and easier to remain seated where I typically did until the bell rang.

After lunch we returned to Sacred Heart, but the stark image of the lunch tables—both here and back home—stuck with me. I wondered what I would miss by remaining at my limited, comfortable table, so I went out of my way to sit next to a boy from Pembroke in the van on the ride back. His name was Mike. When we passed by Lorenzo Smith Elementary, I asked about his friends there, and as we drove by Martin Luther King Jr. Park, I asked if he ever played baseball there. He responded with brief, awkward answers to my questions, but he seemed most intrigued by this new game of "ass-up" that someone mentioned to him earlier that day.

* * *

Very few, if any, other pronouncements from the United States Supreme Court maintain a status as revered as that of *Brown v. Board of Education of Topeka.* Circumventing the sovereignty of numerous state governments and overturning sixty years of the court's own jurisprudence, Chief Justice

Earl Warren led the tribunal in 1954 to hold that the U.S. Constitution forbids racial segregation in schools.[1] In its analysis the court expressly refused to consider how those people who adopted the Fourteenth Amendment in 1868 would view the question of integrated schools.[2] Nor did it look to the role of public education in 1896 when the court's predecessors in *Plessy v. Ferguson* affirmed the principle of "separate but equal" in all public accommodations, including railcars, theaters, and schools.[3] Times had changed:

> Today education is perhaps the most important function of state and local governments. Compulsory school attendance laws and the great expenditures for education both demonstrate our recognition of the importance of education to our democratic society. It is required in the performance of our most basic public responsibilities, even service in the armed forces. It is the very foundation of good citizenship. Today it is a principal instrument in awakening the child to cultural values, in preparing him for later professional training, and in helping him to adjust normally to his environment. In these days, it is doubtful that any child may reasonably be expected to succeed in life if he is denied the opportunity of an education. Such an opportunity, where the state has undertaken to provide it, is a right which must be made available to all on equal terms.[4]

In other words, education was not just a public accommodation; it was *the* public accommodation. Soon thereafter, the court ordered school districts in Kansas, South Carolina, Virginia, Delaware, and the District of Columbia to open their doors to black students and additionally to formulate plans that would actively integrate the schools "with all deliberate speed."[5]

In the remote southeastern corner of rural Kankakee County, however, black and white young people had been attending school together for years. A limited degree of integration already existed at the elementary school level in Pembroke Township as early as the beginning of the twentieth century. As the black population of Pembroke grew following World War II, overall enrollment and the percentage of black students grew significantly. Pembroke's numerous schoolhouses were eventually consolidated into a new building under a single, predominantly black elementary school district.

A greater degree of integrated schooling occurred at the high school level. Well before *Brown v. Board*, St. Anne Community High School was fed not only by the elementary schools in St. Anne and outlying areas but those in Pembroke as well. This high school was an uncommon example of rural integration, but the situation was not always harmonious. Educational achievement sometimes lagged, facilities became overcrowded, brawls broke out, and support for the school dwindled in both communities. Some pressed for more state funding, enlarged buildings, or greater distribution of the students at schools throughout the county. Others argued that a separate high school for Pembroke was the answer. Thus, as school districts across the country deliberately sped toward desegregation, parties in St. Anne and Pembroke, on more than one occasion, pushed for plans that substantially amounted to *de facto* resegregation. Under these plans, each community would govern and tend to its own. Each time though, leaders concluded that such plans for separation were financially unsustainable or constitutionally forbidden, so the effort to find the right conditions for racial harmony continues.

In *Brown v. Board*, the Supreme Court also refused to consider nineteenth-century sensibilities with respect to public education because "in the South, the movement toward free common schools, supported by general taxation, had not yet taken hold [then]." Instead, "education of white children was largely in the hands of private groups. Education of Negroes was almost nonexistent, and practically all of the race were illiterate."[6] This disparate pattern continued in the South into the twentieth century. When black farmers in the Deep South looked northward for greater opportunities, the promise of public schools and upward mobility was a prime basis of attraction.

Like many aspects of the migrants' lives in the North, expectations outshined reality. Since 1874 Illinois law opened schools in the state to all people regardless of color—at least on paper. But local leaders proved creatively intransigent. In one instance around the turn of the twentieth century, black parents in downstate Alton, Illinois, sued successfully for the admission of their children into a better-funded white school through litigation. However, bolstered in confidence by the U.S. Supreme Court's blessing of separate but equal systems in *Plessy v. Ferguson*, Alton school officials interpreted the state court's integration orders narrowly and allowed only the children named in the lawsuit into the white schools. The administration stalled and resisted broader application, causing the litigation to bounce around the state's circuit, appellate, and supreme courts for eleven years until the plaintiffs' resources to maintain the litigation (as well as other desegregation strategies in Alton that included boycotts and sit-ins) were exhausted.[7] Similar disparities existed in Chicago where schools in black neighborhoods often had substandard facilities and resources.[8]

In the rural outpost of Pembroke, school conditions were poor for black students as well as the decreasing number of white students that lived in the township during the early twentieth century. Under the Land Ordinance of 1785, the federal government had divided all public lands (including what would become the Northwest Territory) into square units composed of thirty-six sections of one square mile each. One section in each unit was reserved for public education.[9] Some places ignored this requirement, but Pembroke's early school system generally adhered to the subdivision. Small, one-room schoolhouses were built throughout the township with names that included Carrie Marie, Doney, Fairmore, Gobin, Mathers, North Hopkins, and Tallmadge.[10]

Eight grades of students learned in the same room, with the first through fourth graders going to classes in the mornings and fifth through eighth graders going in the afternoons. According to Merlin Karlock, who attended the Mathers School, the younger students quickly learned not to respond to a question that one of the older students could not answer or they would face repercussions after class. Although each building had a school bell to mark the beginning of classes, they lacked indoor restrooms and plumbing, hot lunch programs, and any sort of meaningful library.[11] Many of the teachers were unqualified or uneducated themselves.[12] Some of the one-room schools were attended exclusively by white or black students, but many contained a mixed population.[13] Gertrude Higginbottom was the only black girl in her schoolhouse of twenty people. When asked if she experienced racism there, she stated, "Well, yes. But you know, we stayed tight-lipped."[14]

Lorenzo Smith, one of Pembroke's first black teachers, arrived there in 1945.[15] After serving in the armed forces during World War II, Smith started teaching at one of the small schoolhouses with an enrollment of twenty-eight children.[16] Committed to a philosophy of promoting self-help through hard work and discipline, Smith taught all eight grades for five years before the number of students expanded and a second teacher was hired for his building.[17]

The one-room schoolhouses in Pembroke operated under the control of several different school districts. In the mid-1950s when the black percentage of the population grew considerably, Smith began to push for a consolidation of Pembroke's districts in order to marshal greater talent and resources.[18] Smith was joined by Ida Busch, also one of Pembroke's early black teachers, and Wesley Higginbottom, Gertrude's brother-in-law and a member of one of the local school district boards.[19] In 1957 the schools were reorganized into Pembroke Community Consolidated School District 259, which was governed by a school board directly elected by local voters.[20] Shortly thereafter in 1959, District 259 retired the schoolhouses and opened a large new facility, Central Elementary School, close to the Blacktop.[21]

Smith was named superintendent of District 259, and he faced difficulties due to lack of resources almost immediately.[22] Many families did not own automobiles, and the nascent district did not have any buses. "It was a struggle," said Sandra Gidding Mays. "I mean the kids had to walk."[23] Within a few years District 259 organized bus service for its students, but given the long distances between homes and the poor condition of roads throughout Pembroke, cost for maintaining and running the buses was high. In another instance, what began as a strike over pay and class size by District 259's teachers on April 29, 1970, quickly expanded to a united walkout by the custodians, cooks, and bus drivers that lasted almost two weeks. Only after wages were renegotiated and Smith agreed to bargain with a new union representing the custodians did classes resume.[24]

The scarcity of resources was caused in part by Illinois' school financing system. Like most states, Illinois finances its school districts primarily through local property taxes, which meant that Pembroke's ability to raise revenue for education from within the township was very limited. A large portion of the township's people resided in inexpensive mobile homes, and as a result, in 1972 District 259 was ranked second to last in Illinois based on the amount of taxable property per student.[25] Namely, Pembroke's District 259 had only $6,666 per student while Grade School District 256, which served neighboring St. Anne, had a tax base of $33,616 per student.[26] Although District 259 received considerable funding from the state, the formula for determining the amount of state aid was based upon average daily attendance rather than enrollment. Thus, truancy, a persistent problem in Pembroke, harmed not only the children missing classes but the school's overall budget as well.[27]

Smith's reputation as a strict disciplinarian earned him some disapproval in the community.[28] Others criticized Smith and the school board for a lack of transparency. After receiving public complaints in January 1972, the state evaluated the district and issued a report citing a lack of open atmosphere among the board, administration, faculty, staff, and community as the main problem within the district. It noted that twenty-two "special meetings" were called "some at peculiar hours and without proper notice," and further recommended that District 259 be placed on a probationary status.[29]

Before the end of the school year, the state evaluators returned to Pembroke and found "general improvement in a number of areas," so they decided not to put District 259 on probation. This did not placate those in the community who remained heavily displeased with Smith. In June 1972 local resident Gloria Caldwell asked two representatives of Reverend Jesse Jackson's Operation PUSH in Chicago to attend a meeting in her home and help organize against Smith. Seventy Pembroke residents attended and launched a petition for Smith's removal. Caldwell also wrote to the state questioning Smith's credentials, but the state office of registration and certification responded by assuring that Smith had the necessary certificates for teaching and administration.[30]

Smith clearly had his detractors, but several actions demonstrated his willingness to self-sacrifice and think creatively for the benefit of his students. For example, when federal funds became available to launch Project Head Start with a program targeting literacy rates, Smith recognized that only school districts promising to match the funds were eligible for the grant. Knowing the tight limits of his budget, Smith opted to forgo the $1,500 that he would receive as administrator of the program in order to secure the federal money. An article in the *(Kankakee) Daily Journal* reported that "Pembroke got Project Head Start, and Smith got a no-pay summer job."[31] Smith also recruited volunteers from Olivet Nazarene University in nearby Bourbonnais to serve as tutors.[32]

As Pembroke's population increased rapidly in the 1960s and 1970s, Smith led District 259 to expand and construct more facilities. He successfully lobbied for the construction of two schools to accompany Central Elementary: George Washington Carver and Whitney Young, the latter of which was ultimately renamed to honor its principal Ida Busch. Central Elementary was also renamed in the 1960s to honor Martin Luther King, and again in 1972 when it became Lorenzo R. Smith Elementary School.[33]

Despite the additional buildings, enrollment continued to exceed capacity. Lorenzo Smith Elementary was built for only 430 students, but at the time it was renamed, it had to accommodate over seven hundred.[34] In the autumn of 1974 the average class size in District 259 was forty-five. Smith continued to press for more resources, arguing that "once [the children] are in our district, our responsibility is to serve them. . . . It's simply impossible to give them the kind of help they need without more classrooms."[35] Less than two years later, Smith Elementary broke ground on additions that included fifteen more classrooms, a science lab, and a full-sized gymnasium. The state paid almost 1.2 million dollars, and Pembroke voters approved a bond issue by referendum that raised another five hundred thousand dollars.[36]

On August 13, 1980, Smith suddenly died at the age of sixty-one from coronary thrombosis. Over four hundred people attended the funeral held at Smith's longtime home of worship, Greater St. Paul Baptist Church.[37] Hopkins Park mayor Alex Jones discussed the loss: "I'm just upset. I've been with him so many years. He's like my brother. Our family relationships go so many, many years back. He was so helpful in the community. He always had time for you." Township supervisor Robert Hayes described Smith as "one of the greatest men as far as Pembroke is concerned that's ever lived." Hayes continued, "I saw him take one-room schools and build them into learning institutions. . . . I would say it's a great loss to Pembroke Township's education system."[38]

Decades before *Brown v. Board* was decided, the Supreme Court held that schools could be segregated as long as they had comparable accommodations. Yet Smith and teachers like him continued to fight for equal resources in the township's elementary schools even decades after *Brown*.

Pembroke may have been isolated from the rest of Kankakee County in aspects like jobs, economics, infrastructure, media, and culture, but the township has been directly connected to its neighbors through secondary education (grades nine through twelve). At St. Anne Community High School, interaction among teenagers from St. Anne and Pembroke was unavoidable.

During the early twentieth century, Pembroke was not part of any particular high school district. If students desired, they could attend the public schools in St. Anne, Momence, or elsewhere, but many simply stopped going to school altogether. In 1940 Pembroke had fewer than seven hundred people, but it was growing,[39] and the school districts in St. Anne and Momence speculated at the time that the territory would be a taxable source of income in the future. Momence acted first and commenced annexation proceedings. St. Anne countered by filing a lawsuit against Momence arguing that Pembroke was geographically closer to St. Anne and should fall within its school district. According to Merlin Karlock, "It was a bitter fight with some people coming to blows over it." Momence prevailed at the trial level, but the decision was reversed on appeal. The St. Anne district, which already included surrounding territory in the small communities of Wichert and Papineau, won the right to annex Pembroke, thereby creating St. Anne Community High School District 302. Karlock added that some in St. Anne would later regret that decision.

Robert Themer, a reporter for the *Daily Journal*, went to high school at St. Anne during the early 1960s. Although he has since written extensively about exceptional aspects of the Pembroke community, he saw nothing irregular about the state of affairs at St. Anne High School while attending. According to Themer, the audiences at student events, plays, and concerts were always filled with parents and grandparents. Football games on Friday nights were regularly followed by lively celebrations at restaurants in town, but he recalls now that even though the student body was nearly half black by 1960, those celebrations rarely included students or families from Pembroke. "Through young, white eyes, it seemed Small Town America at its best," wrote Themer.[40]

Jean Jackson remembered her high school experience differently. Jackson spent her first two years at Wendell Phillips High School, a predominantly black and relatively well-financed school in Chicago, before her family moved to Pembroke in 1959. She recalled that a wide variety of resources at Wendell Phillips were not available at the smaller institution: "When I came to school out here at St. Anne, they did not offer a foreign language, they didn't have a pool, and they didn't have an activity night. It was just very, completely the opposite."[41]

It was also Jackson's first experience attending school alongside a large percentage of white students. "There were a lot of racial problems," said Jackson. She recalled that cheerleaders were picked according to a popular vote of the students. One year a girl from Pembroke tried out for the team, and according to Jackson, "Even though we knew we were underdogs, we did know there was enough of us that if we all voted for her, that she would have to be on the team. I mean . . . you didn't have to be that smart to figure that out." Despite Jackson and her friends' efforts, the young woman did not make the team. "Some of the teachers didn't care about us and they let us know they didn't care about us," said Jackson.[42]

By the 1950s and 1960s a significant achievement gap existed between white and black students at St. Anne. A report commissioned by the Kankakeeland Community Action Program found that of the black students entering St. Anne in 1956, only 30.6 percent graduated, while 78 percent of the white students graduated.[43] Also, as Pembroke continued to grow, St. Anne High School became increasingly crowded, and relations between black and white students became hostile. During the late 1960s and early 1970s several violent conflicts broke out, and the school was sometimes shut down for the day, and even for as long as two weeks.[44] Eventually administrators asked police officers to walk the halls during the school day.

In 1975, shortly after the public rejected a proposed tax increase for school expansion, the state closed the high school due to safety code violations related to the overcrowding.[45]

When the school reopened nine days later, the administration was forced to revert to an old form of instruction similar to that of the one-room schoolhouses. Juniors and seniors attended classes between 7:40 A.M. and noon, freshmen and sophomores went from 12:06 P.M. to 4:20 P.M., and no one received lunch. For a brief period, shifts were shortened even further so that some students went to school only on Tuesday, Thursday, and alternate Friday mornings and the rest went on Monday, Wednesday, and the other Friday mornings—a total of only eight to twelve hours of instruction per student per week. Although the Illinois Board of Education approved the plan, the high school was put on probationary status until the split shifts ended five years later.[46]

As conditions at the high school deteriorated, the District 302 school board looked to the courts to address its problems. The board hired Robert E. Manley, an attorney educated at Harvard Law School with significant experience in matters of school desegregation. Manley had represented school boards as plaintiffs and defendants in places such as Denver, Washington, and his hometown of Cincinnati. He also published a number of articles on desegregation strategies, arguing that neither the status quo nor coerced busing would do much to improve public education for all. Instead Manley advocated strategies that involved large, consolidated districts or federations of several districts to offer numerous choices and elective busing to students and their families. Manley's credentials and experience in the urban context were extensive, but they could not automatically be applied to the rural situation at St. Anne High School.[47]

In July 1976 District 302 filed a lawsuit in U.S. District Court for the Central District of Illinois, naming 130 parties as defendants, including the governor, secretary of state, state and county education officials, and eleven school districts throughout Kankakee and Iroquois Counties, as well as their superintendents personally. Notably, St. Anne Grade School District 256 was also a named defendant.[48] Standing on the precedent set over twenty years before in *Brown v. Board*, the District 302 complaint alleged that the defendants "have collaborated in gerrymandering white residential areas out of the St. Anne Community High School District in order to decrease the number of white students within [the] District and thereby are a substantial cause of segregation."[49] District 302 sought to prove that the defendants, through their rules, regulations, and official actions, were creating an increasingly segregated environment at St. Anne High School, where the student body at the time was 75 percent African American.[50]

Defendant school districts in the area reacted with varying degrees of umbrage. The attorney representing the Momence school district, which was itself 11 percent black, responded with frustration. "I'm bitter about this case. I'm bitter anytime someone sues an innocent party for no good reason."[51] The superintendent from Sheldon, which is located twenty-five miles from St. Anne in eastern Iroquois County and had practically no black population, stated defensively,

> I have only been in the district a little bit over a year, and there is no way they can say that as an individual I conspired to segregate that school. If [District 302 superintendent Henry Slinker] is looking to all 11 districts to get his problems solved, that's one thing. But if it's in reference to individuals, I can't see where he has used a correct means.[52]

Others intimated as to what sort of remedy and impositions might result from the lawsuit. While State Superintendent Joseph Cronin publicly recognized that a countywide desegregation plan could be necessary,[53] Ralph Miller, an attorney representing the Bradley-Bourbonnais district, which had only a small black population at the time, employed hyperbole. Miller stated that District 302 filed its suit for "notoriety," and should it be successful, "we could be busing students from Cairo to Waukegan if we're not careful," pointing to municipalities at the southern and northern extremities of Illinois.[54]

One of the few voices to validate motivations behind the lawsuit was that of defendant Joseph Doglio, superintendent of the Kankakee school district. When asked if he would have filed a similar claim, he replied in the affirmative. Doglio commented, "I think their concern is legitimate. Some districts are placed in a position, for whatever reasons, (that) have a greater percentage of lower-economic groups or minorities that impact an area because of the way the district boundaries are drawn." However, Doglio, whose district was 44 percent black, also noted, "I can't imagine any judge coming up with a remedy that would make Kankakee have a higher percentage of minorities than what it has now."[55]

In November 1978 the suit overcame a major legal hurdle when Judge Harold Baker held that District 302 had adequately alleged a legal claim against the defendants in their complaint and that the lawsuit should be heard on the merits. Judge Baker accordingly denied the defendants' motions to dismiss and set a schedule anticipating a trial by 1980.[56] In

February 1979 Pembroke District 259 filed an intervenor petition seeking to join District 302 as a plaintiff and arguing that any interdistrict desegregation plan should consider Pembroke's elementary schools as well. The Kankakee County Office of Education opposed the petition saying that it would "muddy the waters," but Judge Baker disagreed and granted it.[57] The drive for a judicially imposed desegregation plan appeared to be gaining momentum.

Outside of the courts though, the people of St. Anne were not united on how to resolve the issues at its community high school. At the same time that Robert Manley and the District 302 school board were focused on a litigation strategy for implementing *Brown v. Board*, other residents of St. Anne prepared a plan that would separate their high school students from Pembroke's. This group, informally known as the "Committee of Ten," met regularly, examined conditions at the existing schools, and consulted with an education expert from Northwestern University.[58] Under the committee's "detachment" proposal, a new high school district would be created largely from territory in St. Anne's elementary school district. Pembroke would remain in District 302, as would the existing high school building that was located miles away from Pembroke within St. Anne village limits. By specifically carving the new district to exclude the existing high school, the plan did not need approval of voters in Pembroke. Only those under the new district's jurisdiction needed to vote in a referendum—thereby rendering passage of the plan more likely.[59]

In June 1978 the Committee of Ten officially filed a petition for its proposal with the Kankakee County Regional Office of Education.[60] The school board president of District 302 initially stated that the detachment proposal might help the ongoing federal lawsuit "by showing the urgency of the matter."[61] But eventually the board determined to oppose the detachment plan. County officials held ten hearings that created nine hundred pages of transcript on the viability of the proposed districts.[62] In April 1979 trustees of the county board of education voted unanimously against the Committee of Ten's petition, citing testimony indicating the newly proposed district would be 93 percent white and the remainder of the existing district would be entirely black. According to District 302 board president LeRoy DeYoung, "For a governmental body to make a district 100 percent black would be illegal." Lorenzo Smith saluted the plan's rejection and said, "It was a gutsy decision and a fair and honest opinion for the kids."[63]

All the while, District 302's federal lawsuit moved forward, and parties commenced the discovery process by taking depositions. But as the trial date and other court deadlines were pushed back, motivations to continue the suit waned.[64] Enrollment at St. Anne High School had dropped, thereby diminishing some of the overcrowding and racial tensions, and in 1979 the school was able to end its cost-saving program of split shifts.[65] District 302 also hired a new superintendent, Terrance Ryan, whose public statements about the lawsuit were less than enthusiastic. Ryan told the *Daily Journal* that he assumed the position after the suit was filed, and despite what he viewed as great strides taken by the school, he was obligated by his board to pursue the litigation. Also weighing on District 302 were the ever-increasing bills from attorney Robert Manley. Five years after the suit was filed, legal costs for District 302 alone were estimated to be $155,000.[66]

In January 1982 Tunis Hoekstra, a St. Anne resident with no children then enrolled in the school system, gathered signatures from three hundred individuals petitioning the board to drop the suit. In an earlier interview Hoekstra stated, "We have had problems (in the school). In the past three years, with the present administration, that school is 100 percent better. . . . There's law and order there."[67] Against the counsel of Manley, who believed the lawsuit would still yield benefits, the board voted to drop it.[68] The court dismissed the case in October 1982.[69]

Perhaps the federal suit compelled a brief respite from conflict at St. Anne High School, but the underlying issues were not eliminated. As Robert Themer noted, "Little connection remains between [the high] school and the predominantly white residents of St. Anne Elementary School District." The people of St. Anne did not buy into the high school as they did the elementary school where parent groups, booster clubs, and other volunteer support remained vibrant and strong.[70] Many families with financial means (in both St. Anne and Pembroke) opted out of the troubled school and sent their children to one of the private high schools in Kankakee.

This lack of support for St. Anne High School was demonstrated by the St. Anne community's reluctance to approve any tax increase for District 302. Even when the high school strained under safety code violations from disrepair and overcrowding, voters outside of Pembroke refused to invest any more money in the district. Between 1965 and 1994 voter initiatives for a tax increase failed nine times—usually with majorities in Pembroke, where most of the students lived, favoring the increase, but with opposition in St. Anne, Wichert, and Papineau, where most of the taxable property was. In one instance, St. Anne voters consented to the elementary school district's first attempt to raise taxes while simultaneously voting against raising taxes for the high school district.[71] Finally, in November

1994 voters approved a tax increase for District 302 by a vote of 718 to 665. Pembroke still was the only portion of the district with a majority of votes in favor.[72]

Tensions again flared in 1996 with the firing of Genova Singleton, a black administrator at St. Anne High School who was popular in the Pembroke community, and who would later serve as Pembroke Township supervisor. She had taught in Pembroke District 259 for fifteen years before she was hired as principal of St. Anne High School in 1993.[73] Three years later the school board voted first to remove Singleton for stated reasons of administrative and disciplinary deficiencies and second to hire two white men as the new principal and superintendent to lead the high school. Both votes were split four to three along racial lines and sparked a month of protests and boycotts by students from Pembroke. At an open meeting held later that year in Pembroke to express concerns over the removal, District 259 board member Willie Ross stated, "The students will not have an advocate as they did with Singleton."[74]

As old disagreements resurfaced in a new generation, leaders returned to the concept first developed by the Committee of Ten—separate schools for the separate communities. This time, however, the primary impetus to split the districts came not from St. Anne, but from Pembroke. Frustrations mounted with St. Anne's perceived unwillingness to support and fund the high school while still maneuvering to control it.

Pembroke's wish for its own community high school, a clear manifestation of Pembroke's desire for self-governance, was not new. While Lorenzo Smith opposed the detachment proposal submitted by the Committee of Ten, he expressed similar ambitions on at least one occasion. According to a 1960 profile of Smith by the *(Kankakee) Daily Journal*, "He sees in the future another great benefit for the community however—establishment of a high school in Pembroke Township."[75] Moreover, as with the St. Anne community, Pembroke's support for a high school eight miles outside of Hopkins Park was never as strong as the support for the elementary schools within Pembroke. Those schools in District 259 benefited from volunteer involvement by parents, churches, and other community institutions. In some ways this controversy paralleled the late nineteenth-century experience of black leaders in Brooklyn, Illinois, who first integrated its schools but then acceded to white demands and voluntarily resegregated them.[76]

Soon after Genova Singleton's dismissal from St. Anne High School in 1996, Dr. Billy Mitchell, superintendent of Pembroke's elementary schools and a supporter of plans for separate high schools, publicly renewed his position. He argued that Pembroke would do a better job of educating its own children because the commitment would be greater: "The school ought to be the center of any of these small communities." Creating two separate high schools, per Mitchell, would be merely pragmatic.[77]

He also defended the Committee of Ten and individuals from St. Anne that supported a two-district plan. In an interview Mitchell said, "I don't think those guys are racists for wanting their own school. If that school was for that community, they would support it and it would be alive with people using it. There's nothing for anybody there now." Mitchell argued that the existing high school, which had a graduation rate of only 64.6 percent compared to 80.7 percent statewide, was not serving either community. Like many in St. Anne, Mitchell voted against a proposed tax increase for District 302 earlier that year, and he also chose to send his children to Bishop McNamara, the Catholic high school in Kankakee.[78]

In December 1996 the District 302 board voted to instruct its superintendent, Jerry Newell, to consider plans for district realignment, or what had become known as the "Billy Mitchell Proposal." Newell stated the Mitchell Proposal "seems to be a remedy" to the ills at St. Anne. He continued, "If the communities don't come up with a plan, someone else will come in here and do it for you. And it may not be what either community wants."[79] In April 1997 the voters of District 302 rejected a proposed bond issue of $705,000 for the high school—again supported in Pembroke but rejected everywhere else in the district. High school administrators then informed all but five teachers that their contracts may not be renewed, and the school announced that it would further pare down the curriculum and eliminate all sports programs.[80]

The District 259 elementary school board in Pembroke responded to the failed bond issue by unanimously passing a resolution in support of breaking up District 302.[81] District 259 also prepared to file a petition for a new district with the Regional Office of Education and explored the availability of school construction funds from the state.[82] The financial hurdles were too great, however. The state offered some funding, but not nearly enough to build or operate a high school in the cash-strapped district. According to Mitchell, constructing a new school in Pembroke was a "dead issue."[83]

The issue was nonetheless revived in 2001 when the state awarded a $7.6 million grant to District 302. The prospect of new funding activated those in favor of separate districts, and the elementary school boards in both St. Anne and Pembroke voted to pursue such a plan. Mitchell was asked whether the state should support the creation of a predominantly black district, and he responded, "Why not? All-white districts are formed every day."[84]

As officials negotiated how to divide the grant money between two districts, a number of voices against the separation plan spoke up from within the St. Anne High School student body. Sophomore Dawn Duby gathered ninety-one student signatures opposing a division—almost a third of the school. Duby explained her position:

> I don't think we should have one white school district and one black school district. We need to learn to get along with other races and cultures. If we separate the races in high school, then how will we ever know about one another? I would hate two separate districts. I enjoy the school like it is now.[85]

Duby's position won the day when the state announced that the $7.6 million grant could only be used for the existing district's high school.[86] Without the promise of funding, Pembroke District 259 determined again that plans for neither a new high school nor a new district could move forward.

District 259 has continued to change in other ways. During the 1980s and 1990s the population in Pembroke leveled off and subsequently began to decrease. In 1993 District 259 had 673 students, but by 2003 the number had fallen to 386. Without the enrollment figures it once had, Pembroke could no longer pay the operating costs for three schools. The school board closed George Washington Carver in 2002 and Ida Busch the following year.[87] Since then only Lorenzo Smith Elementary has remained open in District 259. Enrollment generally continues to trend downward, and as of 2015, District 259 instructs 285 students ranging from preschool to eighth grade (up from 275 in 2014). The racial makeup is no longer uniformly black, though it remains heavily so at 85.3 percent, with 2.5 percent white, 9.1 percent Hispanic, and 3.2 percent of two or more races. Of the students, 89.8 percent are designated as low-income.[88]

Students at Lorenzo Smith are required to wear uniforms of navy pants and white collared shirts. They walk through hallways adorned with posters promoting auditions for productions of *The Wiz*, information on how to work in the school's recording studio, and several pictures of President Barack Obama—as a young boy sitting next to his father, as a basketball player wearing his old Punahou High School jersey, and as a grown man speaking to his own daughters.[89] Six banners hang from the gymnasium walls, each promoting a specific virtue: Fairness, Respect, and Responsibility on one side of the room, and Trustworthiness, Caring, and Citizenship on the other.

Standardized test scores are behind Illinois averages, but the percentage of students that met or exceeded state standards rose from 36 percent in 2002 to 61 percent in 2012. Comparatively, the state figure was 83 percent in 2012. (Under the more rigorous Common Core State Standards adopted in 2013, the percentage of students meeting and exceeding expectations in 2014 was 33 percent in District 259 and 59 percent in Illinois generally.[90]) The school celebrates improvement not only with the students and teachers but also with people inside and outside the Pembroke community. According to former state representative Lisa Dugan, "When they reach a goal, they have dancing for the afternoon. They invite everybody. I come in. The mayor comes in. It's a real big deal for them."[91]

At St. Anne Community High School, where enrollment is now 259 students, test scores have also improved. The percentage of students meeting or exceeding state standards climbed from 19 percent in 2002 to 40 percent in 2011, although it dropped to 29 percent by 2014. (For secondary education, the state figure was 51 percent in 2011 and 54 percent in 2014.[92]) The high school has become more racially balanced at 35.9 percent white and 41.3 percent black. A growing Hispanic component of the district now represents 15.4 percent of the student body, and 7.3 percent has a mixed racial background.[93]

The school also has reactivated its sports programs, and in March 2008 the boys basketball team, composed of students from both St. Anne and Pembroke, achieved historic success: by defeating Nomokis High School by a score of 67–61 during the Class 1A state championship game at Peoria's Carver Arena, the team brought the first and only men's state basketball title to Kankakee County.[94] According to Steve Soucie, a sports writer for the *Daily Journal* and a 1992 graduate of St. Anne High School,

> The string of car headlights seemed to stretch for miles on Saturday night, maybe even all the way back to Peoria. And as the procession of fire engines, police cars, school buses and other vehicles began its victory tour through the three diverse and sometimes divided communities of the St. Anne school district—St. Anne, Hopkins Park, and Pembroke—those beacons only grew in number. The lights shone brightly and directly on the most successful basketball team in Kankakee area history—the St. Anne Community High School Cardinals.[95]

Notably, the Cardinals' achievement has been rivaled only by the Bishop McNamara High School women's team, led by Lorenzo Smith Elementary

Table 7.1. Education Statistics

	Hopkins Park	Pembroke Township	St. Anne Township	Momence Township	Yellowhead Township	Kankakee County	Illinois	United States
High School Graduate or Higher (%)	67.2	71.0	83.4	80.4	92.9	86.8	87.6	86.3
Bachelor's Degree or Higher (%)	7.4	10.1	10.9	11.2	14.5	17.6	31.9	29.3

Source: U.S. Census Bureau, *2010–2014 American Community Survey 5-Year Estimates: Selected Social Characteristics in the United States* (2015), http://factfinder2.census.gov.

School alumnae Khadaizha Sanders, which won the county's first women's title in 2015.[96]

According to data compiled between 2010 and 2014, a gap persists between the percentage of those graduating high school in Hopkins Park and Pembroke Township and those in neighboring areas, as well as broader jurisdictions (table 7.1). But the percentage of those with bachelor's degrees, at least in Pembroke, is relatively comparable to other surrounding townships, and other signs of progress are evident. The severe discord at St. Anne High School has abated, extracurricular activities have resumed, and test scores have risen.

Demographics will shape the future of Pembroke's school system and have already compelled Pembroke leaders to embrace new strategies at the elementary school level. As of the fall of 2013, the sole remaining elementary school in the township was renamed the Lorenzo R. Smith Sustainability and Technology Academy—not only in order to target a curriculum around Pembroke's potential as a twenty-first-century rural community, but also to become eligible for increased federal and state funding in these areas.[97] A continued drop in the township's population could very well lead to the closure of Lorenzo Smith, which would likely result in a combined elementary school district that resembles the high school district.

Even in spite of the practical difficulties, the desire for a separate high school in Pembroke is still very much alive. When Samuel Payton, then mayor of Hopkins Park, stated at a village board meeting during the height of the economic recession in 2009 that his "biggest wish" was for Pembroke's teenagers "to come home" to their own high school, members of the audience responded like they were at church: "Amen, Amen." Alternatively, High School District 302 may continue as a small, rural institution linked by a complicated and sometimes messy history of integrated education. In past decades the high school has seen its overcrowded halls erupt out of racial hostility. But it has also seen ninety-one young people affirm that their education was enriched and their constitutional rights fulfilled because they could get up from their own lunch table and learn with other students who were not like themselves.

8

Building on Sand

Later that evening, we returned to the Sacred Heart basement for dinner. I filled my plate, grabbed a bottle of water, and found an open seat next to a few people, including Adam. Although we had not been close before, I felt comfortable engaging him today as if I had known him for years. Adam was holding a nice, new basketball in his lap. There was a hoop down the road from the church, so I asked Adam if he was going to organize a pickup game. Adam said he hoped to. We chatted about sports briefly before conversation at the table turned to accounts of the group's various projects throughout the township, which were now winding down.

One person explained her role at "The Brickyard," a small stone patio and fire pit our group constructed next to the garden planted by Sacred Heart's resident nuns. She noted that, despite the poor quality of the soil, the nuns worked to cultivate all sorts of vegetables and fruits in their garden because there was no supermarket in Hopkins Park.

Another talked about "Sunshine Shelter," the garage of a woman named Callie Jones, which he helped to repaint. Ms. Jones, who was over ninety years old, had decided that the building should be a bright marigold color. When she wasn't serving the teens homemade lemonade, she grabbed a brush herself and joined the volunteers.

Adam described "Rat Patrol"—an effort to clean up a yard covered with a knee-deep layer of trash. Garbage had collected there for several months because the homeowner couldn't afford the waste-

removal service available to the community. Adam said that he met the owner, an elderly man who confessed that he couldn't keep up with cleaning the refuse, especially when other people began leaving theirs on his lawn as well.

Before I could mention my experiences of cutting through "The Jungle" or pushing around "Black Gold" in a Bobcat, Michelle called me back into the kitchen. She was standing with Adam's older sister, Angela. "We heard that you like to draw," said Michelle. I was slightly surprised because my artwork, which often consisted of sketches in the back of a chemistry notebook, was something that I generally kept to myself. Michelle explained that one of the final projects of the trip was to design and paint a mural on the cinder-block wall located between the back of the church and the nuns' house. Angela would be taking the lead, and they were looking for people who could help. Intrigued but still slightly nervous to put my drawing on display, I said yes.

After the nightly revival session, I joined Angela and two other friends, K.T. and Brad, to survey our workplace. The wall stood immediately behind the area now covered with rich, black topsoil. This odd, three-sided structure was approximately four feet tall and unattached to anything but the concrete slab beneath it. It may have once been a barbeque pit or the foundation of a small building, but regardless of its former purpose, it looked incomplete. While the rest of the teen group gathered to write in their journals, we got a head start on the mural. The sun set well before we finished covering the wall with two coats of white paint.

* * *

Allen "A.J." Jones might have been on to something. At age two his family moved to Hopkins Park where his relatives had been community leaders for generations. Jones's grandmother was Barbara Smith-Jones, the township supervisor from 1989 to 1997, and his uncle, Walter Jones III, served as mayor of Hopkins Park from 2011 to 2015.[1] After high school the youngest Jones moved around a bit. He attended classes at Southern Illinois University but after a few months decided to leave. He moved to Texas where he found work, but soon thereafter he found himself with less money than when he arrived. So he returned home at age twenty-two and took a job at Wildwind Senior Estates, a facility managed by his uncle that provides subsidized housing to senior citizens in Pembroke. According to Jones, "I don't plan on going nowhere. I keep coming back here." That sentiment, however, in no way reflected a lack of ambition. Jones noted that many people in Pembroke lack laundry machines. "They either wash their clothes by hand or go into Kankakee or Momence," he said. Having identified this consumer need, Jones said he hoped to take a few business classes and then open a laundromat in Hopkins Park.[2]

In pursuing his project, Jones will face many of the same obstacles that have impeded economic development in Pembroke for decades. His natural client base, much of which does not have a car, will need to travel lengthy distances on bad roads to use his facility. A long history of catastrophic fires in the area will drive his insurance premiums upward, and without any natural gas lines, heating his facility will require propane gas and a correspondingly higher overhead. Further, he will be subject to property tax rates that are generally higher than the other rural areas around Pembroke. Jones himself recognizes a major obstacle to his plans: financing. "People have great ideas," he said, "but they've got no money to do it."

Around the turn of the millennium local and state leaders launched an effort to remove some of those obstacles and provide Pembroke with the unprecedented resources of a major capital project. A proposed women's prison promised to bring stronger infrastructure, more tax dollars, and increased foot traffic to the area. While some within the community questioned whether they really wanted a massive jail in their backyard, the deal-making hometown governor, George Ryan, made it a personal goal to help the impoverished community through the project. Yet building on the sands of Pembroke would again prove difficult. Even after the state broke ground and laid the prison's foundation, raising everyone's hopes, the heavy winds of Illinois politics caused the ground beneath that foundation to shift.

A review of economic statistics suggests that Allen Jones was indeed fortunate to have his job at Wildwind. The estimates in tables 8.1 and 8.2 show that unemployment rates in Hopkins Park (25.1 percent) and particularly Pembroke Township (32.2 percent) greatly exceed those of the larger political subdivisions. Some local officials, including former Hopkins Park mayor and current Kankakee County board member Samuel Payton, report that the figure has grown as high as 40 or 45 percent in the recent past.[3] These conditions are even more striking when one considers the number of people over the age of sixteen who are not in the labor force—either because they

Table 8.1. Employment Statistics

	Hopkins Park	Pembroke Township	Kankakee County	Illinois	United States
Total population above age 16	408	1,704	88,144	10,170,489	248,775,628
Number in labor force	167	863	55,623	6,718,857	158,965,511
Percentage in labor force	40.9	50.6	63.1	66.1	63.9
Number unemployed	42	278	5,823	669,561	14,504,781
Unemployment rate (%)	25.1	32.2	10.5	10.0	9.1
Number employed	125	585	49,729	6,032,031	143,435,233
Employed above age 16 (%)	30.6	34.3	56.4	59.3	57.7

Source: U.S. Census Bureau, *2010–2014 American Community Survey 5-Year Estimates: Selected Economic Characteristics* (2015).

are retired or have given up on actively seeking work. While approximately 55 to 60 percent of all people over the age of sixteen in the United States, Illinois, and Kankakee County have jobs, this figure is only about 31 percent in Hopkins Park and 34 percent in Pembroke. Also notably, the percentage of persons claiming disability status is greater than surrounding areas—30.1 percent in Hopkins Park and 28.5 percent in Pembroke versus 16.1 percent in Kankakee County, 10.6 percent in the state of Illinois, and 12.3 percent in the United States.[4]

Income statistics offer similarly drastic differences. Not only do local average income levels fall beneath their outside counterparts, much larger portions of Hopkins Park and Pembroke live in extreme poverty.

Employment and income remain low largely because of the numerous impediments to development, the combination and interactions of which are not found in many other communities. On top of poor soil quality, high crime rates, and educational barriers discussed in earlier chapters, the community faces other hurdles that have likely stalled economic growth.

Water

Commercial agriculture does not fare well in Pembroke not only because the sandy soil lacks essential nutrients but also because it cannot retain water for long. In order to make use of the land, farmers must artificially

Table 8.2. Income Statistics

	Hopkins Park	Pembroke Township	Kankakee County	Illinois	United States
Median income ($)	16,618	25,466	51,000	57,166	53,482
Mean income ($)	23,563	32,822	63,556	78,521	74,596
With income below $10,000 (%)	30.9	21.6	7.6	7.2	7.2
With income below $15,000 (%)	45.3	29.9	12.8	11.8	12.5
With income below $25,000 (%)	61.8	48.9	23.3	21.8	23.2

Source: U.S. Census Bureau, *2010–2014 American Community Survey 5-Year Estimates: Selected Economic Characteristics* (2015) and U.S. Census Bureau, *2010–2014 American Community Survey 5-Year Estimates: Selected Social Characteristics* (2015), http://factfinder2.census.gov.

irrigate it by pumping groundwater into the fields. When area farmers began installing irrigation systems in the early 1980s, nearby landowners noticed a significant drop in the water table. Although Hopkins Park had water lines installed by that time, most outlying areas of Pembroke rely on wells for water. During times of drought these wells go dry.[5] Illinois law grants priority to residential water needs over agricultural needs, but despite legislative reforms to protect residents' water rights, the problem of dry wells persists.[6] Further, the water available is often of suspect quality—particularly that pumped from cheaper, shallow wells.[7] A number of homes and businesses in Pembroke have improper drainage and disposal systems that can contaminate the water, which, according to Howard Jones, "sometimes looks like tea."[8] Pembroke elementary school superintendent Dr. Billy Mitchell confirmed that the school district has at times resorted to buying bottled water "due to the foul smell" of what came from the faucet.[9]

Gas

Natural gas first came to Kankakee County in 1931 when a pipeline was constructed from Texas to Chicago. A local extension also served Kankakee, St. Anne, and Momence, but Pembroke was not included.[10] Even as the population grew, homes and businesses remained too diffuse to justify an extension of the infrastructure. Hopkins Park, which is more densely populated than Pembroke, still has only 165 people per square mile, as compared to Momence with 2,416 and St. Anne with 2,464.[11] In a 1993 study the Nicor Gas company estimated that it would cost $1.3 million to make Hopkins Park serviceable, and that figure today would be significantly higher due to drastically higher steel prices.[12] Without natural gas, nearly 65 percent of people in Pembroke heat their buildings using propane; others resort to wood, oil, or electric space heaters.[13]

Fire

Brush fires may preserve the black oak savannas by preventing the overgrowth of greenery, but they also threaten the manmade structures of the area. Such fires can originate naturally from lightning strikes, but others occur when people without natural gas use unsafe electric space heaters to keep warm or when they burn trash instead of employing a private hauling service they can't afford. The blazes have consumed thousands of acres and taken several homes, businesses, community buildings, and even lives.[14] Pembroke has also had difficulty maintaining an adequately resourced and staffed fire department. When fire ripped through six hundred acres during a single night in October 1995, Pembroke had to rely on thirteen other fire departments in the area to help bring the fire under control.[15] As a result of the fires, residents often have difficulty finding private insurers willing to cover their homes at affordable prices—or sometimes at any price.[16]

Transit

Charles Draine, a former county board member representing Pembroke, once described his town's roads as "rivers, trails, and adventurous roller coasters."[17] Due to the porous nature of the sandy soil, gravel roads deteriorate quickly, thereby making it more important to pave over the roads with asphalt. It is, however, an expensive process.[18] In recent years additional stretches of road have been upgraded, but they remain treacherous for those living in more remote locations. Arthur Collins explained that when the weather gets bad, "you just stay home."[19] For those with automobiles, the impact of rising gasoline prices is especially harsh. The spread-out nature of the community means that residents must drive several miles for commonplace tasks. Many cannot afford gasoline or car insurance and must rely on neighbors, friends, or ShowBus, the rural public transportation provider whose service must be requested at least a day in advance, for travel.[20]

Health

The provision of health care to the rural community has also involved challenges. Despite a recent focus on organic produce in Pembroke's farming community, fresh fruits and vegetables are still more elusive than the chips, donuts, or soda pop sold at one of the Blacktop gas stations. Indeed, a 2005 study conducted by the University of Illinois at Chicago found Hopkins Park to be the most overweight community in the Chicago area.[21] A higher percentage of people in Pembroke had no health insurance (24 percent) than in the state of Illinois (13 percent) and in the United States (15 percent), according to data compiled before the enactment of the Affordable Care Act.[22] Further, the prevalence of drugs necessitates a specialized care for addiction. Health services are available at a clinic in Hopkins Park owned by one of the hospitals in Kankakee. Several local physicians have taken it upon themselves to dedicate time at this clinic or on their own, but even they can only be present in Pembroke for a fraction of each week. Emergency situations also prove difficult to address, as the round trip for an ambulance to the closest hospital in Kankakee is over thirty-five miles, and every route in or out of Pembroke crosses railroad tracks.

Taxes

Property tax levels in Pembroke are generally higher than in nearby rural areas of Kankakee County. In 2014 the taxable rate for property in Hopkins Park was 12.1 percent of assessed value, as compared with 11.1 percent in St. Anne (St. Anne Township), 9.7 percent in Aroma Park (Aroma Township), 8.6 percent in Sun River Terrace (Ganeer Township), 8.5 percent in Momence (Momence Township), and 7.7 percent in Irwin (Otto Township).[23] Rates in the unincorporated portions of these townships compare similarly. At times various districts within Pembroke have levied the maximum rate permitted by the state.[24] Although land values are generally lower in Pembroke and the differences in actual tax liabilities may be less substantial, the difference in rates likely discourages some outside investment.

Crime and Corruption

Crime rates likely deter economic investment and development in Pembroke. At least during the past several years, the per capita incidence of several types of crimes in Pembroke, including homicide, aggravated assault, and burglary, has significantly exceeded that of Kankakee County as a whole.[25] Unfortunately, corruption and mismanagement by those in authority have also shaken public confidence. Pembroke officials have been accused (often by each other) of lacking transparency, destroying or misplacing official records, or failing to account for public funds and spending.[26] Such claims are fueled by the fact that a relatively high proportion of public money has gone to pay administrative costs as compared with other municipal authorities in the area.[27] Further, in the past Pembroke and Hopkins Park have received state grants that were not used for the purpose indicated on the application. The state requires such grants to be repaid. After calling for the return of $1.4 million in the early 2000s, the state refused to provide any more funds until some degree of confidence and oversight was established.[28] In 2005 township government was shut down entirely when missed payments led to the rescission of Pembroke's liability insurance coverage.[29]

Although prosecutors at times have been reluctant to go after the small community already beset by extreme poverty, recent Pembroke leaders have not been spared. In May 2012 township supervisor Larry Gibbs resigned from his position after pleading guilty to income tax evasion.[30] Then the FBI raided the township office in September 2013, citing "an ongoing investigation into corruption in Pembroke."[31] This led to the arrest and guilty plea of Gibbs's appointed successor, Leon Eddie Mondy, for defrauding the township of more than $60,000 that he used for gambling.[32] In any event, the specter of crime and corruption can be as destructive as the acts themselves when people hold back on initiatives that would be otherwise worthwhile.

By the end of the twentieth century, Pembroke's plight was no longer unknown. People like Robert Hayes, Elvia Steward, and Lorenzo Smith had worked hard to put their community on the map, and people outside it began to take notice and pursue various empowerment initiatives. For example, Pembroke participated in Great Society programs in the 1960s, received special attention from the federal Small Business Administration in the 1970s, and launched volunteer Habitat for Humanity efforts starting in the 1980s.[33] The most extreme poverty, however, has so far proven intractable.

Pembroke also drew the attention of ServantCor, a small health-care system founded by Catholic nuns that ran hospitals across northern Illinois. The sisters wondered if Pembroke could benefit from the "healthy communities" movement, which recognized that, in addition to quality medical care, good health requires strong communities with economic vitality. In the mid-1990s they decided to create a pilot program in Pembroke and asked one of their young executives, Craig Culver, to take charge. Culver spent years as a community organizer, working with individuals in Pembroke to identify needs and then leveraging public and private resources throughout the state.[34] These efforts helped to convene the Pembroke Township–Hopkins Park Community Partnership, or the Partnership for short, which grew to include over 250 member organizations and individuals from Pembroke and nearby areas.[35] Resources leveraged through the Partnership were not exclusively financial as initiatives included the creation of a farmers' market in downtown Kankakee to support Pembroke's growers and a government official shadowing program that paired Hopkins Park leaders with other municipal managers in the county to exchange ideas and best practices. The Partnership remained active during the first years of the twenty-first century and explored many options for development, but particularly those ideas originating in Pembroke.[36]

Several years earlier, Pembroke officials began discussing the possibility of bringing a major capital project to the area. In 1993 township supervisor Barbara Smith-Jones met with a representative of the Illinois Department of Corrections (IDOC) about the potential construction of a state prison in Pembroke. But when the staffer asked what the community could offer the state in terms of incentives, Smith-Jones concluded that Pembroke could not compete and decided not to apply.[37] The Partnership thought the idea had merit and began working with leaders in the private and public sector to prepare a new bid.[38] In April 1997 township supervisor Rose Covington and Hopkins Park mayor David Leggett submitted an application to IDOC to be considered along with forty other Illinois communities. Although Covington and Leggett made a presentation to IDOC officials after being named one of eight finalists, IDOC eliminated Pembroke from consideration in July 1997.[39] However, when the following year's state budget called for the construction of two new prisons to ease overcrowding, Pembroke was prepared to renew its bid, and this time Pembroke had an ascendant Illinois pol behind its cause.[40]

George Ryan Sr. was a pharmacist from Kankakee where, according to the *Chicago Tribune*, his "immersion in hardball, take-no-prisoner politics occurred."[41] In 1962 Ryan served as campaign manager for the state senate candidacy of county GOP chairman Ed McBroom, and in 1966 Ryan himself was appointed to the county board with McBroom's blessing. Ryan met Pembroke's Hollie McKee and Robert Hayes, both Republicans who also served on the county board. As Ryan rose in political rank, Pembroke became part of his constituency, which kept him mindful of its struggles.

Ryan was elected a state representative in 1972, Speaker of the House in 1981, lieutenant governor in 1982, secretary of state in 1990, and eventually governor in 1998.[42]

With a significant connection to clout in Springfield, efforts continued back in Kankakee County to build support for the prison bid. On October 7, 1999, the Partnership organized a bus tour that stopped in towns throughout the county and brought people to Hopkins Park.[43] Supervisor Covington and Mayor Leggett attended along with neighbors from the township to show support.[44] According to one Pembroke resident, the rally of approximately six hundred was the largest group of black and white people together that he could recall ever gathering in the township.[45]

Tony Perry, a local real estate developer and personal friend of Governor Ryan, helped create a strategic plan for the prison and led several presentations to state agencies. After the rally he wrote a letter published in the *Daily Journal*: "That memorable night will be remembered as a moment when all of Kankakee County wrapped its arms around the community of Pembroke and said with one voice, 'You deserve this tremendous economic opportunity. We will work with you to make it happen.'"[46]

Supporters of the eighteen-hundred-bed prison projected that it would herald numerous benefits, including 250 temporary construction jobs and 950 permanent jobs that would staff the facility.[47] The local community college agreed to hold job-training sessions at Lorenzo Smith Elementary so that Pembroke residents would be ready for those jobs once they arrived.[48] Moreover, once Hopkins Park annexed the prison grounds, the eighteen hundred inmates would be considered residents, which would significantly increase the amount of state motor fuel taxes and income taxes allocated to the village.[49] The increased number of visitors to the prison would ensure constant maintenance for roads and economic demand for a budding retail base. Finally, the prison would warrant construction of a natural gas line that could connect to homes and businesses in the community. According to Governor Ryan, the project "would be a big shot in the arm for Pembroke Township."[50]

Not all within Pembroke believed the prison would be the windfall promised. At the same time the Partnership garnered support, several residents organized the Pembroke Advocates for Truth (PAT) around a stated goal to "research and inform locals as to facts and realities" concerning the prison.[51] Some argued that the countywide rally earlier that month was merely "an illusion of support" since only a small fraction of the attendees actually lived in Pembroke.[52] In response, PAT organized its own public forum to permit voices in opposition to be heard.[53] Longtime Pembroke resident Ardella Perry also wrote a letter to the editor of the *Daily Journal*, questioning whether the promised jobs would actually go to Pembroke residents. According to Perry, who lived close to the proposed site, "I am not impressed that I have to pass a prison each time I leave home or that my grandson will have to pass by a prison before he sees his grandmother."[54]

Opponents viewed the prison as a loss of self-determination in the community. A flyer announcing the formation of PAT posed the question, "We need businesses and industries that reflect the philosophy and vision we share as a community. This is Our Town . . . What would we like to see in it?" PAT argued that the prison was "forced upon" Pembroke, and they vowed to "remove foreign control." Rather than focusing efforts on the prison, they should be directed to other needs of the community, such as improving the public library, building a high school, and promoting organic agriculture.[55] Florence Carroll questioned the motives behind the prison and wrote that supporters were only looking to profit from a development that would "totally change the whole way of life of the Pembroke area—and hardly for the betterment of all."[56]

Some sentiments in opposition were racially charged. Reverend Louis Barnes viewed the October rally as gravely ominous: "When the whites wanted to hang a black man in Mississippi, I saw them bring a hundred white folks to the hanging. When the state wanted to locate a prison in a black community, I saw them fill this building with white folks."[57] A publication called the *Soul Saving Center Newsletter* argued, "The American justice system is unfair to African-Americans, and many of our people are in prisons unjustly. . . . To gain any benefit by the imprisonment of mothers and children is like the Africans who sold us to the white man for their personal gain."[58]

The black community of the area, however, was not wholly united against the prison. In addition to numerous Pembroke residents, the Kankakee County chapter of the NAACP announced its support based on the expected jobs and improved infrastructure.[59] Regardless, the opposition mobilized many in Pembroke, and PAT's membership quickly grew from 15 township residents to approximately 250—a fact noticed by local politicians.[60] According to Supervisor Covington, the prison meant "jobs for the community. . . . I see it as a blessing. I just hope it doesn't divide the community."[61]

On December 8, 1999, the state announced that it had chosen Pembroke as the site for a new $90 million women's prison. In front of a sign that read

"Win Win Situation. Jobs-Roads-Housing-Opportunities," Governor Ryan appeared with other local officials at a gathering of four hundred people in the Lorenzo Smith gymnasium. The governor spoke to the crowd about knocking on Pembroke doors during his 1972 campaign for state representative when there were few paved roads and taverns had dirt floors. "I have lived here all my adult life," he said. "I've known about the poverty, and I wanted to help." Governor Ryan stated that he would rather build schools than prisons, "but if we must build prisons, then I'm glad to see one come to this community."[62] Pembroke school board member Roosevelt Smyly agreed: "It's sensational news. It means a great opportunity for all Pembroke Township residents if they prepare to take advantage of it."[63]

Although some within PAT expressed their disappointment, local reaction to the prison announcement was largely positive.[64] Then on January 6, 2000, the *Chicago Tribune* raised questions about the propriety of Tony Perry's role with the prison development, reporting that he stood to gain $33,000 in real estate commission fees if it moved forward. During the months before the announcement, Perry had purchased options on three potential prison sites north of Hopkins Park that he could exercise before selling the land to the state, thereby profiting from the public project. The *Tribune* article also noted that Perry chaired one of the first major fundraisers for Ryan's gubernatorial bid and personally gave $19,000 to Ryan's campaign fund.[65]

Also reported in the article, Perry had supposedly stated that it was Governor Ryan who asked him to go to Pembroke to help with their bid, but Ryan's spokesperson later denied that the governor sent anyone on his behalf.[66] Ryan nonetheless defended Perry saying there was nothing illegal or immoral about the deal or the commission fee: "He went out and bought an option on land, like he would do for anything else."[67] Supervisor Covington, whose support for the project had begun to wane, said the fee may not be illegal, but it was unwarranted. According to Covington, "We all went around trying to get the 160 acres the state needed for the prison; this was not just Tony Perry involved here, so why is he making a dime on it?"[68] Three days after the *Tribune* article highlighting Perry's involvement first appeared, he announced that he would forgo the $33,000 fee.[69]

Criticism resurfaced in April 2000 when it was reported that the Hopkins Park Planning Commission had hired Perry as a grant writer without approval of the village board. The contract would have paid Perry $5,000 per month through January 2002, but it was signed only by Perry and Mayor David Leggett.[70] Perry said that when he signed, he understood Leggett to have the necessary authority, but without approval as a budget line item or a majority vote by the village board, the contract was invalid. Supervisor Covington asserted that township authorities had been pushed out of prison discussions because they did not sign an agreement like Mayor Leggett did.[71] Governor Ryan's office also weighed in, saying that the village should not pay Perry because the state had consultants available to aid Hopkins Park with preparation of the bid.[72] Village board members subsequently questioned the need for any paid grant-writing agreement.

Additionally, community leaders increasingly expressed a concern first raised by PAT—that Pembroke would not benefit from infrastructure improvements at the likely site in northern Pembroke Township. IDOC preferred that the natural gas line to the prison come from Momence, but this cheaper path would not go through Hopkins Park.[73] There was also little reason to improve many township roads when prison traffic would come from Route 17 to the north, again bypassing Hopkins Park to the south. According to Genova Singleton, a member of the township board at the time, "The bottom line is if we don't want the prison there, we should go and say 'Mr. Governor, you didn't do it right—you need to go back and put the prison where we want it.'"[74]

These fears faded in September 2000 after the state completed its appraisal of the proposed prison site. State law requires the Illinois Capital Development Board (CDB) to approve land purchases for major projects. When the state's appraisal valued the site much lower than the price to which the state initially agreed, the CDB rejected the site.[75] This blunted momentum for the prison but did not stop it. In November 2000 a CDB spokesperson stated that it would willingly discuss other, less expensive site proposals.[76] IDOC extended at least seven more offers to landowners that did not attract willing sellers, but the governor remained committed.[77] "I've got to tell you. I'm going to be very persistent on putting that [prison] in Pembroke," he said while speaking at a Lincoln Day dinner in Kankakee.[78]

Word of a pending new deal surfaced in April 2001. Supervisor Covington stated at a township board meeting that officials in Springfield had asked her not to disclose many details, but that the state was negotiating to purchase land south of the village.[79] On May 4, 2001, the *Daily Journal* reported that the CDB had approved the purchase of 120 to 140 acres between the Hopkins Park Blacktop and the state line, a location that would create more traffic through the village to reach the site. The CDB also affirmed that the state would pay to construct natural gas lines that would go through the village.[80]

Following the terrorist attacks of September 11, 2001, the economy began to stall nationwide. State comptroller Dan Hynes reported that conditions might delay the funding of the state's capital projects, and Governor Ryan committed to cutting $50 million from the annual budget, which was achieved in part by not opening a recently completed maximum security prison in Thomson, Illinois. Despite this, local state legislators continued to affirm that the Pembroke prison would move forward.[81]

On September 24, 2002, a groundbreaking ceremony was held for the prison. By that point, plans called for a $104 million facility with an operating budget of $54 million that would fund 750 permanent jobs. Two years of anticipated construction would also create 300 more jobs. Although the governor did not attend, State Representative Phil Novak, a Democrat, stated at the groundbreaking, "When Ryan took office, he met with local legislators. His first question: 'What can we do for Pembroke?'"[82] When Illinoisans went to the polls for the 2002 election, contractors had already begun surveying the site and laying the prison's foundation.[83]

Governor Ryan, however, was not on the ballot that year, having announced fifteen months earlier that he would not seek a second term.[84] The governor was hobbled from the start of his administration by allegations of corruption and malfeasance during his tenure as Illinois secretary of state. In November 1994 six children were killed in a car crash involving an unqualified truck driver. The incident prompted a federal investigation revealing that the driver received his license through bribes paid to employees in then-Secretary Ryan's office.[85] In April 1999, three months after Governor Ryan's inauguration, six of these employees were indicted.[86] Prosecutors did not connect Ryan to the incident, but their investigation expanded into the secretary's office and how it was used to raise campaign funds. The investigation ultimately led to the conviction of seventy-nine people. Although Governor Ryan made history through several of his initiatives—issuing a complete moratorium on the death penalty in Illinois, becoming the first sitting U.S. governor to meet with Cuban president Fidel Castro, and helping Chicago mayor Richard M. Daley pass a state ban on assault weapons—these were all overshadowed by his own fraud and racketeering convictions and the resulting sentence of six and a half years in federal prison.[87] Ryan reported to prison in November 2007, and in January 2013 he was released to spend the remainder of his term under home confinement in Kankakee.[88]

In his stead, Illinois voters chose a new chief executive that would ultimately meet a similar, if not more infamous, demise. After Rod Blagojevich was elected governor in 2002, legislative leaders more openly expressed skepticism about Ryan's hometown prison. State senator Pat Welch of Peru, co-chair of a bipartisan commission charged with making budget recommendations, predicted a $2 billion shortfall in the coming year. He suggested that, in order to relieve prison overcrowding, the state should reopen Sheridan Correctional Center, which was located in his own legislative district and recently closed by Governor Ryan. Welch also recommended that the state reexamine the Pembroke prison.[89] "I think it will eventually be built but I don't think it will be on as fast a track," Welch said.[90] Local representatives including Novak and State senator Debbie Halvorson protested and argued that conditions in Pembroke were uniquely dire and warranted completion of the prison.[91]

Back in Pembroke construction continued, but concerns and doubts about the women's prison had already taken a toll. Township supervisor Rose Covington was defeated by Genova Singleton in the spring of 2001. Covington blamed the loss on her early support for the prison, but according to her, "That's OK. I stand by my principles on that. I know we need economic development in the community." Hopkins Park mayor David Leggett was also voted out and replaced by Reverend Jon Dyson in the spring of 2003. Singleton and Dyson both generally supported the prison, but took issue with certain aspects of the project.[92] The new leaders also had less connection to the Partnership, which had helped to launch the initial discussions about the prison. The Partnership remained active behind several other initiatives but lost steam when changes at ServantCor eliminated Craig Culver's full-time organizing role in Pembroke.

Worries mounted that prison spoils would go to people outside of Pembroke when a locally owned hardware shop was not offered a contract to help with construction. This attracted the attention of Reverend Jesse Jackson, who spoke at a January 2003 public forum held in Reverend Dyson's Church of the Cross. Jackson asked the crowd, "A new jail in Pembroke is going to be a boom for whom?" In addition to community members and volunteers from Jackson's Operation PUSH, the meeting was also attended by Representative Novak and a state senator from Chicago named Barack Obama.[93]

Discussions of putting the Pembroke prison on hold were more than speculation. On April 9, 2003, the *Daily Journal* announced that Governor Blagojevich ordered a halt to construction. In support of the decision, Senator Welch stated, "From what I've read in the paper, the town itself isn't benefiting that much from this construction. [A] few gas stations, maybe a Casey's, maybe a fast-food restaurant."[94] While Blagojevich's office stated the following week that prison overcrowding had stabilized and that the state did not have funds to complete construction, Representative Novak noted that the governor's proposed budget still contained $700 million for other capital projects.

When construction stopped, IDOC officials estimated that the prison was 10 percent complete.[95] Approximately $13.2 million had already been spent leveling the ground, laying the foundation, placing sewage and plumbing systems, digging a retention pond, and building an entrance road.[96] Contractors also claimed that the state owed them a total of $40 to $50 million for work done and supplies purchased.[97]

In May 2003 the Illinois House and Senate passed legislation that restored $75.8 million to the budget specifically for the Pembroke prison.[98] But in a press conference shortly thereafter Blagojevich stated, "It begs the question of why you need . . . new prisons when you have five prisons that are under-utilized or not utilized at all. So you know where this discussion is leading."[99] On August 22, 2003, Blagojevich signed a budget retaining the $75.8 million, but he later confirmed through a spokesperson that he would not use the funds to finish prison construction.[100]

Although the prison was dead, the Blagojevich administration launched its own initiative to address extreme poverty in Pembroke. TEAM Illinois (an acronym for Together Everyone Achieves More) was designed to focus the efforts of thirty-three different state agencies to serve the needs of particularly poor communities.[101] The initiative targeted places like Cairo at the southern tip of Illinois, Savanna in the northwest, and the Englewood neighborhood in Chicago, but according to Supervisor Singleton, Pembroke Township was at the top of the Governor's list.[102] She added that the Blagojevich administration had been in close contact with her since stopping work on the women's prison.[103]

On July 21, 2003, Pembroke hosted another "groundbreaking" ceremony, this one attended by Blagojevich and Reverend Jackson, not to launch any physical construction, but to inaugurate the promise of "significant investment" by TEAM Illinois. In his remarks Blagojevich stated, "We want to be able to come back here in three years and say 'This is what we've done in Pembroke.' We are committed not to just say 'hello' and never come back." Jackson expressed his satisfaction with the prison's demise, calling it "a plan to lock them up, not lift them up."[104]

In line with the governor's goal, TEAM Illinois helped to coordinate a lengthy list of public services and events for Pembroke, including job fairs and training, health clinics, road repair, computer equipment upgrades, tire shredding, park improvements, and grant-writing workshops.[105] Efforts continued into Blagojevich's second term and included a visit from Lieutenant Governor Pat Quinn in 2008 to commemorate the opening of the Pembroke Township Credit Union and a deposit-only ATM in the village hall.[106] In January 2009 Blagojevich was impeached and removed from office for soliciting bribes in exchange for political appointments. Quinn then became governor, and he was elected for a full term in 2010, but he did not direct much attention toward his predecessor's proposals for Pembroke. Governor Bruce Rauner, who defeated Quinn in 2014, announced a program in January 2016 intended to connect minority entrepreneurs with private capital, but he has not pressed for any specific initiatives in Pembroke.[107]

The TEAM Illinois website, however, was still online as of April 2016 and displayed a list of achievements in and goals for Pembroke. Among the projects described as "ongoing" are installing natural gas lines, training and outfitting the fire department, establishing a reliable water treatment system, and converting one of the unused elementary schools into a historical tourist center.[108] Former township supervisor Larry Gibbs recognized that TEAM Illinois did provide many needed services, but the initiative never had any significant money behind it. The program instead meant to coordinate the various state agencies and make use of existing resources.[109] According to former roads commissioner Albert Sutton, TEAM Illinois took credit for helping to pave roads using money that had already been allocated to the township.[110]

Construction never resumed on the prison. A year after Blagojevich gave the stop order, the *Daily Journal* described in a follow-up article: "Foundations are overgrown and building materials are still scattered around the site."[111] By 2009 the state legislature gave Hopkins Park permission to lease the property from the state at a cost of $1 per year. The village could then sublease it to potential developers, and a pamphlet promoting the land noted that it could be used for organic farming, industrial facilities, or commercial use.[112] But even today the *Journal*'s description of the tract remains accurate.

The women's prison would have been a major capital infusion to the area, unlike any other during the township's history. It probably would have led to significant infrastructure improvements, including, finally, a natural gas line to Hopkins Park. Yet it also seems clear that the prison could not have conveyed all it promised. For example, even though the state finished the supermax prison in 2001 in Thomson, another economically depressed area of Illinois, it was not opened.[113] In October 2012 the federal government agreed to purchase the Thomson prison from the state, but one can only hypothesize whether the Pembroke prison would have ever opened or found a willing buyer if construction had been completed.[114]

While many of Pembroke's stories are so surprising, intriguing, or remarkable as to shock the listener into disbelief, the prison narrative is predictably disappointing. It began with people inside and outside the community hoping to build up Pembroke, and they decided on trying to build something in Pembroke. That something was big—so big that many worried it would change the community itself. The project found a powerful sponsor who took it as his own. But when he fell, so did the project, and so did those initial hopes. What might be the most discouraging aspect of the story is that this pattern has happened before and has repeated itself so quickly.

The other stories from Pembroke, however, describe individuals who have faced constant setbacks but pushed forward: Hollie McKee failed twice before his election as the township's first black supervisor; Barbara Bratton rebuilt the Sacred Heart Re-sale Shop after a fire; and Allen Jones returned home to Pembroke and planned for his community's future. These accounts prove the resilience of Pembroke. So whatever the reason was for the prison's downfall—be it miscalculation, turf battles, lack of broad community support, statewide corruption, or mere chance—it is unlikely to stop the community from trying to determine what its next forward step will be.

9

Nature Preserved

Early Thursday morning, Angela, K.T., Brad, and I looked upon our blank cement-block canvas. Our minds churned with half-formed visions of symbols and colors to represent the hopeful theme of our time in Pembroke. We had all the time, talent, and paint that we would need to complete our task. All that remained was figuring out how to use them.

Angela took out a piece of paper from her pocket. "I should have been paying more attention last night at the revival," she said, "but I had an idea." She unfolded a sketch she had done in pencil. It contained a building on top of a curved hill—a simple and obvious depiction of the Sacred Heart chapel and the grassy rise on which it sits. The building itself only took up a fraction of the sketch area because Angela had kept the rest open to our collective creativity.

Our primordial ideas quickly evolved into words. We pointed at various spots on the sheet and discussed the possibilities. "We could add that tall bell pole here," said Brad. "And we can put the new Sacred Heart sign here," I said. "How about a sun behind the church? Its colors could fan out into the rest of the sky, from one end of the mural to the other," suggested K.T. We sat down at a picnic table and translated our ideas into a more detailed sketch. Angela again opened up the process to us and asked which sections each of us would like to work on. We divvied up the tasks and quickly got started.

The work wasn't as tough as chopping through leafy overgrowth or picking up months of trash, but it wasn't exactly comfortable either. Standing, kneeling, or sitting cross-legged, we labored for hours in front of the cinder blocks. It didn't matter though. We were content. As we outlined our design in pencil and added our first colors to the wall, we talked freely about the mural and other creative projects that we had already completed or hoped to complete one day. We moved from one detail to the next, at times running to the front of the real Sacred Heart chapel to get a better perspective of our subject matter. I worked on Brad's idea for the bell pole by using several mixtures of paint to shade the bell and make it jump from the wall. K.T. retrieved a sponge and began the complicated process of coloring the sky. We formed a bond while we worked and created together.

We were in a zone, away from our normal world back home, as well as away from the unfamiliar world of Hopkins Park. But soon the strangeness of our environment snapped us back to its reality. No one noticed the group of wild pigs walking around the church until they were within twenty feet of us. Though we all jumped, they didn't seem bothered by our presence. We looked around for an owner, but there wasn't one in sight. The hogs just strolled past us and continued down the road like they were on a daily commute.

We continued into the early afternoon, painting while everyone else ate lunch. Only when Ken approached us to let us know the group would soon be leaving did we cap our paint cans and rinse our brushes. Ken told us that we were going to visit the home of one of the church's first parishioners, Arthur Collins.

Our vans followed gravel roads to a dirt driveway leading into a thick oak forest. At the end was a small trailer that was rusting around the corners and sagging at the middle. Ken knocked on the door, and after a moment Mr. Collins appeared in well-worn slacks and a plaid shirt. He had cloudy, blue eyes that widened only slightly at the sight of forty people before him. Mr. Collins smiled and offered to show us around, leading us to a leveled tree trunk for wood chopping. "That's what I use to heat the trailer," he said. Then he pointed to a nearby bucket, "I get my water from the well down the way. I used to have two wells, but one froze over, and I could never get it to go again."

Arthur Collins seemed to know exactly what would surprise us most about his home, and he took pride in showing it off. When

someone asked if he ever thought about moving, he quickly re-
sponded with a youthful excitement, "I like it right here. I wouldn't
want to be anywhere else."[1] Before we left, Mr. Collins took out his
harmonica and played a rich, moving song against the backdrop of
the black oaks and his makeshift habitat. At that moment I had to
agree with him.

* * *

The survival of a unique environmental habitat in Pembroke—wild hogs
and all—is purely accidental. Nature prepared the black oak savannas,
but it was the unintended consequences of human actions that actually
protected them. In many respects their preservation happened unknow-
ingly *because* of people, rather than in spite of them.

At the end of the nineteenth century, governmental leaders drained the
Grand Kankakee Marsh in Indiana for purposes of agricultural improvement, but not in Illinois where drainage would have harmed agriculture
further down river. Fifty years later the private developers of Pembroke
subdivided the land into tiny plots that fit through statutory loopholes
and escaped the costly development requirements of Illinois land use law.
This also kept anyone from compiling a large enough tract to make it
worthwhile to artificially transform the land into something more fertile.
While neighboring areas were changed into rows and hedges, the original
swamps and savannas of Pembroke survived. Commercial and agricultural
interests saw few reasons to invest capital in Pembroke, and the real estate
market correspondingly valued the land at threadbare levels. For precisely
this reason, people from Chicago without much of an income could purchase the small parcels, and they arrived without the resources needed to
alter the habitat. Rather, they created a community that—like the Native
Americans before them—embraced and coexisted with their surroundings.

Until today no one needed to conserve the land deliberately—it just
happened. However, it remains to be seen whether preservation can or
will continue in Pembroke. Threats to the black oak savannas still exist.
Even though many living inside and outside Pembroke now appreciate the
unusual value of the savannas, they do not always agree on how best to
preserve and promote Pembroke's unique ecological identity. Outside environmental groups advocate stricter methods of conservation like perpetual
use restrictions to maintain the oaks' survival, but the people of Pembroke

worry about forever losing control of the land on which they chose to build their homes years ago.

Conservation nonetheless presents an opportunity for Pembroke. If efforts are successful, the result will be a lasting, exceptional ecosystem. Pembroke will possess a unique natural beauty that many will long to experience. Indeed, people would likely travel long distances and pay money to do so. Economic development often means disaster for the surrounding environment, but in Pembroke an appropriately preserved habitat could be the driver needed for an economic boost. Development may not take an expected or traditional form, but in a community where preferences often resemble those held by Arthur Collins, development should not necessarily do so. For the black oak savannas to survive and for the community to embrace them as a source of uplift, conservation (and other development efforts) will require the interactions of insiders and outsiders.

Proponents of preservation are not new to the Kankakee River Valley. Even the initial push to drain the river in Indiana met with opposition. Some came from scientific studies, including one presented in an 1892 article of the *Engineering News*, which recognized the ability of the river to store water and prevent floods downstream. Many landowners of the time also opposed dredging. In San Pierre, Indiana, four hundred farmers and landowners met in 1897 to protest drainage of the valley, claiming that further efforts would cause more destruction than benefit. In addition, naturalist Amos Butler issued an early warning in his 1898 book *The Birds of Indiana*, where he noted the impact the dredge would have upon the native species' habitat.[2] Author Earl Reed also recognized the environmental harm in *Tales from a Vanishing River*, a fictional narrative that sought to capture life in the Grand Kankakee Marsh before—as the title suggests—it was gone.[3]

By the 1930s much of the marsh in Indiana had been eliminated and replaced with farmland. Several individuals began pushing for restoration, recalling the hunting grounds of the old swamp with a wistful remorse. In 1934 writer and zoologist William Bridges promoted a state plan to revitalize the marsh with his article, "They Say the Kankakee Is Coming Back: Indiana Has a Practical Plan for Restoring a Hundred Thousand Acres of Famous Marshland to a Wildlife Paradise."[4] Bridges wrote,

> There was never anything quite like the old Kankakee marsh in northwestern Indiana—the Grand Marsh they called it in its great days sixty

years ago. Never anything else and never will be. The superabundance of its feathered game and fur and fish was next to unbelievable. I have heard old men recall the mighty rush of wings as clouds of ducks rose before the guns of the market hunters, listened to their description of creaking wagons hauling hundred-pound bales of mink and otter and 'coon and muskrat skins into the railroad towns, and pictured through their memory the flat bottom boats that sometimes sank under loads of bass and perch and pickerel.[5]

The federal government also proposed creating a forest preserve for hunting and other recreational uses in 1938.[6] Eleven years later the U.S. Fish and Wildlife Service (FWS) purchased eight thousand acres in neighboring Newton County, Indiana, where the FWS would establish the Willow Slough Fish and Wildlife Area.[7]

Certain plant and animal species indigenous to Pembroke were not categorically identified until the late 1970s. Carl Becker, the manager of national heritage projects for the State of Illinois, conducted a natural areas inventory in 1978 by examining a dune close to Leesville in southeastern Pembroke Township. According to a colleague, "Carl's shoelace came undone. As he bent aside, he found a very rare orchid that was thought to have been extirpated from the state."[8] Conservationists from outside Pembroke began to take greater notice of the uncommon flora and fauna.

Although professional naturalists had not identified or inventoried the natural community, Pembroke residents already possessed an intimate knowledge and appreciation of their surroundings. Life in Pembroke during the early and mid-twentieth century often revolved around the understanding and enjoyment of nature. At age seventy-six, lifelong resident Leela Mae Eason told a story about picking wild mushrooms as a girl. Her harvest contained specimens of what she could recall being safe to eat, but she still sought her mother's approval when she returned home. "I had quite a few," said Eason. "But after she went through them, she had thrown out all but ten. Yeah, you gotta know about the mushrooms."[9]

Both public and private entities undertook official conservation initiatives. The public efforts initially concentrated on areas immediately outside of Pembroke Township, including the Hooper Branch Savanna Nature Preserve in Iroquois County, which was established by the Illinois Department of Natural Resources (IDNR) in 1986. In the mid-1990s the public agencies began looking at Pembroke as part of a federal project prospectively named the Grand Kankakee Marsh National Wildlife Refuge.[10]

In 1996 the FWS announced the proposal for this massive refuge covering areas of Illinois and Indiana.[11] After designating over fifty thousand acres as focus areas, the FWS planned to purchase between twenty-three thousand and thirty thousand acres of land scattered across these areas to establish a refuge. About ten thousand acres would be within Pembroke Township. The proposal announced that the FWS would acquire land only from willing buyers and pay certain relocation expenses.[12] Once purchased the FWS could issue land use regulations in line with the conservationist and restorative purposes behind establishing the refuge.[13] The stated top priority was to save the black oak savannas as one of the most endangered ecosystems in the United States.[14]

Lightly put, the Grand Kankakee Marsh proposal was not received well in Pembroke Township. Even the women's prison, which was put forward around the same time, did not generate the united hostility and opposition that the federal wildlife refuge did. During the spring and summer of 1998 grassroots efforts mobilized around the notion that the federal government meant to seize control of Pembroke. A flyer circulating throughout the community implored citizens to attend a township board meeting on April 23, 1998, and stated, "Wake Up. Is your land in danger of being taken by the US FWS?" According to one account of the meeting, a "large, sometimes unruly crowd" arrived seeking answers.[15]

Four years prior, Barbara Smith-Jones, then township supervisor, and other local officials willingly met with conservation leaders. Smith-Jones appeared supportive of preservation efforts at the time and expressed an interest in setting aside three hundred acres of Pembroke land to attach to another conservation area.[16] One election cycle later, Smith-Jones's successor, Rose Covington, strongly opposed the much larger refuge plan— a position she made clear at the April 23, 1998, meeting. There an FWS representative attended to argue his case for conservation, but Covington repeatedly refused to grant him the floor to speak. According to opponents' materials distributed for the meeting, "The proposed Grand Kankakee Marsh National Wildlife Refuge is really a plan by the Department of the Interior and others to take over Pembroke Township."[17]

Much of the criticism against the plan was based on the fear that the FWS would collect the territory through the exercise of eminent domain. Federal law gives the FWS the ability to use this authority to acquire land for public use,[18] but the FWS has asserted that its policy was not to exercise this power. It would only do so when the identity of the actual owner of the land was questioned, to determine fair market value, or in circumstances that present an immediate threat to the natural environment.[19] Given the stated priority of the refuge to save a highly endangered habitat, some suspicions regarding public takings may have been legitimate. In any event, the FWS's assurances did not quell rumors of forced relocation.[20]

Whether they would be forced off the land by eminent domain or not, those of Pembroke with limited means felt the pressures of financial reality when approached by the FWS with an offer to buy the land. Interested purchasers were not always available in Pembroke, so if a landowner faced financial problems sometime in the future, there was no guarantee he or she would be able to divest the land for cash. Thus, even though federal law limited the FWS to pay only the fair market value of the land, which in Pembroke may not be much, many took advantage of this rare opportunity to liquidate their property assets.[21]

The refuge also could have hurt the already dire public coffers in Pembroke. As federal property, parcels acquired by the FWS would not be subject to local property taxes. Under the federal Refuge Revenue Sharing Act, assuming Congress appropriated sufficient funds, the FWS could reimburse local governments with some of the lost revenue.[22] But according to the act's formula, only if the FWS collected money through high admission fees or hunting fees could the local authorities possibly recover all of the lost tax revenue from the proposed refuge.

Supervisor Covington found nontraditional allies when opposing the refuge, including Pembroke and Hopkins Park officials, the Kankakee County Farm Bureau, Momence businessmen, and landowners in the small, unincorporated community of Thayer, Indiana.[23] These critics successfully delayed and ultimately prevented the establishment of the refuge. In May 1998 U.S. senator Dick Durbin met with local leaders in Hopkins Park, and afterward he sought a delay from the FWS to further solicit public opinion on the project.[24] Congress eventually authorized the creation of the refuge but allocated no money to it. The proposal remained dormant for years[25] and only recently was revived with a plan that focuses on the periphery of Pembroke.

Private groups have had more success in dedicating smaller, targeted conservation areas. The Nature Conservancy, founded in 1951, is a leader in these efforts. The Conservancy's efforts span the globe, but it has taken a special interest in protecting the black oak savannas.[26] Rob Littiken, the Conservancy's Kankakee Sands project manager, has lived close to Pembroke in Indiana. He described the Nature Conservancy as a science-based organization dedicated to saving nature in all its forms for future generations to experience and enjoy.

In the face of environmental threats, the Nature Conservancy often employs active measures. Littiken and his team annually engage in a systematic, hand-picked harvest of the prairie grass and wildflower seeds in order to spread and cultivate them in a targeted area.[27] They have also introduced new plants when deemed beneficial to the ecosystem, but they limit the transplants to those whose seeds are found naturally within fifty miles of the new location. Additionally, the Conservancy works with local fire departments to conduct controlled burns of approximately five hundred acres of the savanna each year.[28] These help to maintain the balance of trees and grasses, as well as to prevent the spread of harmful, nonnative species. They also reduce the flammable material that fuels the uncontrolled burns that can consume homes and other structures throughout Pembroke.[29]

The Nature Conservancy protects natural environments using more passive measures that include the acquisition of private property rights and the official dedication of property as a state nature preserve. Through the first method, the Conservancy simply buys land like any private owner. Although it could ban entrance altogether, the Conservancy permits public access for hiking and study while restricting certain damaging activities on their land. The Conservancy also pursues alternative arrangements that keep residents on their land while preserving its ecology. By selling a "conservation easement" to the Conservancy, a landowner agrees to submit to restrictions on how it uses the land and an affirmative obligation to retain its natural character.[30] The Conservancy may also engage in "sellback" transactions in which a landowner sells a parcel to the Conservancy who in turn sells it back at a higher price but adding restrictive covenants that "run with the land" to guarantee future preservation. According to its bylaws, the Conservancy cannot pay more than fair market value for any property. Rob Littiken explained this provision as a means to "avoid the appearance of impropriety . . . so people don't think we are using land purchases to give a kickback or give sweet deals to certain individuals." The Conservancy has also acquired land through participation in foreclosure auctions, which occur with unfortunate frequency in Pembroke.[31]

The Conservancy's other primary method for land preservation involves the dedication of the land as a nature preserve under the Illinois Natural Areas Preservation Act. Pursuant to that law, if a designated state commission deems land to have retained its natural character, a private landowner can dedicate it as a preserve. The land is then protected from "impairment, disturbance or artificial development."[32] The owner can individualize the dedication to define rights, duties, and uses in line with preservation of the habitat, but the dedication must be for perpetuity.[33] The owner may amend the dedication only after receiving state approval that the change would be consistent with the overall purposes of the Preservation Act.[34]

The Nature Conservancy owns five such preserves within Pembroke or nearby. Mskoda Land and Water Preserve sits on 649 acres in St. Anne Township where it was dedicated in 2004.[35] One year later the Nature Conservancy dedicated Pembroke Savanna Nature Preserve, consisting of eighty-six acres and "the best example of dry sand savanna in all of Illinois," as described by the Illinois Nature Preserves Commission at the time of dedication.[36] This preserve, located only a mile from the Blacktop, connects with Mskoda to cover the largest dune formation in the area. In May 2009 the Nature Conservancy dedicated a third preserve, the Carl N. Becker Savanna Nature Preserve. Its sixty-eight acres are located near Leesville, very close to the same dune where the preserve's namesake found the rare orchid thirty years prior.[37] In 2013 the Conservancy dedicated five acres also near Leesville as the Callie Mae Spraggins Savanna Nature Preserve and seventy-seven acres in northern Hopkins Park as the Hopkins Park Nature Preserve.[38] In addition to certain activity restrictions, the Conservancy designs public entrances and trails on its lands away from environmentally sensitive areas.

By amassing land for conservation, the Nature Conservancy prevents agricultural interests from buying the savannas and converting them into something more suitable for farming. It also ensures that some fires are able to maintain the savanna. While too many fires are problematic, their total absence also poses complications. When cultivating crops, farmers reduce the frequency of fires on their land by regularly removing the dried leaves and husks that serve as kindling and by digging irrigation ditches between fields, making a blaze less likely to spread to neighboring territory. With fewer fires, taller trees can grow and overtake the ground plants, quickly turning the remaining savanna into a forest. This has already occurred in Indiana, where savannas became patches of thick forest nestled in between corn and bean fields.[39] In this sense, development affected even the land that remains undeveloped.

The Nature Conservancy also seeks to keep out one of the most immediate environmental threats through their land-acquisition strategy. All-terrain vehicles (ATVs), when driven on the delicate sand savannas, can potentially destroy within a matter of years a habitat that took millennia to form.[40] The dunes make for a fun, rugged off-road course, but the ATVs' tires rip apart the savannas. Because of the light and porous nature of sand, only a small amount of force is needed to uproot the surface plants that grow in it. Dune grasses would naturally cover almost all of the sandy hillsides, but a single rider can create large, visible scars that reveal the sand beneath. Further, the dunes only stay in place because of the surface vegetation. When an ATV removes the vegetation, winds quickly pick up the vulnerable sand, thereby cutting an even deeper scar into the savanna.[41] Many riders do not live in Pembroke, but some do, and they use the ATVs for recreation or simply as a less-expensive means of transportation better suited to the terrain. By prohibiting this activity and others like horseback riding, the Conservancy seeks to avert damage to the dunes.

In a mailing sent to members of the Nature Conservancy in early 2009, people from across the Midwest were invited to "join us as we explore Pembroke Savanna, one of the rare oak savannas of the Kankakee Sands."[42] The draw of these activities has already brought many to the area that may not have otherwise heard of Pembroke Township. They have hiked through the Becker Preserve and climbed sand dunes in the Mskoda Preserve. Indeed, one of the primary benefits anticipated from the proposed women's prison was the increased amount of traffic in Pembroke as people visited and worked there. The natural attractions of Pembroke's backyard could also bring in greater traffic, even without the installation of a large prison that faced severe local opposition. More guests to the township would warrant infrastructure improvements, and the heightened needs for food, gas, banking, lodging, and more would be able to support a commercial base in Pembroke. An environmental tourism industry potentially could take hold in Pembroke, particularly given its close proximity to one of the largest urban centers in the country.

For that to occur, the Pembroke community itself would need to buy into conservation efforts—an investment that many are reluctant to make. Residents worry about what the permanent legal restrictions and impermanent eco-tourists will do to the community. Much like opposition to the proposed state prison, concerns about conservation efforts are rooted in two related fears—a loss of self-determination and a threat of exploitation.

With respect to self-determination, the Pembroke identity was forged from people like Basu who proudly made the choice to become independent and self-sustaining in this isolated community. Basu, who moved from Chicago to Hopkins Park in the 1980s, stated, "We want to be people in the country."[43] Even those born in Pembroke, like Larry Barnes, proudly track their continued presence in the community to a specific decision made by their parents or grandparents. Barnes returned to Pembroke after serving as a U.S. Marine throughout the world. "This is my family's land," he said, "and I'll be here now to take care of it."[44] The people of Pembroke see within themselves a virtuous independence that comes from owning land and remaining connected to it. According to Barnes, "Our land is like gold because it's how we can prosper." Basu agreed. "You can be in the city and buy a high-rise condo. But that's just air, not land. You can't grow food out of air," he said.

Rather than preserve the land, many worry that conservationism will roll through Pembroke like a well-funded bulldozer, upending the established community and its identity. Many longtime inhabitants have already chosen to sell their land to the Nature Conservancy—a fact that concerns Basu. "The Conservancy wants to buy, and some people are selling," he said. "They don't see that the chunk of cash they get is short term, but it only lasts a while. Not like the land, which produces endlessly."

The sheer amount of land amassed by the Conservancy—1,800 acres or 5 percent of Pembroke Township as of 2016—evokes powerlessness, a sentiment on display years prior at an October 2009 Hopkins Park village board meeting.[45] One woman rose during the open forum portion to complain about the increasing amount of land being purchased quietly by outside groups: "They're steady buying, and we can't do nothing about it. We need ATVs in the community. We're in the country. We need them to get around. They're good for the kids, to keep them busy." Samuel Payton, mayor at the time, agreed. "What they're doing is not illegal, but they're buying up Pembroke," he said. "We need to put some kind of mechanism together, so we can be aware. We need to get organized." The assembly responded in support, "Amen. Amen."

Because Pembroke is predominantly black and conservation advocates are predominantly white, the perceived loss of control and identify is often viewed in racial terms. According to former township supervisor Larry Gibbs, "They don't need to preserve us. We're doing a fine job of it now. What we've done is working. Leave it alone. The Caucasian community always thinks it needs to save us."[46] Basu, a community leader in the push for sustainable agriculture, sees clear similarities between the current residents and the original Native American inhabitants. He explained, "Nobody needed to tell them to maintain the land. They were already doing it." To him it is ironic that white people now seek to protect the land from those living on it. The people who got rid of the buffalo are the same ones who are now trying to bring it back. That ain't right."

With respect to the threat of exploitation, history lends itself to a suspicion within the community that conservation efforts may be a mere subterfuge. Many recall other moments when people were promised the benefits of a new initiative but soon found themselves lost beneath it. Basu sees comparisons to Pembroke not only in the Native American experience but also in the broader African American experience. "We've seen it before. They ran people out of town with their highways, development, and gentrification." This theme was echoed by Reverend Jesse Jackson in 2003 when he came to Pembroke to speak about the halted women's prison. He stated, "All of a sudden, Pembroke is on the map because it got a contract to build this jail. Here comes the old tax man, and right behind him the real estate man . . . the land grabbers."[47]

Many view the conservation restrictions placed upon the land as a type of exploitation itself. Rather than permit inhabitants to use the land as they choose, it is reserved as a sanctuary for others to view. This is reflected in comments made by Allen Jones: "What good is the land when you have to be a spectator from the outside?"[48] Basu similarly noted a distinction between those who use the land for recreation and those who use it for living.

Residents also fear that preservation efforts may be a ruse to achieve other motives. At the October 2009 village council meeting, an audience member asked, "What is it they're after? The oaks?" One of the village trustees responded, "You know it's something under the ground they're after." Although oil wells dug during the 1930s came up dry, the widespread belief survives that one will eventually find a lucrative oil deposit under Pembroke.[49] Less speculatively, geological surveys indicate that a material known as feldspar, which is found in the township's sand, could realistically be excavated and processed for the manufacture of glass.[50] The mere possibility of these two resources causes people in Pembroke to regard outside preservation efforts with pointed skepticism.

It is unfortunate that the conservationists and Pembroke residents often seem far apart, because in reality they share many of the same interests and goals. Like the conservationists, the people of Pembroke respect the land—they retain a fundamental understanding of and appreciation for the natural environment. In addition to being a lifelong resident of Pembroke, Leela Mae Eason has been a long-time member of the Audubon Society. She enjoys impressing her houseguests by opening the window and identifying Pembroke's birdlife by their calls, distinguishing the sounds of house wrens, blue jays, canaries, cardinals, brown thrashers, catbirds, and whippoorwills. At the age of nine Pasama Kweli began planning Earth Day activities that have continued as an annual tradition on her parents' farm in Pembroke.[51] Moreover, public meetings often discuss proposals by which the community may advance green initiatives, such as solar panels for home use. According to former supervisor Gibbs, "People would take them, even if it costs a bit more."

From the residents' perspective, the shared goals of environmental protection fall apart when the local community is not involved in the discussion. Comments made by Flood Wade of Hopkins Park regarding the dedication of the Becker Savanna Nature Preserve reflect such sentiments: "These white guys come out here and buy up our township. Then they hold a dedication and name it after another white person and then don't even invite our community to witness the event."[52] Even more so, the proposal to create a permanent thirty-thousand-acre federal wildlife reserve was a nonstarter among the longtime residents. Johari Cole-Kweli sees the problem with failing to involve the community. She explained, "They want to come in with 'you should do this,' and 'we can do that.' They try to paint their own pictures, rather than sitting down with the community and asking, 'What would you like to see? Here are our resources. How can we help you find that vision?'"[53]

From the conservationists' perspective, common goals break down due to misperceptions. The Nature Conservancy's Rob Littiken has said his biggest obstacle is false information taken within the community as truth. He once had to quell the rumor that the Conservancy was introducing rattlesnakes to the local ecosystem. More consistently Littiken has had to assure residents that he is not a government agent and that the Conservancy does not and cannot use the power of eminent domain to amass territory. The conservationists have also been unsuccessful so far in convincing everyone in Pembroke as to the need for protecting the savannas from the tear of ATV tires.

Both may be right in their analysis. At their roots these two obstacles—exclusion and misperception—are related because they both arise from a lack of sustained communication. For joint efforts to occur, conservation groups and any other economic development attempt will need to include the people of Pembroke in every step of the process. Those initiatives must recognize and embrace the distinct history, culture, and preferences of the area.

But correspondingly, the community would need to be open to the resources and expertise that conservationists and other outsiders can offer. The community would thus avoid the pitfalls of insularity that cloud objectivity and lead to the rejection of a good idea simply because it has never been done in Pembroke before.

Some uncomfortable disagreements may occur, but the goals of the two groups are not mutually exclusive. Rather, their shared interests represent an existing foundation from which a strategy of community development and empowerment could emerge. The most important investment for these efforts will be time. Conservation and economic development, like most aspects of community planning, must begin with only the rough sketch of an idea, not a lengthy, detailed proposal. It has to be discussed and drafted, then discussed and redrafted again. Several iterations of sustained dialogue are necessary for the outsiders to remedy misperceptions and for the insiders to believe in the plans.

In the case of conservation, already it seems the two groups have recognized this need and hope to build upon cooperative efforts. For example, Littiken has taught a course for local children with community leader John Howard about the unique aspects of the Pembroke ecosystem. The village and township have also invited the Nature Conservancy to attend their community festivals where the Conservancy can distribute educational material about the Pembroke ecosystem. Even more recently and significantly, the Nature Conservancy has joined with several community leaders, as well as the U.S. FWS, the Field Museum of Chicago, and other groups, to conduct a collaborative quality-of-life survey and to develop a long-term sustainability plan that incorporates and promotes Pembroke's cultural and ecological value. By opening numerous avenues of communication and dedicating a significant amount of time to their discussion, the groups hopefully will develop a plan that sustains the black oaks and provides an economic boost to Pembroke.

10

Pembroke Today and Tomorrow

The mural was nearly complete. We just needed to add a few colors to the sky and some detailing on the church. As we returned from Arthur Collins's trailer, the four of us also decided to sign the back of our handiwork each with the picture of a wild hog to commemorate our earlier visitors. Working on the finishing touches, I could hear the smack of a basketball against the ground. I turned my head and saw young Duke with the shiny leather ball that Adam had been holding at dinner yesterday. Duke was awkwardly attempting to dribble the ball between his legs, and Adam was standing a few feet away to offer coaching advice each time the ball struck Duke's calf or knee.

"Looks like your brother showed Duke a new move," I said to Angela.

She responded, "Yeah, and gave him something to perfect it with too."

Angela explained to me that Adam had asked their mother earlier in the week to bring one of his old basketballs from home so that he could give it to Duke. When she returned with a ball, Adam realized that she had mistakenly brought his pricey NBA-regulation ball that he had bought only a couple weeks ago rather than a used one. Even though Adam's summer leagues would resume shortly after we returned from Pembroke, he gave the new ball to Duke anyway.

When we finished painting the curled tails of our respective pigs, we stood back and looked at the new prayer garden with a sense of accomplishment. The satisfaction on our faces, however, barely rivaled Adam's the first time he witnessed Duke nail the crossover dribble.

It was our last evening in Pembroke, and Sacred Heart did not have a revival scheduled, but parishioner Agnes Strong DeLacy was willing to come to Old Hopkins Park anyway and sit for my second interview of the week. There is a good chance that she was more interested in driving over to meet us than actually sharing her insights, as the ninety-four-year-old woman had just purchased her first new car: a bright purple Dodge Neon that looked as cheerful as the driver herself.

Ms. Strong DeLacy told us that she grew up on a farm in rural Mississippi. As a teenager she moved to Chicago where she lived for fifteen years before relocating once more to Leesville. "We didn't have electricity and running water," she said of her new home. "We had a lamp and kerosene."[1] The primitive conditions mattered little to Ms. Strong DeLacy who was elated just to have a garden again. There she grew vegetables for her family, and when the town built a canning factory for public use, she began pickling goods to sell. "They had big vats and salt," she explained. "Trucks would come and take [the goods] on to Chicago." Although the factory closed a few years later, she continued to sell her produce up north.

We learned that Ms. Strong DeLacy's passion for gardening was connected to her family background. Her great-grandmother had been forced to work on a farm as a slave, but three generations later, Ms. Strong DeLacy owned her own land and cultivated it using horticultural skills passed down her ancestral line. This history was a source of strength and confidence for Ms. Strong DeLacy and enabled her to speak comfortably with us about sensitive issues that might otherwise be avoided.

She said that too often during her lifetime she had felt the sting of racial prejudice, but she nonetheless believed harmony was possible because we had too much in common. "I don't care how black your hair is, how red it is, how brown it is," she said. "If you live long enough, it's going to turn white." To her, problems arise when people "don't want to listen to each other. . . . We have to listen to what people say, and think about it."

Ms. Strong DeLacy was also at ease speaking about her own mortality: "Don't wait until I'm dead to come put all these flowers on me." Instead, we should bring them to her now because "those people in the graveyard can't smell them." Before the interview ended, Ms. Strong DeLacy asked us to take out a piece of paper. "Put down your names," she said, "and when I get to God, I'll tell Him to look out for you all."

We walked back to the church basement. All of the other teens had gone inside for the evening. But enough sunlight remained to see Ms. Strong DeLacy get in her colorful, new vehicle and drive past Duke, still dribbling in the road.

* * *

Pembroke Township hosted a centennial celebration in 1977 with several days of festivities that commemorated the community's past, but one speaker chose to look to days ahead. Andrew Hargrett was the executive director of the Kankakeeland Community Action Program (KCAP), a non-profit organization first financed by President Lyndon Johnson's Economic Opportunity Act of 1964.[2] KCAP, like other efforts initiated outside of Pembroke, sought to identify needs and available resources for community development. Prior to his KCAP role, Hargrett attended Atlanta University and worked as a social research analyst with the Chicago Commission on Youth Welfare.[3] Hargrett himself was an outsider to Pembroke Township, but he embedded himself within it and came to understand its distinctive character. Shortly before the end of his tenure with KCAP, he offered a loose set of predictions at the centennial celebration in a speech called, "Pembroke in the Year 2000."[4]

He first stated that one of the nation's biggest problems was its "large decaying cities." He believed that "sometime between now and the year 2000, America is going to stiffen its backbone and really try to do something about this mammoth problem." Hargrett noted that many were allured by the excitement of cities, but too often "the better life escapes them." Instead, Pembroke could be part of a workable solution: "There will be a large number of satellite communities, possibly 50 to 100 miles from the city, and they would be federated with the city, and the people who are seeking a better life in the city can come to these satellite communities." These places, according to Hargrett, "will remain small, possibly never more than 20 to 25,000 people. And I can see Pembroke become a satellite city."

On energy, he cited a government official who cautioned that "the fuel which we use in operating our automobiles could possibly run out within the next 30 years." Therefore, the country would turn to large-scale public transit. "I think that we will begin studying this industry when the rich and poor alike start using mass transportation. Therefore, I think that whatever type of equipment we use will move from Chicago to Pembroke Township within possibly 30 minutes," Hargrett said.

On industry, he said that "there are many, many people working in automobile factories; however, the automobile industry will go out of existence. The industry will be of developing food and will serve and provide food for the entire world—not only for Kankakee County and Pembroke Township, but for the entire world." Hargrett anticipated an increased demand for protein, and specifically shrimp from the South Pole. "Pembroke will get into that whole area of protein," said Hargrett. "And when it gets into that area, it will develop an international community because it will have to have connections at the South Pole."

Finally, Hargrett discussed the interaction between Pembroke and its federated city to the north: "Every time that Pembroke looks out, it looks at somebody that doesn't need Pembroke." However, in the future, "Chicago will need Pembroke, and Pembroke will need Chicago." Cities will look to Pembroke for their physical and spiritual nourishment, and Pembroke will benefit as it brings in new skills from the cities. He ended the speech with a hope that "in the year 2000 . . . some of you younger ones can compare notes of what I said."

The year 2000 has passed, and while forecasts of midwestern bullet trains and Antarctic shrimp markets have not yet materialized, certain aspects of Hargrett's vision clearly exist in Pembroke today.

He predicted that many people would leave the large cities in search of a better, simpler life—a motivation that compelled much of Pembroke's expansion during the mid-twentieth century when migrants left the crowded, hostile blocks of Chicago for the vacant five-acre lots of Pembroke. Census statistics nonetheless suggest that this trend has reversed direction in recent decades (table 10.1). Although census workers may fail to count many people who live in backwoods trailers and shacks, the correction of any such discrepancies would not likely change this pattern showing that the population of Pembroke, like most of rural America, is currently sliding.

Table 10.1. Population Statistics

	1980	*1990*	*2000*	*2010*
Hopkins Park	673	601	711	603
Pembroke Township	4,693	3,320	2,784	2,140

Source: U.S. Census Bureau, *Twenty-Third Census of the United States, 2010 Census Summary File 1: Total Population*, http://factfinder2.census.gov; U.S. Census Bureau, *Twenty-Second Census of the United States, Census of Population and Housing, 2000*; U.S. Census Bureau, *Twenty-First Census of the United States, Census of Population and Housing, 1990*; U.S. Census Bureau, *Twentieth Census of the United States, Census of Population and Housing, 1980*, https://www.census.gov.

Nevertheless, migration to Pembroke has not ceased, as a steady stream of people continues to flow down from Chicago. Each person is looking for a better life and brings new skills to the community. Samuel Payton used to be president of the Rosemoor Community Association in his Chicago neighborhood where he also founded the local Parent Teacher Association. Upon retiring as a high school business manager in 2005, Payton brought his predilection for involvement to Hopkins Park, where he became mayor in 2007 and Pembroke's representative on the Kankakee County Board in 2014.[5] As mayor, Payton invited every new resident to a village board meeting and added a specific agenda item of recognition and welcome to the community.

Another community leader, Sharon White, was an electrical engineer developing voice-recognition software for a telecommunications company in the Chicago suburbs. In 2003 she moved to Pembroke where she began writing grant applications for the township and growing organic vegetables next to her home. After harvesting her first crop, she planned to do double the next year. White subsequently became the chief executive for the cash-strapped township following her election as supervisor in April 2013.[6]

Johari Cole-Kweli and her husband Shardi Kweli are also migrants to Pembroke. Before moving there she was a researcher for the Illinois Institute of Technology and for Eli Lilly and Company; he was an information technology professional.[7] Both were thriving in Chicago, but in the mid-1990s they changed course and moved their family to Pembroke. The couple continued to exercise their technical skills by opening a resource center for computer education in Pembroke that has trained over four hundred people, certified several platform specialists, and hosted a successful robotics team for Lorenzo Smith Elementary School students. Cole-Kweli proudly noted a woman from the Chicago suburbs once attended a software class at the center: "She heard they were cheap and so good, so she came."

Hargrett also predicted that Pembroke's future was tied to initiatives to reduce energy use and produce healthy food. The community has realized this forecast with a growing emphasis on sustainable, organic agriculture. Many in Pembroke may not have the financial resources to purchase the chemicals, equipment, or land needed to engage in large commercial operations, but they can engage in smaller projects that are more intensive in terms of time, labor, and creativity. In lieu of herbicides, Sharon White has spent time each day pulling weeds from her field of watermelons, jalapeños, sweet peppers, radishes, and cabbages.[8] Basu and his wife Pam have compensated for the lack of nutrients in the soil, not by adding chemical fertilizers, but by rotating a far wider variety of crops than the usual corn and soybeans.[9]

Pembroke farmers have acted collectively to encourage growth by achieving larger economic scales of production. One of the efforts of the Hopkins Park–Pembroke Township Community Partnership in the late 1990s was to create a cooperative of thirty families that could pool resources for seed, fertilizer, equipment, and bringing goods to market.[10] Another organization, Pembroke Farming Families, was an offshoot of antipoverty nonprofit Heifer International and helped residents become farmers or expand into new areas of production. If a vegetable farmer wanted to raise chickens the organization would provide that farmer with a batch of baby chicks. The following year that farmer was required to pass along a new batch of chicks to another family.[11] Additionally, Pembroke has partnered with the University of Illinois Extension Service to offer farming classes.[12] Produce from Pembroke now appears at farmers markets throughout the region, and recent efforts have connected Pembroke to "food deserts" in the South Side of Chicago where fast food is much easier to find than fresh produce.[13]

The agricultural community has also become a source of innovation. In addition to their efforts to expand computer literacy in Pembroke, Johari Cole-Kweli and Shardi Kweli have developed new technologies through their agricultural operations.[14] According to Cole-Kweli, who has taken advanced microbiology coursework at the Massachusetts Institute of Technology, "the benefit of technology is combining it with everything else." She and her husband have done so by constructing an experimental greenhouse on their farm that functions during the winter by harnessing heat generated from compost. Cole-Kweli has also worked to develop online payment systems for farmers and served on a state task force that crafted legislation promoting local produce in public institutions.[15]

Relatively recent migrants Dr. Jifunza Wright Carter, a practicing family physician, her husband Fred Carter, a former trucking executive, and their son Akin established the Black Oaks Center for Sustainable Renewable Living in Pembroke in 2006. Projects on their "eco-campus" have included constructing agricultural buildings with recycled materials, energy diversification through the use of a bio-diesel van, and sustainability camps for children. In December 2012 the Black Oaks Center announced that it was accepting applications to train new farmers in the community.[16] In line with Andrew Hargrett's predictions, these initiatives all demonstrate Pembroke's potential not only to benefit from a green economy but also to meaningfully contribute to it.

Modern Pembroke continues to embrace its identity as a rural, black community by hosting distinctive events and institutions. The Basus built a museum and cultural center on their farm to display numerous artifacts, books, films, dolls, and art that highlight the heritage, achievements, and contributions of black Americans, as well as how the white majority has portrayed the black minority over the years. Visitors can also walk the farm's fields to pick vegetables and fruits for themselves or purchase the natural jams, butters, oils, tinctures, and soaps that Pam Basu manufactures from the farm's crop. In recent years the Basus have hosted several festivals closely connected to Pembroke's cultural history, including the Herb Festival, a springtime celebration of the township's natural bounty; the Juneteenth Celebration, marking the end of slavery in all parts of the United States; and Garvey Fest, an August commemoration of the black nationalist leader Marcus Garvey who promoted autonomy and self-reliance as a means of racial uplift.[17]

The Pembroke Rodeo, which celebrates its forty-first anniversary in 2016, has been another popular yearly event bringing thousands to the township.[18] After witnessing his first rodeo at Chicago Stadium close to his home in the city's West Side, Thyrl Latting, at the young age of twelve, saved his money and purchased his first horse in 1943. Within a few years he was traveling throughout the country as a bull rider and steer wrestler. Upon retiring from active competition at age thirty, Thyrl formed Latting Rodeo Productions, Inc. to put on shows throughout the country. His son Mike, who attended the University of Southern Colorado (now Colorado State University–Pueblo) on a rodeo scholarship and eventually became principal of Ida Busch School in Hopkins Park, now serves as president of the production company and continues to host the annual rodeo at the family's ranch just outside of Pembroke Township.[19] Along with the other ranch and horse stable owners of Pembroke, the Lattings have made a concerted effort to promote stories of early black cowboys. According to Mike Latting, "Black kids go to basketball games. They go to football games because they have a sense of belonging. Our kids are not aware of rodeo as entertainment. They don't know their culture had just as much to do with settling the west as anyone else's."[20] Just as Andrew Hargrett envisioned, Pembroke serves the outside world as a repository for lesser known African American history and traditions.

Hargrett's speech contained not only predictions of what Pembroke would look like today but also a normative vision of what it should look like tomorrow. Hargrett expressed his idea about where and how Pembroke should focus its efforts, but as prior experiences have demonstrated, such as with the proposed state prison and the planned federal wildlife refuge, people have different ideas about growth and development. Indeed, there is not one vision for Pembroke, but many. For Pembroke to determine its future, it would be useful for the community to first catalogue the details of those visions—no matter how discordant they may be.

Fortunately, similarities and patterns of ideas for the ideal Pembroke have already emerged from perspectives within the community:

- "Sure, we want to bring in some economic development and the amenities that go with it, but we don't want to lose those parts that make Pembroke great, that make people want to move out here in the first place. We have to make sure of that." Sharon White, Pembroke Township supervisor.[21]
- "I never want to make this community Chicago, or to take away the beauty that the Nature Conservancy is trying to preserve, take away the fresh air, take away the ability to grow your own food. . . . But in the same token, I want jobs, a thriving school, a place kids can go for recreation, a full-fledged library." Samuel Payton, former Hopkins Park mayor and current Kankakee County board member.
- "It has to involve some business development while still leaving the rural aspect rural. . . . The Amish do it. They use their horses and carriages to work. We need to develop those Amish skills." Reggie Stewart, owner of Run-Away Camp and deacon at Christ Deliverance Church.[22]

- "We'd like to see some development in small areas; an industrial park would be fine, [but] we want to keep it where people can make a living using the natural resources they have. Arts, crafts, horseback-riding tours—people will come to see that beauty. There's only 1 percent left of black oaks in the world. Why not utilize that?" Johari Cole-Kweli, Iyabo Farms.[23]

Each of these voices describes a balance between promoting modern amenities and retaining the natural qualities of the land. People will disagree as to where exactly the dividing line should be, but the priorities above offer a general direction of development and a basis for continued discussions and planning.

As Pembroke finds its way forward, outsiders like Hargrett, who are not originally from the community but care about its success, will have an important but complicated role. Up to now, much outside contribution has involved the donation of money, food, clothing, or other provisions. In 2002 the *New York Times* brought national attention to Pembroke with a poignant article, called "In Trenches of a War of Unyielding Poverty," that detailed the situation of a hungry six-year-old boy: "The cupboards were bare. The food stamps were exhausted, the staples from the local food pantry depleted."[24] After reading the story, a group in New Jersey organized an effort to send a box of groceries to sixty Pembroke families each month. Others from places as distant as Utah and Maine or as different as Massachusetts and Texas contacted the group and asked how they could start their own program for the community.[25] Generosity fed the hunger of the young boy's family and several like his.

Even so, outsiders cannot ignore that such efforts, on their own, might lead to unintended and even harmful consequences, such as people relying exclusively on charitable donations. Sister Mary Beth Clements of Sacred Heart Mission has spent years living and serving in the community, but it causes her stress when she witnesses scenes at local food depositories where scuffles break out over who gets the best meats or cheeses. "It can bring out the desperation of people and create chaos that feeds into poverty, moving backward," said Clements.[26] Others within the community agree. According to former Township Supervisor Larry Gibbs, "We need help, but we don't want handouts forever. We need jobs so we can help ourselves. This is about self-determination and self-sufficiency."[27] Basu has said that a reason he commemorates Marcus Garvey each year is that Garvey promoted independence and self-reliance, and that all people—particularly those in Pembroke—can benefit from those principles.[28]

The story of Brenda Tucker, a volunteer for the Northern Illinois Food Bank, one of several food pantries to provide regular assistance in Pembroke, highlights the complexity of the issue. Unlike many residents of Hopkins Park, Tucker hated her first visit from Chicago to the country: "All the flies and mosquitoes would eat me up till I look like I had chicken pox or measles." Her family, however, continued to bring her to the country to visit her aunt. Tucker eventually relented and came to appreciate the peace and fresh air. She moved to Hopkins Park in 1983 but continued to commute every day to her job at a hospital pharmacy in Chicago's Tri-Taylor neighborhood. She explained, "I'm still a city girl, but now, I'd rather be here. That's why I try to keep it city living country style."[29]

In November 2007 Tucker was diagnosed with an untreatable form of glaucoma that caused her to lose her vision completely in one eye and partially in the other. "When that happened," said Tucker, "it messed up my whole world. All I'd known was to get up and go to work." Unable to function in her job, Tucker left the hospital, but payments from federal disability insurance did not begin until six months later. She described her situation during the interim: "For those months I was living off the food pantry."

Since that time Tucker has volunteered with the Northern Illinois Food Bank each month when it delivers a trailer filled with groceries to Pembroke. People signing up the day before receive a box full of groceries. Unfortunately, abuses of the system occur: some people sign up in both Pembroke and other areas, such as Kankakee, and receive multiple boxes days apart. Organizers have sought to prevent this by screening people, and Tucker believes that she is there to prevent such problems. According to her:

> I wanted to stop some of the corruption. [Other volunteers] were taking a lot of stuff, giving it to their friends. . . . I stayed because those people at the end might be the people who really need it, and I wanted to make sure those people got something. I needed to be there because I was one of them at the end.

Pembroke has foundations upon which it can build a self-reliant economy, but an unemployment rate of over 30 percent means that the community has not yet achieved that status. People like Brenda Tucker are suffering right now. After expressing his own concerns about scenes at the food bank, former mayor Samuel Payton recognized that "what they're doing, there is a need for it." A large portion of Pembroke is currently struggling with the severe ills of poverty, and a donation of money or material goods does feed the hungry and shelter the homeless for the time being.

Nonetheless, those truly interested in Pembroke's future cannot resort exclusively or even predominantly to such efforts. Systemic change will require more than simple donations. It will take more creative investments of time, talent, and humility—time to gain understanding and build relationships within the community, talent to substantiate the community's goals with targeted expertise, and humility to step back and let the community chart its direction. James Theuri, a Kenyan-born professor with a doctorate in plant pathology has offered agricultural classes to Pembroke residents through the University of Illinois Extension Office. Though aware of instances when the efforts of other outsiders were received coolly, he has had a largely positive experience. "You cannot come in here and say, 'I want to help you,'" said Theuri. "They want to hear that you are coming to partner with them."[30]

In the late 1990s the Hopkins Park–Pembroke Community Township Partnership chose an apt name for their group, intending it to be "an informal alliance guided by the wishes of the community."[31] Although ServantCor's Craig Culver exerted significant personal energy to recruit over 250 members into the Partnership and to learn their individual reasons for joining, he repeatedly and consistently affirmed his role as a partner.[32] Culver also may have sat on the Partnership's steering committee, but a majority of the committee's five members came from Pembroke.

Full meetings of the Partnership were overwhelming at times with so many people and so many issues on the table, but slowly opportunities for mutual exchange took shape. According to Culver, they located strengths of the community, leveraged various resources in the needed directions, and thereby created the community's own currency. This model allowed the Pembroke community to determine its own path without walling itself off to important, meaningful contributions from the outside world.

The Partnership also promoted a participatory model of planning within the member institutions of Pembroke. For example, at Culver's suggestion, Sacred Heart hosted a parish-wide discussion to articulate the faith community's priorities for the next few years. The resident nuns solicited responses in the church bulletin and eventually held a vote for the congregation that selected the following priorities: youth, outreach, and permanence of the parish. Culver then could go through his database of Partnership members to pair Sacred Heart with an ongoing educational initiative or an upcoming community festival.[33]

Future efforts should emulate the philosophy and model of the partnership, but also take note of its downfall. Progress stalled when Culver was transferred away from his role in Pembroke. Without an individual or an organization to provide a daily focus on orchestrating the connections within and extending outside the community, those networks tended to deteriorate. While financial resources will not solve every problem in Pembroke, they are needed to maintain a vehicle of partnership and mutual exchange through which those problems can be solved.

Andrew Hargrett presented a hopeful vision of the community, but over three decades later, Pembroke has a population less than half of its size at the time of Hargrett's speech. Also, the community now has a median age eight years older than the rest of the country—44.1 years compared to 37.4—so it makes demographic sense that two of the three schools in the township have been closed for lack of students.[34] Further, the fact that Sacred Heart parishioners listed permanence as a top priority shows their own concern over seeing fewer and older people in the pews. Perhaps Hargrett's vision and those of others in Pembroke today are overly optimistic. Pembroke's future could be more similar to places like Beech, Roberts, and New Philadelphia—the rural, black villages established in the Midwest during the nineteenth century only to be abandoned a few decades later.

Pembroke, however, has already endured such doubts for more than a few generations. Since its founding the community built and rebuilt itself to persevere. When Pap and Mary Tetter and other settlers moved to the area, they relied on grueling manual labor to produce food from the sandy ground. They put up homesteads sturdy enough to withstand the cold midwestern winds. The community grew as more migrants moved down from Chicago, but never so large as to prevent an individual from changing the course of the community. To name only a few examples, Lorenzo Smith turned a disjointed collection of schoolhouses into a consolidated school district with modern facilities; Robert Hayes and Elvia Steward belonged to different political parties, but their competing engagement brought office seekers and their attention to Pembroke for the first time; and most recently, Johari Cole-Kweli and Shardi Kweli have put the community online with technology and computer training that will create opportunities for Pembroke in the twenty-first century. During the first decade of that century, approximately 150,000 African Americans moved out of Chicago—many relocating to the city's southern suburbs. If this trend continues and the geographic scope of black Chicagoland continues to grow, Pembroke could once again become a significant migration destination.

Pembroke and its people adapted to changing times and conditions. The community faced down and recovered from drought conditions, catastrophic fires, encounters with the mob, prejudice and bigotry, the assassination of one of its leaders, school shutdowns, government shutdowns, and plenty of economic recessions. Scars from these experiences remind others why Pembroke might be deemed hell on earth. But for the sizeable number of people—young and old—who affirm that they would rather live no place else, there is little left to disturb their view that they have found their version of paradise in Pembroke.

Conclusion: The Good Life

I would face pressure in the coming days: final exams and SATs, then college applications and credit hours, followed by grad schools and job searches, and, ultimately, my career. Each tumultuous step would require steady concentration and a hell of a lot of luck. I had much to look forward to and many opportunities to anticipate, but even those possibilities contributed to a sense of the heavy demands upon me. There was pressure to succeed. Pressure to live up to expectations. Pressure both to fit in and to be myself. Pressure to find my path and to be strong enough, resilient enough, to see it through.

But after a week away in Pembroke, that pressure had evaporated. On this last morning that we would wake up in the basement of Sacred Heart, the group didn't sleep late. Even though we were physically exhausted from a week of labor, we were ready to take advantage of each remaining moment that we had in the town. It was a clear day, and only thin wisps of cloud floated through the sky. As we gathered outside to kick the soccer ball around, the sun rose behind the church in a spectrum of bright light and color—a sight that caused me to think about the mural. I had always assumed we were painting the sunset, probably because most of our painting occurred in the afternoon, but seeing the pinks, yellows, and blues behind Sacred Heart made me reconsider. The church faced the southwest, so the sun would set in front of the building. Our mural depicted the sun behind it. Without knowing, we had painted a sunrise.

Ken called the boys back to the basement where we quickly tore down our untidy barracks. We packed up our belongings, removed the borrowed mattresses, and ran a vacuum to collect the shrapnel from our food fights. The girls finished cleaning their habitat in the rectory, and finally there was nothing to do but relax and wait for our parents to arrive.

After we piled all the mattresses on the side of the church, right next to the small bell tower, the exhaustion of the week finally caught up with us. A few of us climbed on top of the pile to rest. Those people included my old friends who had been by my side for a decade and new friends to whom I had not spoken more than a sentence before this week. We punctuated this interlude with a periodic joke or a comment about going back home, but for the most part we were quiet and content. We had done what Father Tony suggested a few days ago. We had let go of what we thought to be true about Pembroke and ourselves. In place of those preconceptions we found good work to do, good company to enjoy, and a confidence that we could do it again. The pressures of tomorrow were replaced with a relieved excitement for whatever came next.

* * *

On Friday, August 6, 1999, I departed Pembroke with an unanticipated sense of contentment. For a brief period I had achieved that elusive goal desired by all people—the good life, that moment when things seem to fall into place, when all is well. Much philosophical and theological thought has been expended to describe, understand, and obtain the good life. For many religions, including my own Catholicism, the good life is realizing God's will in the direction of one's life, and secular philosophies likewise speak of discovering one's identity and achieving one's destiny.

What was most surprising was where I found that contentment. I found it while calmly relaxing on an old pile of mattresses, but I also found it while swinging a blade over my shoulder to chop down overgrown greenery behind the Sacred Heart rectory. I found it while sleeping in a basement without potable water, listening to a harmonica in front of an old rusty trailer, watching a young boy dribble a basketball on a country gravel road, and spending a week in one of the poorest communities in the country. I had to venture out to a place infamously known for what it lacked in order to experience the good life.

When I returned several years later to research and write this history, I met more people—many who only moved to Pembroke after I left the first time—that echoed this sentiment. Sylvia Patterson used to be a Chicago homemaker, living off her family's proceeds from real estate valued at over a million dollars. Since 2004 though, she has lived on five acres of land in a home valued at fifteen thousand dollars. She said of the yard work, "I'm still fighting to keep it up. I don't know how people with the bigger lawns do it."[1]

By certain estimations of prestige, Patterson has fallen. However, listening to the pride and intensity with which she describes her new life, it is clear she has found herself through her connections to the land in this small, rural village.

Returning from Pembroke I had a new confidence in my identity and my future. Not only was I assured that it was possible for me to attain contentment but I knew a little more about how to get there. Actually, I knew more about what I did *not* need to get there. Pembroke taught me the paradoxical lesson: Despite society's constant drumbeat and exhortations to the contrary, material wealth is not a prerequisite to the good life. Instead, I could find contentment by finding and fulfilling a worthwhile purpose.

For one week my purpose was serving identifiable needs of people in the community. I could commit myself to tasks of landscaping, cleaning, and painting. I made lasting bonds of friendship while creating something with those around me. We could be proud that our mural and prayer garden were now a small piece of Pembroke.

That camaraderie extended not only to the other teens but also to the Sacred Heart parishioners who had also found a meaningful purpose in their interactions with us. Life had given them firsthand experience with the divisions of race, income, and class that still trouble our country. They knew of the exhausting difficulty required to push past differences in order to find common humanity. It was tough, messy work that required them first to understand and embrace their own distinct identities. But they showed us how to take an uncomfortable, awkward step away from familiarity and sit next to someone with a totally different background. We saw what was possible after only a week of these efforts, a partnership exchanging our labor for their wisdom. We were all doing good work by serving the needs of one another.

I returned home to Kankakee and to the pressures of weighty decisions about my future. Yet I was buttressed by the realization that as long as I found good work, as long as I fulfilled a worthwhile purpose, I could find the good life again. I would be okay in facing the demands of college and law school, and then in taking a job at a large firm or government agency if it helped me to serve others in new, complicated, and compelling ways. I could be like Wesley Higginbottom, Gertrude's brother-in-law, who found his identity in commerce. For almost thirty-five years Wes served others' needs as the owner of the only gas station in Pembroke. When he passed away, it left a gaping hole—physically and economically—along Hopkins Park's Blacktop.[2] I also could be like Gertrude, who found her purpose not only by meeting responsibilities at work but also by making time to be a loving parent and an involved community leader. Gertrude gave me a confidence with her guidance: "Whatever your life turns out to be, you're gon' be alright. I know that. I claim that. Whatever you say you do, claim it, and you'll get it. Claim it. It may be hard, it ain't gonna be just right, but claim it."[3]

The effect of my newfound confidence was immediate. A couple months after returning home to Kankakee, Ken and Michelle invited me to go before the congregation of our church and talk about what the week in Pembroke meant to me. Where doubts and insecurities likely would have held me back previously, I stood up and spoke to a crowd of hundreds.

I began by asking the assembly to repeat after me. Then, after stepping back for a moment to compose myself, I recalled the time I had stood before the congregation of Sacred Heart and offered my prayer before a supportive assembly of nodding heads. Gertrude was not here with me in person, but this time I again felt the comfort of her backing, so I let myself go. "Thank you, Jesus!" I yelled. They echoed back. "Praise God!" I announced, and they responded. Eagerly, I told the crowd how common this was within the wood-paneled walls of the Sacred Heart chapel and how its members embraced each ritual of the mass. "Nothing was common, nothing was routine," I said. I also described my work on the mural, the parishioners I interviewed, and the new friends I met while gathering in a circle and kicking around a soccer ball. I had seen a great richness of spirit in the face of material deprivation.

Gertrude once told people from our group, "When the Spirit is inside, you just can't help but let it out. . . . You don't have to say nothing. You'll just be like, wha- wha- what happened?" When I finished speaking and returned to my seat, I understood what she meant. I was taken aback by, and even a bit proud of, my performance. What just *happened* to me? The following week, Father Tony offered his answer to Gertrude's question with a letter published in the church bulletin:

An Open Letter to David Baron

November 7, 1999

Dear David,

I've been meaning to write this letter to you for the past three months and I figure this is as good a forum as any to do it. When you wrote to me after your Hopkins Park mission experience, thanking me for the orientation I gave you all, I was deeply touched. Nothing gives greater joy to a teacher than to witness their students "getting it." And by your letter, you obviously "got" what I was trying to give.

And last Sunday, before the entire congregation of St. Teresa Parish, you proved it. Along with your fellow Youth Group members[,] you shared your moments of transformation. And for our congregation and me personally, it was a sight to behold.

In your talk, after you got us all to shout, "Thank You, Jesus!" you shared with us four moments of insight. Insight is that "aha" experience when all of a sudden you see beyond the superficial, you see what's *really* going on. The four moments of insight were brought on by four catalysts. From your chemistry you know that a catalyst is an element that is introduced into a chemical change to induce the change without really being part of the change itself. (Now you know why I never became a scientist). Because you were willing to be open and vulnerable during your pilgrimage to Pembroke, God introduced to you at least four catalysts for real change. I was touched and honored to have been one of them.

In addition to singing loudly, I introduced you to the notion of paradox. A paradox is not two doctors. It is the wonderful realization that things are not always as they seem. There is a whole other world underneath the visible world and often it is exactly the opposite of what is outwardly manifested. As time goes on you will begin to enter into (you will never fully grasp it) the utter mystery of the cross of Jesus Christ. If you think the paradoxes you saw in Hopkins Park were something, wait till you see what's coming. My prayer for you is that one day you will enter into and see the powerlessness of God's power and the power of Christ's powerlessness as He died upon the cross. That is the *divine* paradox.

David, you will learn that insight builds on insight. Armed with the notion of paradox you were now ready to meet the great Agnes Strong-DeLacy [*sic*], one of God's true works of art. Agnes is a living paradox. She is old, yet no one is younger at heart. She is black but carries all the colors of life in her lived experience. And she may be poor but you saw in her a richness that few millionaires possess. This grand lady was a true catalyst for a profound insight. Grab it. Make it your own. Everything in your culture is going to fight against it for the rest of your life and you know it. You swim in a world that proclaims the bumper sticker, "The one who dies with the most toys, wins" and now you know that is one of the big lies of our society. You now know this in your head. The next step is to know in your heart and have it manifested in your life. And that leads to your third catalyst.

One of the true signs of the work of God in your life is always the element of surprise. Who would have thought that one of your own fellow students would have such a profound effect on you as Adam . . . did. And what did he do? He lived the paradox. He did intend to give away one of his old basketballs to a kid in Pembroke but when his Mom brought him his newest and best ball, he ended up giving that away. And in the process of that simple action he became a catalyst for you.

The last person you mentioned in your talk was you yourself. Good Boy! Right On! While the three that you mentioned danced their dance and did their thing, it was you yourself who were transformed. They didn't do it, you did. They just did their thing. You yourself had to go through the painful process of dropping your old beliefs and securities (in theological terms it's called dying) to open your eyes to a whole new set of sights (it's called rising). No one can make you see. No one can make you better. No one can take the credit for your transformation. It's yours and yours alone. (Now I must warn you, if you accept this fact and it is a fact, then the converse is also true. From here on out you can't *blame* anybody else for your woes, for your own problems. They are yours too. Now there's a scary insight!)

And so the final paradox. You went out to forget yourself on behalf of others and you discovered yourself. Now you've heard that somewhere before, haven't you, David? "The one who holds on to himself will lose himself while the one who loses himself for my sake in the gospel, will find himself."

Happy hunting. Happy losing. Happy finding.[4]

Seventeen years later, memories of my week in Pembroke still arouse a feeling of serene excitement that accompanies the realization of something new and unexpected. In many ways that feeling is even stronger now. I recognized back then that this community was unlike any I had ever seen before, but it would take even longer for me to realize the extent of Pembroke's exceptionalism. Indeed, I had to leave Pembroke and Kankakee to see that. I needed to learn more about the outside world in order to fully grasp how uncommon Pembroke actually was, to see that when America moved in one direction, Pembroke moved in another. And even if this would cause many to regard the impoverished community for its strangeness, I had already seen Pembroke's importance and virtue.

These realizations of paradox, or what Father Tony once called "Teflon moments," have continued to occur in my life, often in places or with people who have no relation to Pembroke. For me, many of those moments certainly have been spiritual in nature, but the lessons of Pembroke carry meaning for believers and nonbelievers alike—just like they do for people of all colors. Agnes Strong DeLacy told me years ago that no matter the color of their skin, their hair would end up white. As her prophecy fulfills itself and I notice the first few gray hairs on my own head, I also see that the significant points of my adult life have brought me closer to consequential, universal truths that I first glimpsed on the outskirts of the prairie.

Notes

Introduction: The Paradox of Pembroke

1. Pew Research Center, *America's Changing Religious Landscape*; U.S. Census Bureau, *QuickFacts: United States*.
2. Gertrude Higginbottom, interview by Saints Patrick and Teresa Teen Group, Project Hearts of Hope, August 1999, tape in possession of author. Quotations from Gertrude Higginbottom in this chapter are from this interview.
3. Lana Higginbottom, interview by author, October 26, 2009, notes in possession of author. Quotations from Lana Higginbottom in this chapter are from this interview.
4. Fernando Higginbottom, interview by author, October 18, 2014.
5. Lee Provost, "County, City Counting on More People Being Counted," *Daily Journal* (Kankakee IL), October 10, 2009; U.S. Census Bureau, *Twenty-Third Census of the United States, 2010 Census Summary File 1*. The response rate to the 2000 Census in Hopkins Park was only 43 percent, and 48 percent in Pembroke Township. That compares with the average of Kankakee County at 69 percent and the national response rate of 68 percent.
6. Lauran Neergaard, "Behind the Poverty Numbers: Real Lives, Real Pain," *Chicago Defender*, September 18, 2011.
7. U.S. Census Bureau, 2010-2014 American Community Survey 5-Year Estimates: Selected Economic Characteristics.
8. U.S. Census Bureau, *2009–2013 American Community Survey 5-Year Estimates: Selected Economic Characteristics*.
9. Eva Grant, interview by author, September 16, 2009, notes in possession of author.
10. David Baron, "Mac Students Participate in Life-Changing Mission," *Bishop McNamara High School Blarney Stone* (Kankakee, IL), September 1999.
11. Barack Obama, "A More Perfect Union."
12. Pat Eckles, interview by author, September 16, 2009, notes in possession of author.

1. Mskoda

1. Janet Cremer, "New Leader's Single Name a Link to African Heritage," *Daily Journal* (Kankakee IL), May 1, 1995.
2. Basu, interview by author, September 16, 2009, notes in possession of author.
3. Cremer.
4. Basu, interview, September 16, 2009.
5. Basu, interview by author, September 11, 2009, notes in possession of author.
6. Basu, interview, September 16, 2009.
7. Betty Flanders, *The Shaping of America's Heartland*, 27–33; Charles Warwick, "Pembroke Township: Lost Corner of the Kankakee Sands," *Illinois Steward*, Summer 2007, 25.
8. Flanders, *Shaping of America's Heartland*, 27–29, 33.
9. Ibid., 31.
10. Ibid., 30; "The Sands of Time," *Illinois Steward*, Summer 2007, 6.
11. Jeffrey O. Dawson, "The Kankakee Torrent," *Illinois Steward*, Summer 2007, 23.
12. Flanders, *Shaping of America's Heartland*, 36–37; "Sands of Time," 6.
13. Flanders, *Shaping of America's Heartland*, 47.
14. Dawson, "Kankakee Torrent," 23.
15. Flanders, *Shaping of America's Heartland*, 40.
16. Dawson, "Kankakee Torrent," 23; Rob Littiken, interview by author, October 26, 2009, notes in possession of author.
17. Flanders, *Shaping of America's Heartland*, 36–37.
18. Littiken, interview.
19. Dawson, "Kankakee Torrent," 23.
20. Susan L. Post, "The Grand Kankakee," *Illinois Steward*, Summer 2007, 4.
21. Robert J. Reber, "Draining the Kankakee Sands—A Story of Contrasts," *Illinois Steward*, Summer 2007, 20.
22. Littiken, interview.
23. Dawson, "Kankakee Torrent," 23; Flanders, *Shaping of America's Heartland*, 37–38, 188–89.
24. Post, "Grand Kankakee," 4–5.
25. Flanders, *Shaping of America's Heartland*, 196–97.
26. Littiken, interview.
27. Warwick, "Pembroke Township," 26.
28. K. C. Jaehnig, "Saving Savanna," *Perspectives: Southern Illinois University Carbondale Research and Creative Activities*, Fall 2008, 2–3.
29. Michael R. Jeffords, "Odds and Ends," *Illinois Steward*, Summer 2007, 35–36.
30. Warwick, "Pembroke Township," 25–26.
31. Jeffords, "Odds and Ends," 36; Fran Harty, "Guest Editorial: The Greater Kankakee Sands Ecosystem," *Illinois Steward*, Summer 2007, 2.
32. Post, "Grand Kankakee," 4–5.

33. Harty, "Guest Editorial," 2.

34. The Nature Conservancy, "Illinois: Kankakee Sands"; Victoria A. Nuzzo, "Extent and Status of Midwest Oak Savanna: Presettlement and 1985," *Natural Areas Journal* 6, no. 2 (1986): 6.

35. Jeffords, "Odds and Ends," 35–36; Robert Themer, "'Nature Friendly' Preserves," *Daily Journal* (Kankakee IL), May 22, 2009.

36. "Sands of Time," 6; Robert J. Reber, "A Wealth of Wildlife: The Early Years," *Illinois Steward*, Summer 2007, 11–13.

37. Charles Warwick, "The People of the Prairie," *Illinois Steward*, Summer 2007, 16–17.

38. Warwick, "People of the Prairie," 17–18; Robert Themer, "Saving Savannas," *Daily Journal* (Kankakee IL), May 22, 2009.

39. Warwick, "People of the Prairie," 16–18.

40. Reber, "Wealth of Wildlife," 13; Andre Engels, "Louis Jolliet (1645–1700) Jacques Marquette (1637–1675)"; A&E Television Networks, "Jacques Marquette."

41. Reber, "Wealth of Wildlife," 11.

42. Second Continental Congress, The Northwest Ordinance of 1787; Staughton Lynd, "The Compromise of 1787," 225.

43. A&E Television Networks, "John Jacob Astor."

44. Reber, "Wealth of Wildlife," 13.

45. Ibid., 13–14; "Sands of Time," 7.

46. Reber, "Wealth of Wildlife," 13–14; Illinois Department of Natural Resources, Office of Scientific Research and Analysis, *Kankakee River Area Assessment, Volume 5*, 40–41.

47. Reber, "Wealth of Wildlife," 14; June Skinner Sawyers, *Chicago Portraits*, 127–28.

48. Illinois Department of Natural Resources, *Kankakee River Area Assessment*, 44.

49. Ibid., 59.

50. Earl H. Reed, *Tales of a Vanishing River* (New York: John Lane Company, 1920), 23–27; Mary Jean Houde and John Klasey, *Of the People*, 380.

51. Illinois Department of Natural Resources, *Kankakee River Area Assessment*, 257.

52. Warwick, "Pembroke Township," 26.

53. Warwick, "People of the Prairie," 18; Troy Taylor, "The Fort Dearborn Massacre."

54. Warwick, "People of the Prairie," 19.

55. Illinois Department of Natural Resources, *Kankakee River Area Assessment*, 59.

56. Warwick, "People of the Prairie," 19.

57. Illinois Department of Natural Resources, *Kankakee River Area Assessment*, 93.

58. Illinois State Archives, "Kankakee County."

59. Chicago and Eastern Illinois Railroad Historical Society, "A Brief History of the Chicago and Eastern Illinois Railroad."

60. Illinois State Archives, "Kankakee County"; Pembroke Centennial Committee, "Pride with Effort."

61. Paul Rix, "Pembroke Township Rich in History," *Daily Journal* (Kankakee IL), May 13, 1977.

62. Houde and Klasey, *Of the People*, 380; Pembroke Centennial Committee.

63. Merlin Karlock, interview by author, September 15, 2009, notes in possession of·author.

64. Reber, "Wealth of Wildlife," 14; "Sands of Time," 9.

65. Karlock, interview; Reber, "Wealth of Wildlife," 15.

66. "Sands of Time," 7, 21–22.

67. Ibid., 8–9.

68. Illinois Department of Natural Resources, *Kankakee River Area Assessment*, 244.

69. Reber, "Draining the Kankakee Sands," 23.

70. "Sands of Time," 9.

71. Jeffords, "Odds and Ends," 35.

2. Pap and Mary Tetter

1. I. Lippincott, "Industry among the French in the Illinois Country," 116; John D. Barnhart, "The Southern Element in the Leadership of the Old Northwest," 186–87.

2. Staughton Lynd, "The Compromise of 1787," 225.

3. Second Continental Congress, The Northwest Ordinance of 1787, art. 6.

4. William Henry Harrison, "Petition of the Vincennes Convention."

5. Legislative Council and House of Representatives of the Indiana Territory, "Petition on Slavery from Indiana," 62–67.

6. Paul Finkelman, "Evading the Ordinance," 22–24, 38–39.

7. Finkelman, "Evading the Ordinance," 41–43; Juliet E. K. Walker, *Free Frank*, 66–67; The New Philadelphia Association, "New Philadelphia: A Pioneer Town."

8. Ill. Const., art. VI, sec. 1–2 (1818).

9. Peter S. Onuf, *Statehood and Union*, 123.

10. Finkelman, "Evading the Ordinance," 49–50; Onuf, *Statehood and Union*, 123–30; Gavin Wright, *Slavery and American Economic Development*, 45.

11. Finkelman, "Evading the Ordinance," 21, 40; Indiana Historical Bureau, "Slavery in Indiana Territory"; University of Virginia, Geospatial and Statistical Data Center, "Historical Census Browser."

12. Dennis K. Boman, "Slavery in Illinois."

13. Stephan A. Vincent, *Southern Seed, Northern Soil*, xiii.

14. Vincent, *Southern Seed, Northern Soil*, 30–31; Walker, 64.
15. Vincent, 38, xii.
16. Ibid., 2, 26, 41–42.
17. Ibid., xvi, 54–56, 98, 112–15.
18. Walker, *Free Frank*, 7, 18, 34–36, 46, 1, 67.
19. National Park Service, "Reading 1: Free Frank McWorter"; National Park Service, "New Philadelphia: A Multiracial Town on the Illinois Frontier."
20. National Park Service, "Reading 2: New Philadelphia"; Roberta Codemo, "History in the Making," *Illinois Times* (Springfield, IL), April 17, 2003.
21. Walker, *Free Frank*, 167–69.
22. Shirley Carlson, *Black Migration to Pulaski County*, 37; Sundiata Keita Cha-Jua, *America's First Black Town*, 31–35.
23. Cha-Jua, *America's First Black Town*, 33–35; Walker, *Free Frank*, 114; National Governors Association, "Illinois Governor Edward Coles."
24. Cha-Jua, *America's First Black Town*, 1, 32.
25. Walker, *Free Frank*, 143–44.
26. Cha-Jua, *America's First Black Town*, 120, 123, 131, 3–6.
27. Carlson, *Black Migration to Pulaski County*, 38; Cha-Jua, *America's First Black Town*, 13, 57.
28. Cha-Jua, *America's First Black Town*, 39; Walker, *Free Frank*, 149–50; Glennette Tilley Turner, lecture at the Kankakee Public Library; Glennette Tilley Turner, *The Underground Railroad in Illinois*, 34.
29. Turner, *Underground Railroad in Illinois*, 6; James T. Ransom, "Underground Railroad Routes in Illinois," 1.
30. "City News Exclusive Report: Residents Fear Nature Conservancy Exploiting Pembroke," *Kankakee (IL) City News*, June 2009.
31. Basu, interview by author, September 11, 2009, notes in possession of author.
32. Merlin Karlock, interview by author, September 15, 2009, notes in possession of author. Quotations from Karlock in this chapter are from this interview.
33. John M. Beck, Irving H. Cutler, and John J. L. Hobgood, "Pembroke Township," 5.
34. Ransom, "Underground Railroad Routes," 1; Turner, *Underground Railroad in Illinois*, 34; National Park Service, "Lincoln Home."
35. Turner, lecture.
36. Beck et al., "Pembroke Township," 5; Virginia Porter, "A Fresh Start in 1852," *Kankakee (IL) Daily Journal*, March 26, 1972.
37. Virginia Porter, "Kankakee County Black History—Tetters Settle Hopkins in 1863," *Kankakee (IL) Daily Journal*, March 27, 1972.
38. Robert Themer, "An Incredible Journey: Pap Tetter's History Is Mysterious and Heroic," *Daily Journal* (Kankakee IL), February 13, 2005.

39. Themer, "An Incredible Journey."
40. "To Honor Elder Citizen," *Pembroke Herald-Citizen*, August 29, 1963; U.S. Census Bureau, *Eighth Census of the United States: Schedule 1—Free Inhabitants, State of Illinois, Iroquois County,* 1860; U.S. Census Bureau, *Ninth Census of the United States: Schedule 1—Inhabitants, State of Illinois, County of Iroquois, Township of Papineau,* 1870.
41. Jihad Muhammad, "ASRI Spearheads an Early Outreach African Humanity/ Scientific Field School Coming 2005!" *ASRI Gazette* 1, no. 1 (Spring 2005), https://www.uic.edu/orgs/asri/images/ASRIGAZZETT1.pdf.
42. Jon Krenek, "Hopkins Haven for Slaves? Project Aims to Find Signs of Underground Railroad," *Daily Journal* (Kankakee IL), January 30, 2005.
43. Muhammad, "ASRI Spearheads an Early Outreach."
44. Themer, "An Incredible Journey."
45. Ibid.; Jon Krenek, "Founder's Kin Shocked by Request," *Daily Journal* (Kankakee IL), January 31, 2005.
46. Lana Higginbottom, interview by author, October 26, 2009, notes in possession of author. Quotations from Lana Higginbottom in this chapter are from this interview.
47. Themer, "An Incredible Journey."
48. Ibid.; U.S. Bureau of the Census, *Thirteenth Census of the United States: 1910 Population, State of Illinois, County of Kankakee, Township of Pembroke.*
49. Arthur Collins, interview by author, October 5, 2009, notes in possession of author.
50. Sister Mary Beth Clements, interview by author, October 18, 2014.
51. "Hopkins Park—A Bit of the Tennessee Hills," *Kankakee (IL) Republican.* The copy of this article is undated, but context places it in the early 1930s.
52. Karlock, interview.
53. Katherine Farnsworth, ed., *Pembroke Local History Book.*
54. Farnsworth, *Pembroke Local History Book.*
55. Porter, "Kankakee County Black History."
56. "Colored Pair Held for Part in Haul by Gun," *Kankakee (IL) Republican News,* June 24, 1931.
57. "Hopkins Park—A Bit of the Tennessee Hills."
58. "New Oil Well Seen in Pembroke," *Kankakee (IL) Daily Republican,* April 18, 1931.
59. "Pembroke Oil Well Project Abandoned," *Kankakee (IL) Daily Republican,* May 16, 1931.
60. "City Connects with Line from Texas Source," *St. Anne (IL) Record,* November 10, 1931.
61. "Hopkins Park—A Bit of the Tennessee Hills." The remaining quotations and information in this chapter are from this resource.

3. The Second Migration

1. Isabel Wilkerson, *Warmth of Other Sons*, 9.
2. James R. Grossman, *Land of Hope*, 3–4.
3. Agnes Strong DeLacy, interview by Saints Patrick and Teresa Teen Group, Project Hearts of Hope, August 1999, tape in possession of author (quotations from Strong DeLacy in this chapter are from this interview); John Hamilton, "Pembroke Foster Grandma to Receive Statewide Award," *Daily Journal* (Kankakee IL), February 20, 2000.
4. Strong DeLacy, interview; "100-Year-Old Still Lives the Good Life," *Daily Journal* (Kankakee IL), March 4, 2005.
5. Hamilton, "Pembroke Foster Grandma."
6. Ibid.
7. "Agnes Strong," *Daily Journal* (Kankakee IL), January 21, 2010; Mary Jean Houde and John Klasey, *Of the People*, 380.
8. Allan H. Spear, *Black Chicago*, 130–32.
9. Grossman, *Land of Hope*, 14, 28–29.
10. Spear, *Black Chicago*, 130–32; Shirley Carlson, "Black Migration to Pulaski County," 40; Grossman, *Land of Hope*, 16–17, 27.
11. Gunnar Myrdal, *An American Dilemma*, 560–61; Robert A. Gibson, "The Negro Holocaust."
12. Grossman, *Land of Hope*, 13, 69–70; Spear, *Black Chicago*, 131–32.
13. Carlson, 37–38; Sundiata Keita Cha-Jua, *America's First Black Town*, 57.
14. Grossman, *Land of Hope*, 74.
15. Spear, *Black Chicago*, 129.
16. Grossman, *Land of Hope*, 74–79, 4, 59, 81.
17. Ibid., 89–90; Spear, *Black Chicago*, 129–30.
18. Grossman, *Land of Hope*, 94–96.
19. Ibid., 1, 113; Spear, *Black Chicago*, 137.
20. Jeffrey Steele, "Railroad Palaces Dot Chicago's History," *Chicago Tribune*, September 20, 1992.
21. Grossman, *Land of Hope*, 113–17.
22. Spear, *Black Chicago*, 48.
23. Grossman, *Land of Hope*, 209, 218.
24. Spear, *Black Chicago*, 22.
25. Ibid., 16–17, 23.
26. Ibid., 22.
27. Grossman, *Land of Hope*, 174.
28. Gary Krist, *City of Scoundrels*, 229, 236.
29. "50 Years in Pembroke: 'Homesteading' in a Great Place to Raise Children," *Daily Journal* (Kankakee IL), August 9, 1998.
30. Cha-Jua, *America's First Black Town*, 77–78, 147–63.
31. Mary Pattillo-McCoy, *Black Picket Fences*, 22–25, 36.

32. John Bowman, "Pembroke Revisited: Beyond a Road Sign, A Mystery to Most Kankakeeans," *Kankakee (IL) Sunday Journal,* July 3, 1966.

33. "50 Years in Pembroke."

34. Houde and Klasey, *Of the People,* 382.

35. Merlin Karlock, interview by author, September 15, 2009, notes in possession of author. Quotations from Karlock in this chapter are from this interview.

36. Linnet Myers, "Dirt Poor," *Chicago Tribune Magazine,* February 28, 1999.

37. Jerry Morgan, "Residents Dispute Realtor's Claim of Good Living at Willow Estates," *Daily Journal* (Kankakee IL), October 16, 1974.

38. Moscickis Realty Advertisement, *Pembroke (IL) Herald-Eagle,* April 10, 1969.

39. Myers, "Dirt Poor."

40. Anne Keegan, "Pembroke: Promise of Good Life Unfulfilled," *Chicago Tribune,* August 28, 1974.

41. Myers, "Dirt Poor."

42. John M. Beck, Irving H. Cutler, and John J. L. Hobgood, "Pembroke Township, 46.

43. Eade v. Brownlee, 29 Ill. 2d 214, 219, 193 N.E.2d 786 (1963); Lisa A. Danielson, "Installment Land Contracts," 91–94.

44. Current protections available to a mortgage holder under Illinois law are codified in 735 ILCS 5/15–1501 et seq. (2016) (previously Ill. Rev. Stat., ch. 110, par. 15–1501 et seq. [1991]) and 735 ILCS 5/15–1601 et seq. (2016) (previously Ill. Rev. Stat., ch. 110, par. 15–1601 et seq. [1991]).

45. Moscickis Realty Advertisement.

46. Eric T. Freyfogle, "The Installment Land Contract as Lease," 293–304.

47. McDonald v. Bartlett, 324 Ill. 549, 588–89, 155 N.E. 477 (1927).

48. Krentz v. Johnson, 36 Ill. App. 3d 142, 145, 343 N.E.2d 165 (1976) (internal citations omitted).

49. Aden v. Alwardt, 76 Ill. App. 3d 54, 59, 394 N.E.2d 716 (1979).

50. 735 ILCS 5/15–1106 (2016) (previously Ill. Rev. Stat., ch. 110, par. 15–1106 [1991]).

51. Ill. Rev. Stat., ch. 109, par. 1 (1953).

52. Ill. Rev. Stat., ch. 109, par. 1 (1957).

53. Beck et al., "Pembroke Township," 67.

54. Ibid., 9.

55. Ibid.

56. Morgan, "Residents Dispute Realtor's Claim."

57. Keegan, "Pembroke."

58. Larry Gibbs, interview by author, September 15, 2009, notes in possession of author.

59. Beck et al., "Pembroke Township," 17.

60. Ibid., 46–47.

61. Reggie Stewart, interview by author, October 12, 2009, notes in possession of author.

4. Welcome to Lamplight City

1. James Piekarczyk, interview by author, October 27, 2009, notes in possession of author. Further Piekarczyk quotations in this chapter are from this interview.

2. Katherine Farnsworth, ed., *Pembroke Local History Book*.

3. "Leesville in Drive to Lure Industry, Firms to Village," *Chicago Defender*, January 19, 1963.

4. Pembroke Centennial Committee, "Pride with Effort."

5. Larry Barnes, interview by author, September 18, 2009, notes in possession of author.

6. John M. Beck, Irving H. Cutler, and John J. L. Hobgood, "Pembroke Township," 25; Kankakee County Planning Department, "Demographics."

7. John Bowman, "Pembroke Revisited: Beyond a Road Sign, A Mystery to Most Kankakeeans," *Kankakee (IL) Sunday Journal*, July 3, 1966.

8. Mary Jean Houde and John Klasey, *Of the People*, 380.

9. Fern Schumer, "The 'Rural South' Looms Just beyond Suburbia," *Chicago Tribune Magazine*, December 13, 1981.

10. Bertha Tetter, letter to author, September 26, 2009, letter in possession of author.

11. Eva Grant, interview by author, September 16, 2009, notes in possession of author. Further Grant quotations in this chapter are from this interview.

12. Farnsworth, *Pembroke Local History Book*.

13. Howard Jones, interview by author, September 15, 2009, notes in possession of author.

14. Schumer, "'Rural South' Looms."

15. Ozroe Bentley, "Publisher View of Official Tour," *Pembroke (IL) Herald-Eagle*, April 23, 1970.

16. Robert Themer, "New Firm to Revive Pembroke Cannery," *Daily Journal* (Kankakee IL), January 21, 1982.

17. Arthur Collins, interview by author, October 5, 2009, notes in possession of author.

18. Farnsworth, *Pembroke Local History Book*.

19. Beck et al., "Pembroke Township," 48.

20. Ibid., 12, 35.

21. Ibid., 3.

22. Ibid.

23. Marvin Balousek and Louise Morgan, "Lorenzo Smith, School Chief in Pembroke, Dies," *Daily Journal* (Kankakee IL), August 14, 1980; Merlin Karlock, interview by author, September 15, 2009, notes in possession of author (further Karlock quotations in this chapter are from this interview); "Portrait Gallery: Lorenzo R. Smith," *Kankakee (IL) Daily Journal*, October 16, 1960.

24. Sr. Mary Cecelia, *Joy: Newsletter of the Sisters at the Martin de Porres Convent at Sacred Heart Catholic Church* 2, No. 3 (1973).

25. "Coronary Thrombosis Caused Smith's Death," *Daily Journal* (Kankakee IL), August 19, 1980.

26. Gertrude Higginbottom, interview by Saints Patrick and Teresa Teen Group, Project Hearts of Hope, August 1999, tape in possession of author.

27. Eva Grant, interview by author, September 16, 2009, notes in possession of author.

28. Pembroke Centennial Committee, "Pride with Effort."

29. Ibid.

30. Sundiata Keita Cha-Jua, *America's First Black Town*, 45.

31. Pembroke Centennial Committee, "Pride with Effort"; Scott Reeder, "Official's Killer Granted Parole," *Daily Journal* (Kankakee IL), January 12, 2001.

32. Ill. Const., art. VII, sec. 5 (1970).

33. Township Officials of Illinois, "TOI History."

34. Pembroke Centennial Committee, "Pride with Effort."

35. Reeder, "Official's Killer Granted Parole."

36. Anne Keegan, "Pembroke: Promise of Good Life Unfulfilled," *Chicago Tribune*, August 28, 1974.

37. Reeder, "Official's Killer Granted Parole"; Ted Watson, "Pot Raid Trips Man Sought in Kankakee," *Chicago Defender*, February 3, 1975.

38. Ted Watson, "Pembroke Official Dies of Wounds," *Chicago Defender*, December 14, 1974.

39. Pembroke Centennial Committee, "Pride with Effort."

40. 65 ILCS 5/11 et seq. (2016) (previously Ill. Rev. Stat., ch. 24, art. 11 [1991]); Ill. Const., art. VII, sec. 6 (1970).

41. Jerry Morgan, "Pembroke: Village Dissolution Sought," *Sunday Journal* (Kankakee IL) April 25, 1976.

42. "Pembroke Dedicates Village Hall Saturday," *Kankakee (IL) Daily Journal*, April 27, 1973.

43. 65 ILCS 5/1-1-2.1 (2016) (previously Ill. Rev. Stat., ch. 24, par. 1-1-2.1 [1991]).

44. Morgan, "Pembroke."

45. Marvin Balousek, "Pembroke's New Officers Pledge to Do Their Best," *Daily Journal* (Kankakee IL), May 1, 1979.

46. Karlock, interview; Agnes Strong DeLacy, interview by Saints Patrick and Teresa Teen Group, Project Hearts of Hope, August 1999, tape in possession of author.

47. Robert Themer, "Leesville: Pembroke's Poor Relation," *Daily Journal* (Kankakee IL), February 21, 1993.

48. Ill. Rev. Stat., ch. 24, par. 3–5 (1955). The modern counterpart of the statute, 65 ILCS 5/2-3-5 (2016), requires a minimum of two hundred inhabitants who do not live in mobile homes to incorporate as a village.

49. "Leesville in Drive"; "Officer's Arrest Stirs Old Controversy," *The Chicago Defender*, October 13, 1962.

50. "Officer's Arrest"; Themer, "Leesville."

51. "Cop School Defendants Told of Their Rights," *Chicago Daily Defender*, May 1, 1963.

52. Themer, "Leesville."

53. Cha-Jua, *America's First Black Town*, 218; Mary Pattillo-McCoy, *Black Picket Fences*, 24–25.

54. Allan H. Spear, *Black Chicago*, 53–57.

55. Booker T. Washington, speech given to Atlanta Cotton States and International Exposition, Atlanta, Georgia, October 18, 1895.

56. Shirley Portwood, "The Alton School Case and African American Community Consciousness 1897–1908," 6–7; Sundiata Keita Cha-Jua, "The Cry of the Negro Should Not Be Remember the Maine, but Remember the Hanging of Bush," 171–75.

57. Cha-Jua, *America's First Black Town*, 138–42.

58. Brooks Jackson, "Blacks and the Democratic Party"; Roper Center, "How Groups Voted."

59. Richard M. Bernard, *Snowbelt Cities*, 65–67.

60. Ozroe Bentley, "General Election Tuesday, Nov. 3," *Pembroke (IL) Herald-Eagle*, October 29, 1970.

61. Farnsworth, *Pembroke Local History Book*.

62. Lisa Hoss, "Ozroe Bentley Leaving Pembroke—A Place He Helped Improve," *Daily Journal* (Kankakee IL), December 23, 1982; Lisa Laney, "Pembroke Eagle to Keep Flying as Historical Record," *Daily Journal* (Kankakee IL), February 24, 1991.

63. Bentley, "General Election Tuesday."

64. Laney, "Pembroke Eagle."

65. "Pembroke Township Board Names New Supervisor," *Daily Journal* (Kankakee IL), December 15, 1974; Robert Hayes, interview by Saints Patrick and Teresa Teen Group, Project Hearts of Hope, August 1999, tape in possession of author.

66. "Pembroke Township Board Names New Supervisor"; Leanne Duby, "Pembroke's Hayes Sees Participation as 'A Red Letter Day,'" *Daily Journal* (Kankakee IL), January 19, 1992.

67. "Pembroke Township Board Names New Supervisor."

68. Ibid.; "DeLaney, Hayes GOP Vice-Chairmen," *Daily Journal* (Kankakee IL), February 29, 1976.

69. Fern Schumer, "Pembroke: A Community without Income, Services, or a Tax Base," *Chicago Tribune*, December 31, 1981.

70. Pembroke Centennial Committee, "Pride with Effort."

71. Robert Themer, interview by author, September 18, 2009, notes in possession of author.

72. Duby, "Pembroke's Hayes."
73. Themer, "New Firm"; Paul Rix, "Cannery Grant Spurs Township: Pembroke Opens Lids to Progress," *Daily Journal* (Kankakee IL), January 23, 1977.
74. Janet Cremer, "Fire Destroys Pembroke Community Building: Lightning May Have Caused Pembroke Fire," *Daily Journal* (Kankakee IL), June 30, 1993.
75. Robert Hayes Advertisement, *St. Martin de Porres Guild Fashion Show Program* (1975), from the archives of Sacred Heart Mission.
76. John Stewart, "Competition Thick in Pembroke," *Daily Journal* (Kankakee IL), January 13, 1993.
77. "5th Pembroke Road Candidate," *Daily Journal* (Kankakee IL), January 14, 1993.
78. Ozroe Bentley, "Comments at Random," *Pembroke (IL) Herald-Eagle*, November 16, 1978.
79. Farnsworth, *Pembroke Local History Book*.
80. Elvia Steward, interview by author, October 26, 2009, notes in possession of author. Further Steward quotations in this chapter are from this interview.
81. Steward, interview; Janet Siwicki, "Elvia Lee Steward—The Roadrunner," *Daily Journal* (Kankakee IL), March 10, 1991.
82. Siwicki, "Elvia Lee Steward."
83. "Elvia Steward," *Daily Journal* (Kankakee IL), August 7, 2014; "Pembroke Eagle Editor, Publisher Ozroe Bentley Dies," *Daily Journal* (Kankakee IL), September 24, 2004; Robert Themer, "Robert E. Hayes, Longtime Pembroke Leader, Dies at 92," *Daily Journal* (Kankakee IL), January 8, 2011.
84. Cha-Jua, *America's First Black Town*, 217–18.
85. David Brooks, "Take a Ride to Exurbia," *New York Times*, November 9, 2004.

5. "A Rip-Roarin' Time"

1. Lana Higginbottom, interview by author, October 26, 2019, notes in possession of author. Further Higginbottom quotations in this chapter are from this interview.
2. Earl H. Reed, *Tales of a Vanishing River*, 23–27; Mary Jean Houde and John Klasey, *Of the People*, 380.
3. Allen Jones, interview by author, September 15, 2009, notes in possession of author; James Piekarczyk, interview by author, October 27, 2009, notes in possession of author; Merlin Karlock, interview by author, September 15, 2009, notes in possession of author. Quotations from Jones, Piekarczyk, and Karlock in this chapter are from these interviews.
4. Houde and Klasey, *Of the People*, 347; Karlock, interview.
5. Houde and Klasey, *Of the People*, 347; Paul Rix, "Pembroke Township Rich in History," *Daily Journal* (Kankakee IL), March 13, 1977.
6. Jones, interview; Karlock, interview.
7. "Federal Dry Agents Raid Thirty Wet Places: Warrants for County Cover Fifty Places," *Kankakee (IL) Republican News*, September 5, 1931.

8. Houde and Klasey, *Of the People*, 347.

9. Sandy Smith and Thomas Powers, "Rackets Rife in Kankakee County Area," *Chicago Tribune*, September 23, 1961.

10. Karlock, interview.

11. Karlock, interview; Lloyd L. General, "Troopers Raid Four Plush Spots," *Chicago Defender*, May 25, 1957.

12. Smith and Powers, "Rackets."

13. Karlock, interview.

14. Sundiata Keita Cha-Jua, *America's First Black Town*, 166–67, 207.

15. "50 Years in Pembroke: 'Homesteading' in a Great Place to Raise Children," *Daily Journal* (Kankakee IL), August 9, 1998.

16. "Close Hopkins Park Playhouses: Vice Fighters Win 1st Round," *Chicago Defender*, May 31, 1953; Lloyd L. General, "Red Light Strip Divides Town," *Chicago Defender*, April 6, 1957.

17. "Hopkins Park Women Plan Fight On Vice," *Chicago Defender*, June 1, 1957.

18. "Citizens Launch Fight against Racial Attacks," *Chicago Defender*, October 31, 1959.

19. General, "Troopers Raid"; "Hopkins Park Vice Foe Beaten," *Chicago Defender*, February 22, 1958; "Tell Murder Plot in Hopkins Park," *Chicago Defender*, June 28, 1958.

20. Sandy Smith, "Mobsters Aiming at Kankakee," *Chicago Daily Tribune*, October 2, 1961.

21. Smith and Powers, "Rackets."

22. Smith and Powers, "Rackets"; Smith, "Mobsters Aiming."

23. Smith and Powers, "Rackets"; "Oust Sheriff in Kankakee; Fined $1,000," *Chicago Daily Tribune*, March 8, 1962.

24. "Oust Sheriff."

25. Smith and Powers, "Rackets."

26. "Ask State to Shut Kankakee Vice: Prosecutor Says Sheriff Won't Do It," *Chicago Daily Tribune*, November 22, 1961.

27. John Bowman, "Pembroke Revisited: Beyond a Road Sign, A Mystery to Most Kankakeeans," *Kankakee (IL) Sunday Journal*, July 3, 1966.

28. Lloyd L. General, "Says Police Raids Miss Target," *Chicago Defender*, June 15, 2015.

29. Bowman, "Pembroke Revisited."

30. Larry Barnes, interview by author, September 18, 2009, notes in possession of author. Further Barnes quotations in this chapter are from this interview.

31. Ibid.

32. "Tavern's License Revoked," *Daily Journal* (Kankakee IL), April 28, 1992.

33. Robert Themer, "Mr. Curt: Fixture on the Front," *Daily Journal* (Kankakee IL), November 21, 2002.

34. Barnes, interview.

35. Themer, "Mr. Curt."

36. John Krenek, "Much-Needed Food Pantry in Hopkins Hits Snag," *Daily Journal* (Kankakee IL), May 18, 2015.

37. Leanne Duby, "1 Dead, 1 Hurt in Pembroke Shooting," *Daily Journal* (Kankakee IL), February 7, 1992.

38. Leanne Duby, "Men Arrested after Invading Pembroke Home," *Daily Journal* (Kankakee IL), July 19, 1993.

39. "7 Are Arrested in Dogfighting Bust," *Chicago Tribune*, August 10, 2009.

40. Ibid.; Kristen Zambo, "Rural Areas Alluring to Dogfighters," *Daily Journal* (Kankakee IL), September 2, 2009.

41. Daniel Egler and Andrew Fegelman, "Buried Alive, Kidnapped Heir's Body Is Found," *Chicago Tribune*, September 6, 1987; Ray Gibson and Wes Smith, "Bungled Kidnap Turned Prison into a Grave," *Chicago Tribune*, September 6, 1987.

42. Egler and Fegelman, "Buried Alive"; Gibson and Smith, "Bungled Kidnap."

43. Egler and Fegelman, "Buried Alive"; Andrew Fegelman, "Three Arrested in Slaying of Kankakee Heir," *Chicago Tribune*, September 6, 1987; "Stephen Small Murder," *Kanwiki*.

44. Egler and Fegelman, "Buried Alive."

45. "Rish Asks for New Judge; Says Judge Was Biased," *Daily Journal* (Kankakee IL), December 4, 2015.

46. Leanne Duby, "Huge Rally to Be Held in Pembroke," *Daily Journal* (Kankakee IL), September 10, 1993; Mike Lyons and Leanne Duby, "Saturday Rally: 'It Was an Army,'" *Daily Journal* (Kankakee IL), September 13, 1993.

47. Lyons and Duby, "Saturday Rally"; Mike Lyons, "7,000 Attend Rally; All Is Peaceful," *Daily Journal* (Kankakee IL), September 12, 1993.

48. Duby, "Huge Rally."

49. Lyons, "7,000."

50. Duby, "Huge Rally."

51. Lyons and Duby, "Saturday Rally."

52. Lyons, "7,000."

53. Lyons and Duby, "Saturday Rally."

54. Lyons, "7,000."

55. Jerry Morgan, "More Control over Gatherings Eyed," *Daily Journal* (Kankakee IL), September 23, 1993.

56. Jerry Morgan, "Area Bullied by Thugs, Huot Says of Rally," *Daily Journal* (Kankakee IL), September 15, 1993.

57. John Hamilton, "Suspected Chemical Dump Found in Pembroke," *Kankakee (IL) Daily Journal*, October 16, 1997; "Toxics Traced to Hoosier Junkyard; Site Unposted," *Daily Journal* (Kankakee IL), November 6, 1997.

58. Jerry Morgan, "Kankakee County Seeking Ways to Recycle Tires," *Daily Journal* (Kankakee IL), December 9, 1990.

59. Jerry Morgan, "Canadian Tire Fire Emphasizes Threat in Area," *Daily Journal* (Kankakee IL), February 25, 1990.

60. Diane Ross, "State Hiring Contractor to Rid Pembroke Township of Tire Pile," *Daily Journal* (Kankakee IL), March 26, 1993; Jerry Morgan, "Tired of the Problem: County Vowing Prosecution of Tire Dumpers," *Sunday Journal* (Kankakee IL), April 10, 1994.

61. Willie Nettles Bey, interview by Saints Patrick and Teresa Teen Group, Project Hearts of Hope 3, Summer 2004, tape in possession of author. Further Nettles Bey quotations in this chapter are from this interview.

62. Leanne Duby, "Deputies Face Mob in Pembroke," *Daily Journal* (Kankakee IL), May 24, 1994.

63. "Sheriff Urges Pembroke 'Watch,'" *Daily Journal* (Kankakee IL), September 17, 1990.

64. Barbara Bratton, "Editorial," *Pembroke (IL) Herald-Eagle*, September 21, 1978.

6. "In the Eyes of the Angels"

1. Nancy M. Williams, interview by Saints Patrick and Teresa Teen Group, Project Hearts of Hope, August 1999, tape in possession of author.

2. Merlin Karlock, interview by author, September 15, 2009, notes in possession of author; Pembroke Centennial Committee, "Pride with Effort: Pembroke Centennial Celebration."

3. Williams, interview.

4. James R. Grossman, *Land of Hope*, 90–91, 94.

5. "The Church History of Greater St. Paul," from the archives of Sacred Heart Mission.

6. Janet Siwicki, "Hopkins Park Woman Builds Church: $235,000 in Savings Goes into Work," *Daily Journal* (Kankakee IL), June 15, 1989.

7. Siwicki, "Hopkins Park Woman"; "Church of the Cross, Hopkins Park, Illinois: 13th Anniversary," from the archives of Sacred Heart Mission (2003).

8. Siwicki, "Hopkins Park Woman."

9. Robyn Monaghan, "Fire Kills Church Founder," *Daily Journal* (Kankakee IL), December 18, 2005.

10. Robert Themer, "Lehmans Leaving Rehoboth Mennonite Church," *Daily Journal* (Kankakee IL), July 30, 1992.

11. "Mark Lehman and Family Return," *Pembroke (IL) Herald-Eagle*, June 22, 1978.

12. Themer, "Lehmans Leaving."

13. Allan H. Spear, *Black Chicago*, 93–95; Mary E. McGann, RSCJ, and Eva Marie Lumas, SSS, "Historical Overview," 4; St. Elizabeth Church, "Father Tolton."

14. Grossman, *Land of Hope*, 173.

15. May Hogan, letter to Reverend Theodore Demarais, from the archives of Sacred Heart Mission (July 25, 1939). Quotations from Hogan in this chapter are from this letter.

16. Barbara Bratton, "A Brief History of Sacred Heart Mission," from the archives of Sacred Heart Mission; Reverend Theodore Demarais, draft letter to Samuel Cardinal Stritch, Archbishop of Chicago, from the archives of Sacred Heart Mission (July 5, 1945).

17. E. M. Burke, letter to Reverend Theodore Demarais, from the archives of Sacred Heart Mission (August 30, 1939).

18. Arthur Collins, interview by author, October 5, 2009, notes in possession of author.

19. Robert Hayes, interview by Saints Patrick and Teresa Teen Group, Project Hearts of Hope, August 1999, tape in possession of author (quotations from Hayes in this chapter are from this letter); "The People behind Sacred Heart," *New Catholic Explorer* (Joliet, IL), June 30, 1989.

20. Bratton, "Brief History"; Collins, interview.

21. Merriam-Webster, "Holy Roller"; Reverend Theodore Demarais, letter to Samuel Cardinal Stritch, Archbishop of Chicago, from the archives of Sacred Heart Mission. The letter is undated, but context suggests the letter was written before June 30, 1941.

22. Reverend Theodore Demarais, letter to Chancellor, Archdiocese of Chicago, from the archives of Sacred Heart Mission (June 30, 1941).

23. Bratton, "Brief History"; Reverend Theodore Demarais, personal notes, from the archives of Sacred Heart Mission; Varnum A. Parish, "Bill for Services Rendered," from the archives of Sacred Heart Mission (September 27, 1941).

24. Reverend Theodore Demarais, letter to Right Reverend Monsignor G. J. Casey, Archdiocese of Chicago, from the archives of Sacred Heart Mission. The letter is undated, but context suggests the letter was written in the autumn of 1942.

25. Samuel Cardinal Stritch, letter to Reverend Theodore Demarais, from the archives of Sacred Heart Mission (January 4, 1943).

26. Bratton, "Brief History"; "Obituary for Barbara Bratton," from the archives of Sacred Heart Mission (October 1990).

27. Bratton, "Brief History."

28. Barbara Bratton, "As I See It" column, *Pembroke (IL) Herald-Eagle*, January 5, 1978; Barbara Bratton, "As I See It" column, *Pembroke (IL) Herald-Eagle*, January 12, 1978.

29. "Mrs. Barbara Bratton," from the archives of Sacred Heart Mission (1966); Marvin Balousek, "A Storyteller with a Pregnant Heart," *Daily Journal* (Kankakee IL), November 29, 1978.

30. "Mrs. Barbara Bratton."

31. Reverend Anthony Taschetta, "Barbara 'Bobbie' Bratton: Remembering Hopkins Park's Grand Matriarch," *New Catholic Explorer*, November 2, 1990.

32. "People behind Sacred Heart"; "Feast of St. Martin de Porres Celebration," souvenir program, from the archives of Sacred Heart Mission (November 5, 1967).

33. "60th Anniversary," souvenir program, from the archives of Sacred Heart Mission (1999).

34. Jeanne Mobley, "Sacred Heart Resale Shop a Miracle Mission," *Daily Journal* (Kankakee IL), April 20, 1984.

35. "Mrs. Barbara Bratton."

36. Bratton, "Brief History."

37. Sacred Heart, "Feast of St. Martin."

38. Nancy J. Ruda, "Helping People Comes from Their Hearts," *Daily Journal* (Kankakee IL), May 17, 1999.

39. Ibid.

40. Howard Jones, interview by author, September 15, 2009, notes in possession of author.

41. Sacred Heart, "Feast of St. Martin"; "25th Anniversary," souvenir program, from the archives of Sacred Heart Mission (1964).

42. "Sacred Heart Church Gains Parish Status," *Kankakee (IL) Daily Journal*, June 7, 1968.

43. Bratton, "Brief History."

44. Sr. Mary Cecelia, *Joy: Newsletter of the Sisters at the Martin de Porres Convent at Sacred Heart Catholic Church* 2, no. 3 (1973).

45. Taschetta, "Barbara 'Bobbie' Bratton."

46. "40th Anniversary," souvenir program, from the archives of Sacred Heart Mission (1979).

47. Bratton, "Brief History" (emphasis added).

48. "People behind Sacred Heart"; "Sister Ignatius Darch, SSCM," funeral eulogy, from the archives of Sacred Heart Mission (May 3, 1984).

49. Cecelia, *Joy*.

50. "Sister Ignatius Darch."

51. *Sacred Heart Newsletter* 1, no. 1, from the archives of Sacred Heart Mission (February 1983); Christian Brothers, "Summer Volunteer Program," from the archives of Sacred Heart Mission (1983).

52. Pew Research Center, *America's Changing Religious Landscape*, 52; U.S. Census Bureau, *QuickFacts: United States*.

53. Farah Stockman, "In Singling Out Nuns, Catholic Church Overlooks Its History," *Boston Globe*, June 12, 2012, http://www.bostonglobe.com; Kent Garber, "What to Do about the Priest Shortage," *U.S. News & World Report*, April 18, 2008, http://www.usnews.com; U.S. Conference of Catholic Bishops, "Demographics."

54. Darren W. Davis and Donald B. Pope-Davis, *2011 National Black Catholic Survey*, 13, 24, 18–19.

55. Pew Research Center, *America's Changing Religious Landscape*, 21, 36.

56. Lydia Saad, "Churchgoing among U.S. Catholics Slides to Tie Protestants," *Gallup*, April 9, 2009, http://www.gallup.com.

57. Cyprian Davis, *History of Black Catholics in the United States*, 259.

58. Ronald D. Harbor, "Constructing an African American Catholic Liturgical Aesthetic," 109.

7. Lunch Tables

1. Brown v. Board of Education of Topeka, 347 U.S. 483 (1954) ("*Brown I*").

2. Ibid., 489–90.

3. Ibid., 492–93 (citing Plessy v. Ferguson, 163 U.S. 537 [1896]).

4. Ibid., 493.

5. Brown v. Board of Education of Topeka, 349 U.S. 294, 301 (1955) ("*Brown II*").

6. *Brown I*, 489–90.

7. Shirley Portwood, "The Alton School Case and African American Community Consciousness 1897–1908," 4, 12, 19–20; Shirley Portwood, "School Segregation in Southern Illinois: The Alton School Case, 1897–1908," 23–26.

8. James R. Grossman, *Land of Hope*, 246–47.

9. Continental Congress, An Ordinance for Ascertaining the Mode of Disposing of Lands in the Western Territory (1785), Library of Congress.

10. Rosalind Jackler, "Statements Taken in School Case," *Daily Journal* (Kankakee IL), March 13, 1979; Katherine Farnsworth, ed., *Pembroke Local History Book*; Merlin Karlock, interview by author, September 15, 2009, notes in possession of author (quotations and citations from Karlock in this chapter are from this interview).

11. Jerry Morgan, "$1.17 Million 'Would Help': Pembroke Seeking School Space," *Daily Journal* (Kankakee IL), June 23, 1974; Phil Angelo, "Karlock Always a Community Advocate," *Daily Journal* (Kankakee IL), January 22, 2016; "Sell 310 Acres of Land in Hopkins Park," *Chicago Defender*, June 28, 1958.

12. Sister Mary Cecelia, *Joy: Newsletter of the Sisters at the Martin de Porres Convent at Sacred Heart Catholic Church* 2, no. 3 (1973).

13. "Hopkins Park—A Bit of the Tennessee Hills," *Kankakee (IL) Republican*. The copy of this article is undated, but context places it in the early 1930s.

14. Gertrude Higginbottom, interview by Saints Patrick and Teresa Teen Group, Project Hearts of Hope, August 1999, tape in possession of author.

15. Marvin Balousek and Louise Morgan, "Lorenzo Smith, School Chief in Pembroke, Dies," *Daily Journal* (Kankakee IL), August 14, 1980.

16 "Portrait Gallery: Lorenzo R. Smith," *Kankakee (IL) Daily Journal*, October 16, 1960.

17. Balousek and Morgan, "Lorenzo Smith."

18. Morgan, "$1.17 Million."

19. "In Loving Memory of Mr. Wesley Higginbothan," from the archives of Sacred Heart Mission (1992).

20. "Hopkins Park Center of School Board Fight," *Chicago Defender,* July 13, 1957.

21. Marvin Balousek, "400 Mourn Death of Lorenzo R. Smith," *Daily Journal* (Kankakee IL), August 18, 1980.

22. Balousek and Morgan, "Lorenzo Smith."

23. Farnsworth, *Pembroke Local History Book.*

24. "Pembroke Goes Back to School," *Kankakee (IL) Daily Journal,* May 12, 1970; "Failure to Negotiate Results in Pembroke School Workers Going On Strike," *Pembroke (IL) Herald-Eagle,* June 3, 1970.

25. Lloyd Elizabeth Fosse, "The Schools of Pembroke: Mired in Hopeless Despair," *Kankakee (IL) Daily Journal,* June 12, 1972.

26. Lloyd Elizabeth Fosse, "Can They Be Remedied? Pembroke's Schools Beset by Ills," *Kankakee (IL) Daily Journal,* June 13, 1972.

27. Fosse, "Schools of Pembroke."

28. Higginbottom, interview.

29. "Pembroke Schools Evaluation Released," *Kankakee (IL) Daily Journal,* January 20, 1972.

30. "Move Begun to Recall Superintendent Smith," *Kankakee (IL) Daily Journal,* June 12, 1972.

31. "Pembroke Revisited," *Kankakee (IL) Daily Journal,* July 7, 1966.

32. John M. Beck, Irving H. Cutler, and John J. L. Hobgood, "Pembroke Township," 21.

33. Fosse, "Schools of Pembroke"; "Coronary Thrombosis Caused Smith's Death," *Daily Journal* (Kankakee IL), August 19, 1980; Trevor Marshall, "A Letter to Miss Busch," *Pembroke (IL) Herald-Eagle,* March 16, 1978.

34. Fosse, "Can They Be Remedied?"

35. Jerry Morgan, "Smith Urges Passage of Pembroke School Referendum," *Daily Journal* (Kankakee IL), August 18, 1974.

36. "Pembroke School Additions Started," *Daily Journal* (Kankakee IL), June 29, 1976.

37. Balousek, "400 Mourn Death."

38. Balousek and Morgan, "Lorenzo Smith."

39. Beck et al., "Pembroke Township," 25.

40. Robert Themer, "St. Anne High—A House Abandoned: School Connection Slight for Blacks and Whites," *Daily Journal* (Kankakee IL), April 21, 1996.

41. Farnsworth, *Pembroke Local History Book.*

42. Ibid.

43. Beck et al., "Pembroke Township," 68–69.

44. Casey Banas, "Dilemma in St. Anne: Bad School or None," *Chicago Tribune*, March 14, 1976; Robert Themer, "School Better Than Its Reputation, but Offers Little Extra," *Daily Journal* (Kankakee IL), April 21, 1996.

45. Banas, "Dilemma in St. Anne"; Rosalind Jackler, "St. Anne Suit: School Puzzle That's Waited Nearly 5 Years," *Daily Journal* (Kankakee IL), March 1, 1981.

46. Banas, "Dilemma in St. Anne"; "St. Anne High School to Phase Out Split Shifts," *Daily Journal* (Kankakee IL), April 3, 1979.

47. "This Attorney Is No Stranger to Desegregation Cases," *Daily Journal* (Kankakee IL), August 8, 1976; Robert Manley, Curriculum Vitae.

48. Marvin Balousek, "St. Anne Suit Costly, Still Year to Trial," *Daily Journal* (Kankakee IL), January 17, 1980; "Papers Served in St. Anne Suit," *Daily Journal* (Kankakee IL), July 29, 1976; "St. Anne Fallout: Lawsuit Leaves Area School Officials Perplexed," *Daily Journal* (Kankakee IL), August 8, 1976.

49. "St. Anne Fallout."

50. Jackler, "St. Anne Suit."

51. Ibid.

52. "St. Anne Fallout."

53. "Countywide School Desegregation Plan Ahead?" *Daily Journal* (Kankakee IL), November 26, 1976.

54. Jackler, "St. Anne Suit."

55. Ibid.

56. Rosalind Jackler, "St. Anne Wins Round in Desegregation Suit," *Daily Journal* (Kankakee IL), November 22, 1978.

57. "Pembroke Elementary Joins Desegregation Suit," *Daily Journal* (Kankakee IL), April 3, 1979; "Pembroke Petitions to Join Desegregation Suit," *Daily Journal* (Kankakee IL), February 4, 1979.

58. Robert Themer, "Unity Isn't Possible; Could Separation Work?" *Daily Journal* (Kankakee IL), April 21, 1996; Rosalind Jackler, "Trustees to Decide Fate of New District Thursday," *Daily Journal* (Kankakee IL), April 3, 1979.

59. Jerry Morgan, "Uncertainty Mounts at St. Anne," *Daily Journal* (Kankakee IL), November 14, 1976.

60. Jackler, "Trustees to Decide Fate"; "St. Anne School Lawsuit to Be Heard in Danville," *Daily Journal* (Kankakee IL), November 19, 1978.

61. Morgan, "Uncertainty Mounts."

62. Jackler, "Trustees to Decide Fate."

63. "St. Anne Decision," *Daily Journal* (Kankakee IL), April 6, 1979.

64. Balousek, "St. Anne Suit"; Jackler, "Statements Taken in School Case."

65. Jackler, "St. Anne Suit"; "Phase Out Split Shifts."

66. "Phase Out Split Shifts."

67. Jackler, "St. Anne Suit."

68. Robert Themer, "St. Anne Drops Bias Suit," *Daily Journal* (Kankakee IL), January 20, 1982.

69. "St. Anne High District Bias Lawsuit Dropped," *Daily Journal* (Kankakee IL), October 19, 1982.

70. Themer, "St. Anne High—a House Abandoned."

71. Janet Cremer, "St. Anne Grade Tax OK'd; High School Nixed," *Daily Journal* (Kankakee IL), March 16, 1994; Janet Cremer, "St. Anne Taxes Rejected," *Daily Journal* (Kankakee IL), November 6, 1991.

72. Janet Cremer, "St. Anne High Tax Hike Approved—Finally," *Daily Journal* (Kankakee IL), November 9, 1994.

73. "Principally, She Likes the Classroom," *Daily Journal* (Kankakee IL), September 12, 1993.

74. John Hamilton, "Few Attend Principal Meeting in Pembroke," *Daily Journal* (Kankakee IL), August 15, 1996.

75. "Portrait Gallery: Lorenzo R. Smith."

76. Sundiata Keita Cha-Jua, *America's First Black Town*, 131.

77. Themer, "Unity Isn't Possible."

78. Ibid.

79. John Hamilton, "St. Anne High Eyes Tax Hike, Realignment," *Daily Journal* (Kankakee IL), December 17, 1996.

80. John Hamilton, "Pembroke High OK'd: Elementary Board Votes Unanimously to Break Away from St. Anne," *Daily Journal* (Kankakee IL), April 9, 1997.

81. Hamilton, "Pembroke High OK'd."

82. John Hamilton, "Pembroke Eyes High School Referendum," *Daily Journal* (Kankakee IL), June 11, 1997.

83. John Hamilton, "Pembroke High a 'Dead Issue'; Costs Cited," *Daily Journal* (Kankakee IL), July 9, 1997.

84. John Hamilton, "St. Anne, Pembroke Seek Separate Schools," *Daily Journal* (Kankakee IL), September 12, 2001.

85. John Hamilton, "St. Anne Students Fight School Split," *Daily Journal* (Kankakee IL), September 28, 2001.

86. John Hamilton, "St. Anne, Pembroke at Building Crossroads," *Daily Journal* (Kankakee IL), October 16, 2001.

87. John Hamilton, "Lacking State Funds, Pembroke Board Decides to Close School," *Daily Journal* (Kankakee IL), March, 12, 2003.

88. Illinois State Board of Education, "PEMBROKE CCSD 259," *Illinois Report Card* (2015).

89. Samuel Payton, interview by author, October 20, 2009, notes in possession of author.

90. Illinois State Board of Education, "PEMBROKE CCSD 259" (2015); Illinois State Board of Education and Northern Illinois University, "PEMBROKE CCSD 259," *Illinois Interactive Report Card* (2012).

91. Lisa Dugan, interview by author, October 21, 2009, notes in possession of author.

92. Illinois State Board of Education, "st anne comm high school," *Illinois Report Card* (2015); Illinois State Board of Education and Northern Illinois University, "st anne CHSD 302," *Illinois Interactive Report Card* (2012).

93. Illinois State Board of Education, "st anne comm high school," (2015).

94. Steve Soucie, interview by author, February 7, 2013, notes in possession of author; Steve Soucie, "St. Anne Celebrates Area's First Basketball State Championship," *Daily Journal* (Kankakee IL), March 10, 2008; Steve Soucie, "Trophy Looks Great in Schoon's Hands," *Daily Journal* (Kankakee IL), March 10, 2008.

95. Soucie, "St. Anne Celebrates."

96. "Sanders More Than Just a Basketball Star," *Daily Journal* (Kankakee IL), January 21, 2016.

97. Johari Cole-Kweli, interview by author, October 2, 2013.

8. Building on Sand

1. Robert Themer, "Hopkins Park Mayor Aims to Change Views," *Daily Journal* (Kankakee IL), April 11, 2011.

2. Allen Jones, interview by author, September 15, 2009, notes in possession of author. Quotations from Allen Jones in this chapter are from this interview.

3. Samuel Payton, interview by author, October 20, 2009, notes in possession of author.

4. U.S. Census Bureau, *2010–2014 American Community Survey 5-Year Estimates: Selected Social Characteristics in the United States* (2015).

5. Bill Norman, "Irrigation Region Groundwater Recovered: Survey," *Daily Journal* (Kankakee IL), July 10, 1990; "Pembroke Water Project," *Daily Journal* (Kankakee IL), August 2, 1991.

6. 525 ILCS 45/5.1 (2016) (any new well pumping over 100,000 gallons per day must be registered); 525 ILCS 45/6 (2016) (Illinois law provides that individuals have the right to make "reasonable use" of ground water, which is defined as "the use of water to meet natural wants and a fair share for artificial wants"); 415 ILCS 55/1 et seq. (2016) (the Groundwater Protection Act coordinates efforts of ten state agencies to protect groundwater).

7. Laurie Goering and Thomas Cekay, "Irrigation Pulls Plug on Resident's Water," *Chicago Tribune*, July 25, 1988.

8. Howard Jones, interview by author, September 15, 2009, notes in possession of author; Sister Mary Cecelia, *Joy: Newsletter of the Sisters at the Martin de Porres Convent at Sacred Heart Catholic Church* 2, no. 3 (1973).

9. "Carver School Uses Bottled Water," *Daily Journal* (Kankakee IL), June 14, 1995.

10. "City Connects with Line from Texas Source," *St. Anne (IL) Record*, November 10, 1931; "Natural Gas for St. Anne about September 1st," *St. Anne (IL) Record*, June 25, 1931.

11. U.S. Census Bureau, *Twenty-Third Census of the United States, 2010 Census Summary File 1: Total Population*; *City-Data*, accessed February 15, 2013, http://www.city-data.com/.

12. Bernard Anderson, manager of community relations and economic development, Nicor Gas, interview by author, September 17, 2009, notes in possession of author.

13. John Stewart, "Pembroke Studies Day Care, Garbage Collection Services," *Daily Journal* (Kankakee IL), April 15, 1992; U.S. Census Bureau, *2010–2014 American Community Survey 5-Year Estimates: Selected Housing Characteristics* (2015).

14. "Fire Destroys Pembroke Community Building: Lightning May Have Caused Pembroke Fire," *Daily Journal* (Kankakee IL), June 30, 1993; "Fire Insurance Too Costly for Pembroke Residents," *Daily Journal* (Kankakee IL), May 4, 1992; Janet Cremer and Kristen Zambo, "Help Sought for Families Victimized by Fires: Firefighter's Home Latest Loss," *Daily Journal* (Kankakee IL), October 7, 2009.

15. Mike Lyons, "Pembroke Ablaze Again," *Daily Journal* (Kankakee IL), October 18, 1995.

16. "Fire Insurance Too Costly"; Carla Sanders and John Hamilton, "29 Homes Lost to Wildfires," *Daily Journal* (Kankakee IL), April 15, 1996.

17. Jerry Morgan, "Proposals Eyed to Remove Old Tires from Pembroke," *Daily Journal* (Kankakee IL), December 28, 1992.

18. Funding for roads comes from a state motor fuel allotment based on the number of miles already maintained in the township and property tax assessments that cannot raise much revenue due to low land values—even when rates have been set at the maximum level permitted by the state. Morgan, "Proposals Eyed"; James Piekarczyk, interview by author, October 27, 2009, notes in possession of author.

19. Arthur Collins, interview by Saints Patrick and Teresa Teen Group, Project Hearts of Hope, August 1999, tape in possession of author.

20. Kankakee County Planning Department, "Showbus."

21. Jeff Lyon, "Attention Deficit," *Chicago Tribune*, September 25, 2005.

22. U.S. Census Bureau, *Selected Economic Characteristics*.

23. Kankakee County Clerk, "County Tax Information."

24. Jerry Morgan, "No Easy Answers to Quagmire Roads in Pembroke Township," *Sunday Journal* (Kankakee IL), April 10, 1994.

25. BAIR Analytics, *RAIDS Online: Regional Analysis and Information Sharing.*

26. John Hamilton, "Papers Missing in Pembroke," *Daily Journal* (Kankakee IL), May 13, 1997; "Oprah Features Pembroke's Plight and Future Hopes," *Kankakee (IL) City News*, October 14, 2005.

27. According to one report from 1981, only one out of every six public dollars went to direct services for the community while the rest paid administrative

costs. Anne Lineve Wead and Peter Young, "Village Overhead Highest in Area: Pembroke Spending Outstrips All Others," *Sunday Journal* (Kankakee IL), December 13, 1981; Fern Schumer, "Pembroke: A Community without Income, Services, or a Tax Base," *Chicago Tribune*, December 31, 1981.

28. Lisa Dugan, interview by author, October 21, 2009, notes in possession of author.

29. Janet Cremer, "Surprise Visit, Oprah Winfrey Tours Pembroke," *Daily Journal* (Kankakee IL), September 28, 2005.

30. "Former Pembroke Township Supervisor Pleads Guilty to Theft," *Daily Journal* (Kankakee IL), September 25, 2014.

31. Jon Krenek, "Another Pembroke Supervisor Is Accused of Fraud," *Daily Journal* (Kankakee IL), July 3, 2014.

32. "Former Pembroke Township Supervisor Pleads Guilty."

33. Schumer, "Pembroke"; "Habitat's 1st 'House Blitz' Saturday: Volunteer Effort in Pembroke Intended to Build Community, Not Just Homes," *Daily Journal* (Kankakee IL), March 18, 1990; Mary Jean Houde and John Klasey, *Of the People*, 420; Ozroe Bentley, "Publisher View of Official Tour," *Pembroke (IL) Herald-Eagle*, April 23, 1970.

34. Craig Culver, interview by author, October 14, 2009, notes in possession of author; Gordon Burnside, "Leveraging Resources for a Better Life," *Health Progress* (November–December 2000).

35. John Hamilton, "Hopkins Park Sees New Effort for Development," *Daily Journal* (Kankakee IL), July 7, 1996.

36. Burnside, "Leveraging Resources"; Culver, interview.

37. "Pembroke out of Running for Super Prison," *Daily Journal* (Kankakee IL), October 1, 1993.

38. Ann Bernard et al., letter to the editor, *Daily Journal* (Kankakee IL), January 17, 2000.

39. John Hamilton, "Hopkins Park among Prison Site Finalists," *Daily Journal* (Kankakee IL), June 8, 1997; "Hopkins Park Locked Out of Prison Sweepstakes," *Daily Journal* (Kankakee IL), July 3, 1997.

40. "Pembroke Township Ready to Renew Prison Bid," *Daily Journal* (Kankakee IL), February 19, 1998.

41. Rick Pearson and Ray Long, "History—and Federal Prosecutors—Will Write Final Chapter in How Ryan Is Remembered," *Chicago Tribune*, January 13, 2003.

42. Pearson and Long, "History"; "The Political Life of George Ryan," *Daily Journal* (Kankakee IL), October 12, 2008.

43. "Buses to Roll in Support of Pembroke Prison," *Daily Journal* (Kankakee IL), October 7, 1999.

44. Burnside, "Leveraging Resources"; John Hamilton, "Rose Denies Plan to Banish Perry from Pembroke," *Daily Journal* (Kankakee IL), January 23, 2000.

45. Robert Themer, "Public Pushes for Pembroke Prison: Estimated 600 People Show Support for Facility, 900 Jobs," *Daily Journal* (Kankakee IL), October 8, 1999.

46. Tony Perry, "Women's Prison" letter to the editor, *Daily Journal* (Kankakee IL), October 21, 1999.

47. Themer, "Public Pushes"; Phil Angelo, "Prison OK'd for Pembroke: Onarga's Bid Loses Out," *Daily Journal* (Kankakee IL), December 8, 1999.

48. Rochelle Simpson, "Job Training for Prison Starts in Week: KCC Will Open Job Center at Lorenzo Smith," *Daily Journal* (Kankakee IL), March 12, 2000; Scott Boehmer, "Prison Job Training Planned," *Daily Journal* (Kankakee IL), December 12, 1999.

49. "Prison Promises to Be Financial Boon to Hopkins," *Daily Journal* (Kankakee IL), October 20, 2000; Robert Themer, "Many Build Hopes on Prison in Pembroke," *Daily Journal* (Kankakee IL), November 22, 2002.

50. Scott Reeder, "Ryan: A Shot in the Arm," *Daily Journal* (Kankakee IL), October 9, 1999.

51. "Pembroke Advocates for Truth," flyer (1999), from the archives of Sacred Heart Mission.

52. "Citizens' Forum Honored," *Insight News* 4, no. 1 (Pembroke Township, IL: July 2000).

53. John Hamilton, "150 Protest Pembroke Prison," *Daily Journal* (Kankakee IL), November 10, 1999.

54. Ardella Perry, "Staged Rally" letter to the editor, *Daily Journal* (Kankakee IL), October 29, 1999.

55. "Pembroke Advocates for Truth"; Mary Baskerville, "Prison, Airport Top Ryan Roundtable," *Daily Journal* (Kankakee IL), May 9, 2000.

56. Florence Carroll, "Other Values," *Daily Journal* (Kankakee IL), December 27, 1999.

57. Hamilton, "150 Protest."

58. "NO PRISON," *Soul Saving Center Newsletter* 1, no. 6 (October–November 2002).

59. Hamilton, "150 Protest."

60. Hamilton, "Hopkins Park among Prison Site Finalists"; "Group Wants Study Done on Women's Prison Impact," *Daily Journal* (Kankakee IL), May 24, 2000.

61. Angelo, "Prison OK'd for Pembroke."

62. John Hamilton, "'Christmas Gift' Prison Seen as Boon to Region," *Daily Journal* (Kankakee IL), December 9, 1999.

63. John Hamilton, "Pembroke's Reaction to Prison Positive," *Daily Journal* (Kankakee IL), December 10, 1999.

64. Ibid.

65. Ray Gibson, "New Prison Benefits Ryan Pal," *Chicago Tribune*, January 6, 2000.

66. Gibson, "New Prison Benefits"; "Developer to Make $33,000 on Prison," *Daily Journal* (Kankakee IL), January 6, 2000; "Governor: No Consultant for Prison," *Daily Journal* (Kankakee IL), June 18, 2000; "Nothing Wrong in Profit: Ryan," *Daily Journal* (Kankakee IL), January 7, 2000.

67. "Developer Won't Take Commission," *Daily Journal* (Kankakee IL), January 9, 2000.

68. Hamilton, "Rose Denies Plan."

69. "Developer Won't Take Commission."

70. "Group Wants Study"; "Hopkins Park, Perry Sued by Ex-Treasurer," *Daily Journal* (Kankakee IL), July 6, 2000; John Hamilton, "Private Pay Pact Raises Questions for Pembroke," *Daily Journal* (Kankakee IL), April 28, 2000.

71. Hamilton, "Private Pay Pact."

72. "Governor: No Consultant."

73. John Hamilton, "Gas Lines for Hopkins Park Still UCDC's Main Concern," *Daily Journal* (Kankakee IL), September 6, 2000.

74. "Hopkins Park Gags Clerk, Prison Foe: Controversial Action Follows Perry Letter," *Daily Journal* (Kankakee IL), February 8, 2000.

75. John Hamilton, "State Rejects Prison Site; Other Pembroke Location Eyed," *Daily Journal* (Kankakee IL), September 26, 2000.

76. "State Works 'Very Diligently' on Prison Site," *Daily Journal* (Kankakee IL), November 28, 2000.

77. Robert Themer, "7 Sites Eyed for Prison, Prices Low," *Daily Journal* (Kankakee IL), November 29, 2000; Robert Themer, "Ryan Determined to Locate Prison in Pembroke," *Daily Journal* (Kankakee IL), November 2, 2000.

78. Lee Provost, "Pembroke Prison Still Promised," *Daily Journal* (Kankakee IL), March 12, 2001.

79. "Prison Site for Pembroke; Hoopeston Out," *Daily Journal* (Kankakee IL), April 11, 2001; "Prison Site to Pembroke's South," *Daily Journal* (Kankakee IL), April 18, 2001.

80. John Hamilton, "Hopkins Park Prison Site Picked," *Daily Journal* (Kankakee IL), May 4, 2001.

81. John Hamilton, "Pembroke Prison Project Still Alive: Legislators," *Daily Journal* (Kankakee IL), January 14, 2002; Roy Bernard, "Hynes: State Finances Shaky," *Daily Journal* (Kankakee IL), October 11, 2001.

82. Jon Krenek, "Prison Spawns Hope: Ryan Sees Brighter Future for Pembroke at Groundbreaking," *Daily Journal* (Kankakee IL), September 25, 2002.

83. "Work Begins on Women's Prison," *Daily Journal* (Kankakee IL), November 8, 2002.

84. "George Ryan Indicted: Events Leading to Ryan's Indictment," *Chicago Tribune*, December 18, 2003.

85. Pearson and Long, "History"; David Schaper, "Former Illinois Gov. George Ryan Heading to Prison," *NPR*, December 6, 2007, http://www.npr.org.

86. "George Ryan Indicted."

87. Pearson and Long, "History"; "Former Illinois Gov. George Ryan Heading to Prison"; Schaper; "U.S. Governor on Cuba Mission," *BBC News*, October 24, 1999, http://news.bbc.co.uk.

88. Annie Sweeney and Ray Long, "George Ryan Set to Move to Halfway House," *Chicago Tribune*, January 22, 2013; Jason Meisner, Annie Sweeney, and Angie Leventis Lourgos, "Ryan Returns Home to Finish Sentence under House Arrest," *Chicago Tribune*, January 30, 2013.

89. Robert Themer, "Many Build Hopes on Prison in Peru," *Daily Journal* (Kankakee IL), November 22, 2002; Scott Reeder, "Proposal Aired to Halt Prison in Pembroke," *Daily Journal* (Kankakee IL), November 21, 2002.

90. Reeder, "Proposal Aired."

91. Themer, "Many Build Hopes on Prison in Peru."

92. Ibid.; H. Gregory Meyer, "Jackson Raises Issues about Pembroke Prison," *Chicago Tribune*, January 27, 2003.

93. Meyer, "Jackson Raises Issues."

94. Scott Reeder, "Governor to Delay, Re-study Pembroke Women's Prison," *Daily Journal* (Kankakee IL), April 9, 2003.

95. Scott Reeder and Stephanie Sievers, "Pembroke Prison Work Halted: Governor Issues Order; Delay Could Be Long-Term," *Daily Journal* (Kankakee IL), April 15, 2003.

96. Karen Mellen, "Pembroke Township Let Down Once Again; Budget Woes Dash Plans for Prison," *Chicago Tribune*, April 9, 2003; Robert Themer, "Pembroke Decision a Month Away," *Daily Journal* (Kankakee IL), October 16, 2003; Village of Hopkins Park et al., "Pembroke Township Development Site, Existing Conditions Report" (October 3, 2007).

97. "Senate Restores Funds for Prison," *Daily Journal* (Kankakee IL), May 23, 2003.

98. Ibid.; Adrianna Colindres, "Prison Halt Ripples Economy: Sub-contractors, Suppliers, Employees All Wait in Limbo Too," *Daily Journal* (Kankakee IL), May 30, 2003; Scott Reeder, "Governor Handcuffs Pembroke Prison Idea," *Daily Journal* (Kankakee IL), August 24, 2003.

99. Scott Reeder, "Guv May Yet Veto Prisons," *Daily Journal* (Kankakee IL), June 3, 2003.

100. Reeder, "Governor Handcuffs."

101. Jon Krenek, "Promises, but No Jobs for Pembroke," *Daily Journal* (Kankakee IL), July 22, 2003.

102. Illinois Department of Human Services, "TEAM Illinois"; Stephanie Sievers, "'Team Illinois' Taps Pembroke," *Daily Journal* (Kankakee IL), July 6, 2003.

103. Sievers, "Team Illinois."

104. Krenek, "Promises."

105. Illinois Department of Human Services, "TEAM Illinois."

106. "Lt. Governor Quinn Salutes Pembroke Township Credit Union on International Credit Union Day," *Standing Up for Illinois*, accessed July 15, 2015, http://standingupforillinois.org.

107. Kim Geiger, "Rauner Unveils Program Aimed at Helping Minority, Female Entrepreneurs," *Chicago Tribune*, January 19, 2016.

108. Illinois Department of Human Services, "TEAM Illinois."

109. Larry Gibbs, interview by author, September 15, 2009, notes in possession of author.

110. Dawn Turner Trice, "Photo Ops Over, Township's Woes Remain the Same," *Chicago Tribune*, February 16, 2005.

111. "Pembroke Prison Site Still Alive as Federal Lock-Up," *Daily Journal* (Kankakee IL), August 23, 2004.

112. Village of Hopkins Park et al., "Pembroke Township Development Site."

113. Christi Parsons, "Illinois the Next Gitmo?" *Chicago Tribune*, November 14, 2009.

114. Rick Pearson, "U.S. Buys Thomson Prison from State for $165 Million," *Chicago Tribune*, October 3, 2012.

9. Nature Preserved

1. Arthur Collins, interview by Saints Patrick and Teresa Teen Group, Project Hearts of Hope, August 1999, tape in possession of author.

2. Illinois Department of Natural Resources, Office of Scientific Research and Analysis, *Kankakee River Area Assessment, Volume 5*, 219–20, 224–28.

3. Earl H. Reed, *Tales of a Vanishing River*; Mary Jean Houde and John Klasey, *Of the People*, 380.

4. Illinois Department of Natural Resources, 330–31; "William Bridges, Writer, Dies," *New York Times*, March 31, 1984, http://www.nytimes.com.

5. Illinois Department of Natural Resources, 330.

6. Houde and Klasey, *Of the People*, 380.

7. "The Sands of Time," *Illinois Steward*, Summer 2007, 10.

8. Robert Themer, "Saving Savannas," *Daily Journal* (Kankakee IL), May 22, 2009.

9. Leela Mae and Charles Eason, interview by Saints Patrick and Teresa Teen Group, Project Hearts of Hope 3, Summer 2004, tape in possession of author.

10. "Sands of Time," 10.

11. Fran Harty, "A Renewed Opportunity for the Greater Kankakee Sands Ecosystem," *Illinois Steward*, Summer 2007, 34.

12. "Sands of Time," 10; Bill Byrns, "Debate over Wildlife Refuge Plan about to End," *Daily Journal* (Kankakee IL), August 16, 1998; "Proposal Critics See Many Flaws," *Daily Journal* (Kankakee IL), August 16, 1998; "Supervisor: Pembroke Opposes Refuge," *Daily Journal* (Kankakee IL), June 4, 1998.

13. 16 U.S.C. § 668dd(d)(1) (2016).

14. U.S. Fish and Wildlife Service, "Proposed: Kankakee Grand Marsh National Wildlife Refuge" (October 7, 1999).
15. John Hamilton, "Pembroke Supervisor Feeds Conspiracy Theory on Refuge," *Daily Journal* (Kankakee IL), May 6, 1998.
16. "Pembroke Land Preservation?" *Daily Journal* (Kankakee IL), August 26, 1994.
17. Hamilton, "Pembroke Supervisor Feeds Conspiracy."
18. 40 U.S.C. § 3113 (2016).
19. U.S. Fish and Wildlife Service, "Land Protection Planning for the National Wildlife Refuge System" (March 2001).
20. "Pembroke Residents Face Forced Relocation," *Insight News* 4, no. 1 (July 2000).
21. U.S. Fish and Wildlife Service, "Land Protection."
22. The FWS would reimburse the greater of (1) 0.75 percent of the land's fair market value, (2) 75 cents per acre, or (3) 25 percent of any receipts collected for operation and management of the land. 16 U.S.C. § 715s(c)(1) (2016). These figures would have to replace the revenues gained from the prevailing property tax rates. The 1999 rates were 8.75 percent in Pembroke and 10.89 percent in Hopkins Park, far exceeding the act's allotted 0.75 percent rate. Kankakee County Treasurer, "Property Search." Moreover, the 75 cent flat fee would only provide more money if the average land value was approximately $8.60 per acre—a dramatically unrealistic value.
23. "Proposal Critics"; John Hamilton, "Feds Expect Little Land Buying in Pembroke Township," *Daily Journal* (Kankakee IL), August 5, 1998; Hamilton, "Pembroke Supervisor Feeds Conspiracy."
24. John Hamilton, "A 1st for Pembroke? Visit by U.S. Senator," *Daily Journal* (Kankakee IL), May 17, 1998.
25. Rob Littiken, interview by author, October 26, 2009, notes in possession of author. Quotations and citations from Littiken in this chapter are from this interview.
26. The Nature Conservancy, "About Us."
27. Themer, "Saving Savannas."
28. The Nature Conservancy, "Red-headed Woodpecker: Preserving a Signature Species of the Illinois Savannas."
29. Littiken, interview.
30. 525 ILCS 33/10 (2016).
31. Robert Themer, "Jackson Warns of Likely 'Land-Grabbers,'" *Daily Journal* (Kankakee IL), January 12, 2003.
32. 525 ILCS 30/3.11 (2016).
33. 525 ILCS 30/9 (2016).
34. 525 ILCS 30/14 (2016).
35. Friends of the Kankakee, Newsletter (July 2008).
36. Illinois Nature Preserves Commission, "Minutes of the 187th Meeting."
37. Themer, "Saving Savannas."

38. Illinois Nature Preserves Commission, "Minutes of the 215th Meeting"; Robert Themer, "More of Pembroke Township Savanna Acres Preserved," *Daily Journal* (Kankakee IL), June 7, 2013.

39. Littiken, interview; K. C. Jaehnig, "Saving Savanna," *Perspectives: Southern Illinois University Carbondale Research and Creative Activities* (Fall 2008).

40. Littiken, interview.

41. Betty Flanders, *The Shaping of America's Heartland*, 197.

42. The Nature Conservancy, "Oak Savannas of Kankakee Sands."

43. Basu, interview by author, September 11, 2009, notes in possession of author. Quotations from Basu in this chapter are from this interview.

44. Larry Barnes, interview by author, September 18, 2009, notes in possession of author. Quotations from Barnes in this chapter are from this interview.

45. Robert Themer, "Kankakee Preserve Baby Step," *Daily Journal* (Kankakee IL), March 28, 2016.

46. Larry Gibbs, interview by author, September 15, 2009, notes in possession of author. Quotations from Gibbs in this chapter are from this interview.

47. Themer, "Jackson."

48. Allen Jones, interview by author, September 15, 2009, notes in possession of author.

49. "Pembroke Oil Well Project Abandoned," *Kankakee (IL) Daily Republican*, May 16, 1931.

50. "Private Groups Eye Feldspar Mining," *Daily Journal* (Kankakee IL), July 17, 1998.

51. Robert Themer, "More Activities Set to Celebrate Earth Day," *Daily Journal* (Kankakee IL), April 24, 2009.

52. "City News Exclusive Report: Residents Fear Nature Conservancy Exploiting Pembroke," *Kankakee (IL) City News*, June 2009.

53. Johari Cole-Kweli, interview by author, October 9, 2009, notes in possession of author.

10. Pembroke Today and Tomorrow

1. Agnes Strong DeLacy, interview by Saints Patrick and Teresa Teen Group, Project Hearts of Hope, August 1999, tape in possession of author. Quotations from Strong DeLacy in this chapter are from this interview.

2. Mary Jean Houde and John Klasey, *Of the People*, 420.

3. "Hopkins Park Residents Get Ready for Big Poverty Bout," *Chicago Defender*, September 25, 1965.

4. Pembroke Centennial Committee, "Pride with Effort: Pembroke Centennial Celebration."

5. "Incumbents Sweep Kankakee County Board Races," *Daily Journal* (Kankakee IL), November 4, 2014; Samuel Payton, interview by author, October 20, 2009, notes in possession of author (quotations from Payton in this chapter are from this interview); Samuel Payton, resume (2009).

6. Sharon White, interview by author, September 15, 2009.

7. Don Terry, "Green Acres," *Chicago Tribune*, July 15, 2007; Johari Cole-Kweli, interview by author, October 9, 2009, notes in possession of author. Quotations from Johari Cole-Kweli in this chapter are from this interview.

8. Sharon White, interview by author, September 15, 2009, notes in possession of author.

9. Basu, interview by author, October 26, 2009.

10. John Hamilton, "Gathering Reviews Pembroke Ag Options," *Daily Journal* (Kankakee IL), August 17, 1998; Linnet Myers, "Dirt Poor," *Chicago Tribune Magazine*, February 23, 1999; Robert Themer, "Local Couple Follows KISS Method of Farming," *Daily Journal* (Kankakee IL), August 15, 2009.

11. Cole-Kweli, interview; Patrick Kampert, "Growing the Business," *Chicago Tribune*, September 7, 2003.

12. Basu, interview, October 26, 2009.

13. Cole-Kweli, interview.

14. Terry, "Green Acres."

15. Cole-Kweli, interview.

16. The Black Oaks Center for Sustainable Renewable Living; Dimitrios Kalantzis, "Growing Hope in Pembroke: Farming Program Promises Jobs, Food," *Daily Journal* (Kankakee IL), December 5, 2012.

17. Basu, interview, October 26, 2009; Basu, interview by author, October 16, 2009, notes in possession of author; Basu Museum and Cultural Center.

18. "Pembroke Rodeo This Weekend," *Daily Journal* (Kankakee IL), May 22, 2014; "Thousands Visit Pembroke and Rodeo," *Pembroke (IL) Herald-Eagle*, June 1, 1978.

19. Elizabeth Williamson, "Riding High When It Comes to Running Rodeos, the Latting Family Knows the Ropes," *Chicago Tribune*, September 19, 1993; Latting Rodeo Productions.

20. Janet Siwicki, "Black Rodeo Has Historic Tone: Pembroke Educator Uses Broncos to Boost Students' Self-Esteem," *Daily Journal* (Kankakee IL). The clipped copy of the article was undated.

21. Sharon White, interview by author, October 2, 2013.

22. Reggie Stewart, interview by author, September 12, 2009, notes in possession of author.

23. Cole-Kweli, interview.

24. John W. Fountain, "In Trenches of a War of Unyielding Poverty," *New York Times*, September 29, 2002.

25. Lisa W. Foderaro, "Hastings-on-Hudson Journal: Shopping for the Family (It's 1,000 Miles Away)," *New York Times*, September 12, 2003.

26. Sister Mary Beth Clements, interview by author, October 18, 2009, notes in possession of author.

27. Dawn Turner Trice, "Area Makes Do, Bad Sewers and All," *Chicago Tribune*, October 3, 2005.

28. Basu, interview, interview by author, September 16, 2009, notes in possession of author.

29. Brenda Tucker, interview by author, October 6, 2009, notes in possession of author. Quotations from Tucker in this chapter are from this interview.

30. Terry, "Green Acres."

31. ServantCor, "Community Networks: The Hopkins Park–Pembroke Township Partnership," *Health Progress* (July–August 2000), 51.

32. Craig Culver, interview by author, October 14, 2009, notes in possession of author; John Hamilton, "Hopkins Park Sees New Effort for Development," *Daily Journal* (Kankakee IL), July 7, 1996.

33. "Sacred Heart Human Services," from the archives of Sacred Heart Mission. The document is undated, but context suggests the letter around 2000.

34. U.S. Census Bureau, *2010–2014 American Community Survey 5-Year Estimates: ACS Demographic and Housing Estimates* (2015).

Conclusion: The Good Life

1. Sylvia Patterson, interview by author, October 7, 2009, notes in possession of author.

2. "In Loving Memory of Mr. Wesley Higginbottom," from the archives of Sacred Heart Mission (September 1992).

3. Gertrude Higginbottom, interview by Saints Patrick and Teresa Teen Group, Project Hearts of Hope, August 1999, tape in possession of author. Quotations from Higginbottom in this chapter are from this interview.

4. Rev. Anthony Taschetta, "Note from the Pastor: An Open Letter to David Baron," St. Teresa Catholic Church Parish Bulletin, November 7, 1999.

Selected Bibliography

Included here are sections for interviews, letters, and lectures; books, journal articles, and online resources; and government records and resources.

Interviews, Letters, and Lectures

Anderson, Bernard. Interview by author. September 17, 2009 (notes in possession of author).

Barnes, Larry. Interview by author. September 18, 2009 (notes in possession of author).

Basu. Interviews by author. September 11, 2009 (notes in possession of author); September 16, 2009 (notes in possession of author); October 26, 2009.

Clements, Sister Mary Beth. Interview by author. October 18, 2014.

Cole-Kweli, Johari. Interviews by author. October 9, 2009 (notes in possession of author); October 2, 2013.

Collins, Arthur. Interview by author. October 5, 2009 (notes in possession of author).

———. Interview by Saints Patrick and Teresa Teen Group, Project Hearts of Hope. August 1999 (tape in possession of author).

Culver, Craig. Interview by author. October 14, 2009 (notes in possession of author).

Dugan, Lisa. Interview by author. October 21, 2009 (notes in possession of author).

Eason, Leela Mae, and Charles Eason. Interview by Saints Patrick and Teresa Teen Group, Project Hearts of Hope 3. Summer 2004 (tape in possession of author).

Eckles, Pat. Interview by author. September 16, 2009 (notes in possession of author).

Gibbs, Larry, and Bertha Moody. Interview by author. September 15, 2009 (notes in possession of author).

Grant, Eva. Interview by author. September 16, 2009 (notes in possession of author).

Hayes, Robert. Interview by Saints Patrick and Teresa Teen Group, Project Hearts of Hope. August 1999 (tape in possession of author).

Higginbottom, Fernando. Interview by author. October 18, 2014.

Higginbottom, Gertrude. Interview by Saints Patrick and Teresa Teen Group, Project Hearts of Hope. August 1999 (tape in possession of author).

Higginbottom, Lana. Interview by author. October 26, 2009 (notes in possession of author).

Jones, Allen. Interview by author. September 15, 2009 (notes in possession of author).

Jones, Howard. Interview by author. September 15, 2009 (notes in possession of author).

Karlock, Merlin. Interview by author. September 15, 2009 (notes in possession of author).

Littiken, Rob. Interview by author. October 26, 2009 (notes in possession of author).

Nettles Bey, Willie. Interview by Saints Patrick and Teresa Teen Group, Project Hearts of Hope 3. Summer 2004 (tape in possession of author).

Patterson, Sylvia. Interview by author. October 7, 2009 (notes in possession of author).

Payton, Samuel. Interview by author. October 20, 2009 (notes in possession of author).

Piekarczyk, James. Interview by author. October 27, 2009 (notes in possession of author).

Soucie, Steve. Interview by author. February 7, 2013 (notes in possession of author).

Steward, Elvia. Interview by author. October 26, 2009 (notes in possession of author).

Stewart, Reggie. Interview by author. October 12, 2009 (notes in possession of author).

Strong DeLacy, Agnes. Interview by Saints Patrick and Teresa Teen Group, Project Hearts of Hope. August 1999 (tape in possession of author).

Taschetta, Reverend Anthony. "Note from the Pastor: An Open Letter to David Baron." St. Teresa Catholic Church Parish Bulletin. November 7, 1999.

Tetter, Bertha. Letter to author. October 26, 2009 (letter in possession of author).

Themer, Robert. Interview by author. September 18, 2009 (notes in possession of author).

Tucker, Brenda. Interview by author. October 6, 2009 (notes in possession of author).

Turner, Glennette Tilley. Lecture at the Kankakee Public Library, Kankakee, IL. February 23, 2006 (transcript in possession of library).

White, Sharon. Interviews by author. September 15, 2009 (notes in possession of author); October 2, 2013.

Williams, Nancy M. Interview by Saints Patrick and Teresa Teen Group, Project Hearts of Hope. August 1999 (tape in possession of author).

Books, Journal Articles, and Online Resources

A&E Television Networks. "Jacques Marquette." *Bio.* http://www.biography.com.

———. "John Jacob Astor." *Bio.* http://www.biography.com.

BAIR Analytics. *RAIDS Online: Regional Analysis and Information Sharing.* Accessed January 23, 2016. http://www.raidsonline.com.

Barnhart, John D. "The Southern Element in the Leadership of the Old Northwest." *Journal of Southern History* 1, no. 2 (May 1935): 186–97.

Basu Museum and Cultural Center. Accessed February 2013. http://basumuseum.org/.

Beck, John M., Irving H. Cutler, and John J. L. Hobgood. "Pembroke Township: A Research Report on Problems and Possibilities." 1966. Kankakee Community College Library.

Bernard, Richard M. *Snowbelt Cities: Metropolitan Politics in the Northeast and Midwest since World War II.* Bloomington: Indiana University Press, 1990.

The Black Oaks Center for Sustainable Renewable Living. http://www.blackoakscenter.org/.

Boman, Dennis K. "Slavery in Illinois: Culture versus Law." Illinois Periodicals Online. Northern Illinois University. http://www.lib.niu.edu.

Burnside, Gordon. "Leveraging Resources for a Better Life." *Health Progress* (November–December 2000).

Carlson, Shirley. "Black Migration to Pulaski County, Illinois 1860–1900." *Illinois Historical Journal* 80 (Spring 1987): 37–46.

Cha-Jua, Sundiata Keita. *America's First Black Town: Brooklyn, Illinois 1830–1915.* Urbana: University of Illinois Press, 2000.

———. "The Cry of the Negro Should Not Be Remember the Maine, but Remember the Hanging of Bush." In *Lynching beyond Dixie: American Mob Violence outside the South,* edited by Michael J. Pfeifer, 165–89. Urbana: University of Illinois Press, 2013.

Chicago and Eastern Illinois Railroad Historical Society. "A Brief History of the Chicago and Eastern Illinois Railroad." http://www.ceihs.org.

Danielson, Lisa A. "Installment Land Contracts: The Illinois Experience and the Difficulties of Incremental Judicial Reform." *University of Illinois Law Review* 1 (1986): 91–125.

Davis, Cyprian. *The History of Black Catholics in the United States.* New York: Crossroad, 1995.

Davis, Darren W., and Donald B. Pope-Davis. *2011 National Black Catholic Survey.* Draft version. 2011.

Engles, Andre. "Louis Jolliet (1645–1700) Jacques Marquette (1637–1675)." *Discoverers Web*. Accessed February 15, 2013. http://www.win.tue.nl.

Farnsworth, Katherine, ed. *Pembroke Local History Book*. 2000. From the files of Eva Grant.

Finkelman, Paul. "Evading the Ordinance: The Persistence of Bondage in Indiana and Illinois." *Journal of the Early Republic* 9, no. 1 (Spring 1989): 21–51.

Flanders, Betty. *The Shaping of America's Heartland: The Landscape of the Middle West*. Boston: Houghton Mifflin, 1997.

Freyfogle, Eric T. "The Installment Land Contract as Lease: Habitability Protections and the Low-Income Purchaser." *New York University Law Review* 62 (1987): 293–320.

Gibson, Robert A. "The Negro Holocaust: Lynching and Race Riots in the United States, 1880–1950." *Yale–New Haven Teachers Institute*. 2014. http://www.yale.edu.

Grossman, James R. *Land of Hope: Chicago, Black Southerners, and the Great Migration*. University of Chicago Press, 1989.

Harbor, Ronald D. "Constructing an African American Catholic Liturgical Aesthetic." In *Let It Shine! The Emergence of African American Catholic Worship*, Mary E. McGann, RSCJ, 87–132. New York: Fordham University Press, 2008.

Harrison, William Henry. "Petition of the Vincennes Convention." 1802. In *Messages and Letters of William Henry Harrison*, vol. 1, edited by Logan Esarey, 62–67. Indiana Historical Commission, 1922.

Houde, Mary Jean, and John Klasey. *Of the People: A Popular History of Kankakee County*. Chicago: General Printing Company, 1968.

Jackson, Brooks. "Blacks and the Democratic Party." *FactCheck.org*. April 8, 2008. http://www.factcheck.org.

Krist, Gary. *City of Scoundrels: The 12 Days of Disaster That Gave Birth to Modern Chicago*. New York: Crown, 2012.

Latting Rodeo Productions. 2016. http://lattingrodeoproductions.com.

Lippincott, I. "Industry among the French in the Illinois Country." *Journal of Political Economy* 18, no. 2 (February 1910): 114–28.

Lynd, Staughton. "The Compromise of 1787." *Political Science Quarterly* 81, no. 2 (June 1966): 225–50.

McGann, Mary E., RSCJ, and Eva Marie Lumas, SSS. "Historical Overview—The Emergence of African American Catholic Worship." In *Let It Shine! The Emergence of African American Catholic Worship*, Mary E. McGann, RSCJ, 1–52. New York: Fordham University Press, 2008.

Merriam-Webster. "Holy Roller." 2015. http://www.merriam-webster.com.

Myrdal, Gunnar. *An American Dilemma: The Negro Problem and Modern Democracy*. New York: Harper & Brothers, 1944.

National Governors Association. "Illinois Governor Edward Coles." 2011. http://www.nga.org.

The Nature Conservancy. "Red-Headed Woodpecker: Preserving a Signature Species of the Illinois Savannas." 2009.

———. "About Us." http://www.nature.org.

———. "Illinois: Kankakee Sands." http://www.nature.org.

———. "Oak Savannas of Kankakee Sands." Letter to Nature Conservancy members and Pembroke community. Spring 2009.

The New Philadelphia Association. "New Philadelphia: A Pioneer Town." http://www.newphiladelphiail.org/.

Nuzzo, Victoria A. "Extent and Status of Midwest Oak Savanna: Presettlement and 1985." *Natural Areas Journal* 6, no. 2 (1986): 6–36.

Obama, Barack. "A More Perfect Union." Transcript of speech given in Philadelphia, Pennsylvania, March 18, 2008. National Public Radio. http://www.npr.org.

Onuf, Peter S. *Statehood and Union: A History of the Northwest Ordinance.* Bloomington: Indiana University Press, 1987.

Pattillo-McCoy, Mary. *Black Picket Fences: Privilege and Peril among the Black Middle Class.* Chicago: University of Chicago Press, 1999.

Pembroke Centennial Committee. "Pride with Effort: Pembroke Centennial Celebration." 1977. Archives of Sacred Heart Mission.

The Pew Forum on Religious and Public Life. *U.S. Religious Landscape Survey, Religious Affiliation: Diverse and Dynamic.* 2008. http://religions.pewforum.org.

Pew Research Center. *America's Changing Religious Landscape.* 2015. http://www.pewforum.org.

Portwood, Shirley. "The Alton School Case and African American Community Consciousness 1897–1908." *Illinois Historical Journal* 91, no. 1 (Spring 1998): 2–20.

———. "School Segregation in Southern Illinois: The Alton School Case, 1897–1908." *Illinois History Teacher,* January 2005.

Ransom, James T. "Underground Railroad Routes in Illinois." *Historic Illinois* 22, no. 6 (April 2000): 1–2.

Reed, Earl H. *Tales of a Vanishing River.* New York: John Lane Company, 1920.

Roper Center. "How Groups Voted." http://www.ropercenter.uconn.edu.

Township Officials of Illinois. "TOI History." http://www.toi.org.

Turner, Glennette Tilley. *The Underground Railroad in Illinois.* Wheaton, IL: Newman Educational Publishing, 2001.

Saad, Lydia. "Churchgoing among U.S. Catholics Slides to Tie Protestants." *Gallup.* 2009. http://www.gallup.com.

Sawyers, June Skinner. *Chicago Portraits.* Chicago: Loyola University Press, 1991.

Spear, Allan H. *Black Chicago: The Making of a Negro Ghetto, 1890–1920.* University of Chicago Press, 1969.

St. Elizabeth Church, "Father Tolton." http://www.stelizabethchicago.com.

"Stephen Small Murder." *Kanwiki*. 2014. http://www.kanwiki.org.

Taylor, Troy. "The Fort Dearborn Massacre: Haunted by History." *Weird and Haunted Chicago*. http://www.prairieghosts.com.

Vincent, Stephan A. *Southern Seed, Northern Soil: African-American Farm Communities in the Midwest, 1765–1900*. Bloomington: Indiana University Press, 2002.

University of Virginia, Geospatial and Statistical Data Center. "Historical Census Browser." 2007. http://mapserver.lib.virginia.edu.

U.S. Conference of Catholic Bishops. "Demographics." http://www.usccb.org.

Walker, Juliet E. K. *Free Frank: A Black Pioneer on the Antebellum Frontier*. Lexington: University Press of Kentucky, 1983.

Washington, Booker T. Speech given to Atlanta Cotton States and International Exposition, Atlanta, Georgia, October 18, 1895. American RadioWorks. http://americanradioworks.publicradio.org.

Wilkerson, Isabel. *The Warmth of Other Sons: The Epic Story of America's Great Migration*. New York: Random House, 2010.

Wright, Gavin. *Slavery and American Economic Development*. Baton Rouge: Louisiana State University Press, 2006.

Government Records and Resources

Continental Congress. "An Ordinance for Ascertaining the Mode of Disposing of Lands in the Western Territory." 1785. Library of Congress. http://memory.loc.gov.

Illinois Department of Human Services. "TEAM Illinois." Accessed April 1, 2016. http://www.dhs.state.il.us.

Illinois Department of Natural Resources, Office of Scientific Research and Analysis. *Kankakee River Area Assessment, Volume 5: Early Accounts of the Ecology of the Kankakee River Area*. 1998. http://hdl.handle.net.

Illinois Nature Preserves Commission. "Minutes of the 187th Meeting." August 2, 2005. http://dnr.state.il.us.

———. "Minutes of the 215th Meeting." September 13, 2013. https://dnr.state.il.us.

Illinois State Archives. "Kankakee County." http://www.cyberdriveillinois.com.

Illinois State Board of Education and Northern Illinois University. *Illinois Interactive Report Card*. 2012. Accessed October 2013. http://iirc.niu.edu.

Illinois State Board of Education. *Illinois Report Card*. 2015. http://illinoisreportcard.com.

Indiana Historical Bureau. "Slavery in Indiana Territory." http://www.in.gov/history.

Kankakee County Clerk. "County Tax Information." Accessed June 4, 2015. http://www.kankakeecountyclerk.com.

Kankakee County Planning Department. "Demographics." 2013. http://planning.k3county.net.

———. "Showbus." http://planning.k3county.net.

Kankakee County Treasurer. "Property Search." Accessed November 11, 2014. http://treasurer.k3county.net.

Kankakee Police Department. "Total Crime Index 2014." 2015. http://www.citykankakee-il.com.

Legislative Council and House of Representatives of the Indiana Territory. "Petition on Slavery from Indiana." 1807. In *The Black Laws in the Old Northwest: A Documentary History*, Stephen Middleton, 180–81. Westport, CT: Greenwood Press, 1993.

National Park Service. "Lincoln Home: The Underground Railroad in Lincoln's Neighborhood." 2008. http://www.nps.gov.

———. "Reading 1: Free Frank McWorter." Accessed February 2013. http://www.nps.gov.

———. "Reading 2: New Philadelphia." Accessed February 2013. http://www.nps.gov.

———. "New Philadelphia: A Multiracial Town on the Illinois Frontier." Accessed February 2013. http://www.nps.gov.

Second Continental Congress. The Northwest Ordinance of 1787. Our Documents: 100 Milestone Documents. http://www.ourdocuments.gov.

U.S. Census Bureau. *Eighth Census of the United States: Schedule 1—Free Inhabitants, State of Illinois, County of Iroquois, Township of Papineau*. 1860. Ancestry.com. http://www.ancestry.com.

———. *Ninth Census of the United States: Schedule 1—Inhabitants, State of Illinois, County of Iroquois, Township of Papineau*. 1870. Ancestry.com. http://www.ancestry.com.

———. *Thirteenth Census of the United States: 1910 Population, State of Illinois, County of Kankakee, Township of Pembroke*. 1910. Ancestry.com. http://www.ancestry.com.

———. *Twentieth Census of the United States, Census of Population and Housing, 1980*. https://www.census.gov.

———. *Twenty-First Census of the United States, Census of Population and Housing, 1990*. https://www.census.gov.

———. *Twenty-Second Census of the United States, Census of Population and Housing, 2000*. https://www.census.gov.

———. *Twenty-Third Census of the United States, Census of Population and Housing, 2010*. https://www.census.gov.

———. *Twenty-Third Census of the United States: 2010 Census Summary File 1: Total Population*. http://factfinder2.census.gov.

———. *2009–2013 American Community Survey 5-Year Estimates: Selected Economic Characteristics*. 2014. http://factfinder2.census.gov.

———. *2010–2014 American Community Survey 5-Year Estimates: ACS Demographic and Housing Estimates*. 2015. http://factfinder2.census.gov.

———. *2010–2014 American Community Survey 5-Year Estimates: Selected Economic Characteristics.* 2015. http://factfinder2.census.gov.

———. *2010–2014 American Community Survey 5-Year Estimates: Selected Housing Characteristics.* 2015. http://factfinder2.census.gov.

———. *2010–2014 American Community Survey 5-Year Estimates: Selected Social Characteristics in the United States.* 2015. http://factfinder2.census.gov.

———. *QuickFacts: United States.* 2014. http://www.census.gov.

U.S. Fish and Wildlife Service. "Land Protection Planning for the National Wildlife Refuge System." March 2001.

———. "Proposed: Kankakee Grand Marsh National Wildlife Refuge." October 7, 1999.

Index

Dave Baron is a constitutional litigator in the City of Chicago's Law Department and a former associate at the law firm of Sidley Austin LLP. He graduated from Harvard Law School in 2009 and the University of Notre Dame in 2006, where he served on the university's board of trustees. Baron now chairs the board of advisors of Old St. Patrick's Church in Chicago and lives in the city's Logan Square neighborhood.

*　*　*